HOW AND WHY BOOKS MATTER

Comparative Research on Iconic and Performative Texts

Series Editor

James W. Watts, Syracuse University

While humanistic scholarship has focused on the semantic meaning of written, printed, and electronic texts, it has neglected how people perform texts mentally, orally and theatrically and manipulate the material text through aesthetic engagement, ritual display, and physical decoration. This series promotes the twenty-first-century trend of studying the performative and iconic uses of material texts, especially as encouraged by the activities of the Society for Comparative Research on Iconic and Performative Texts (SCRIPT).

Published

Iconic Books and Texts

Edited by James W. Watts

Sensing Sacred Texts

Edited by James W Watts

Reframing Authority: The Role of Media and Materiality

Edited by Laura Feldt and Christian Høgel

Forthcoming

Miniature Books: The Format and Function of Tiny Religious Texts

Edited by Kristina Myrvold and Dorina Miller Parmenter

HOW AND WHY BOOKS MATTER:
ESSAYS ON THE SOCIAL FUNCTION OF ICONIC TEXTS

BY
JAMES W. WATTS

SHEFFIELD UK   BRISTOL CT

Published by Equinox Publishing Ltd.

UK: Office 415, The Workstation, 15 Paternoster Row, Sheffield, S1 2BX
USA: ISD, 70 Enterprise Drive, Bristol, CT 06010

www.equinoxpub.com

ISBN-13: 978 1 78179 767 9 (hb) | ISBN-13: 978 1 78179 768 6 (pb) |
    ISBN-13: 978 1 78179 769 3 (ePDF)

British Library Cataloguing-in-Publication Data

A catalogue record for this book is available from the British Library.

Library of Congress Cataloging-in-Publication Data

Names: Watts, James W. (James Washington), 1960- author.
Title: How and why books matter : essays on the social function of iconic texts / James W. Watts.
Description: Bristol : Equinox Publishing Ltd., 2019. | Series: Comparative research on iconic and performative texts | Includes bibliographical references and index.
Identifiers: LCCN 2018024479 (print) | LCCN 2018042574 (ebook) |
ISBN 9781781797693 (ePDF) | ISBN 9781781797679 (hb) | ISBN 9781781797686 (pb)
Subjects: LCSH: Sacred books—History and criticism. | Books—Social aspects.
Classification: LCC BL71 (ebook) | LCC BL71 .W38 2019 (print) | DDC 208/.2—dc23
LC record available at https://lccn.loc.gov/2018024479

Typeset by Queenston Publishing, Hamilton Canada.

Edited by  CAUFIELD COPYEDITING AND TYPESETTING

For Dori,
who started it all

Contents

LIST OF FIGURES

ACKNOWLEDGEMENTS

Chapter 1 "How Books Matter" is a revised version of "The Three Dimensions of Scriptures," *Postscripts* 2 (2006/2008): 135–159, reprinted in *Iconic Books and Texts* (ed. Watts; London: Equinox, 2013), 9–32.

Chapter 3 "Relic Texts" is an excerpt and expansion of one section of "The Three Dimensions of Scriptures," and originally appeared on *The Iconic Books Blog* on June 8, 2012, http://iconicbooks.blogspot.com/2012/06/relic-texts.html.

Chapter 5 "Desecrated Scriptures and the News Media" is an extensively revised and updated version of "Desecrating Scriptures," a case study written with sponsorship from the Luce Project in Religion, Media and International Relations at Syracuse University in 2009, which originally appeared online at http://sites.maxwell.syr.edu/luce/jameswatts.html (no longer accessible).

Chapter 6 "Ancient Iconic Texts" and Chapter 9 "Mass Literacy and Scholarly Expertise" reproduce and rearrange parts of "Ancient Iconic Texts and Scholarly Expertise," *Postscripts* 6 (2010/ 2012), 331–344 = *Iconic Books and Texts* (ed. Watts; London: Equinox, 2013), 407–418 and "Iconic Scriptures from Decalogue to Bible," *Mémoires du livre / Studies in Book Culture* 6/2 (2015), online at http://id.erudit.org/iderudit/1032712ar, http://doi.org/10.7202/1032712ar, published under a Creative Commons Attribution 3.0 Unported License.

Chapter 7 "Rival Iconic Texts" is an extensively updated version of "Ten Commandment Monuments and the Rivalry of Iconic Texts," *Journal of Religion & Society* 6 (2004), http://moses.creighton.edu/jrs/2004/2004-13.pdf, published under a Creative Commons Attribution 3.0 Unported License.

Chapter 10 "Why Books Matter" revises and combines an essay that appeared on *The Iconic Books Blog* on February 20, 2010, http://iconic-books.blogspot.com/2010/02/why-books-matter.html, with material that appeared in "Disposing of Non-Disposable Texts," in *The Death of Sacred Texts: Ritual Disposal and Renovation of Texts in the World Religions* (ed. Kristina Myrvold; Farnham: Ashgate, 2010), 147–159, which is reproduced here by permission of the publisher.

I am grateful to these publishers for permission to reproduce this material in revised form here. I am also grateful to Jason Lewis for giving me permission to incorporate his research on the iconic ritualization of the U.S. Constitution into Chapter 7 (see page 128, note 41).

Introduction: The Iconic Books Project

Books matter to very many people. Of course, they matter to librarians and scholars, authors and publishers, people with professional and economic interests in books. But they also matter to billions of people who treasure their personal book collections, people ranging from wealthy collectors of rare books to young children delighted by the gift of a new picture book. Books matter.

Why do they matter? Answers to this question always start with the books' contents—their stories, arguments, influence, and information. But the example of book collectors, young and old, shows that this is not the whole story. Collectors treasure books as valuable objects—and valuable in more ways than can be measured just by their economic worth.

During the centuries when books and other print media reigned unchallenged as purveyors of information, it was hard to distinguish the value of material media from the value of their contents. The digital revolution of recent years has made distinguishing the medium from its contents, that is, hardware from software, routine with written texts, and with songs and videos too. But to the surprise of tech enthusiasts, books and other written texts still matter to very many people.

So to answer the question "Why do books matter?", we have to look closely at the social functions and significance of written texts. We have to pay attention to their material form and their visual portrayal, their oral and theatrical adaptations, just as much as to the interpretation of their words. It requires us to ask a more technical question: "How do books matter?"

I will begin to answer these questions by starting with the books that matter the most to the most people. They are religious scriptures. More people devote themselves to reading, collecting, decorating, reproducing, protecting, and distributing these books than any others, and they have done so for a very long time. To understand how books matter, it is therefore useful to start with the books that matter the most.

I readily grant that most other books do not share scriptures' value or social functions. But it turns out that scriptures gain their extreme value by exaggerating characteristics of all written texts (Chapter 1). So the discussion in the following chapters starts with and frequently returns to the example of religious scriptures.

The subject and approach of this book grew out of my experiences teaching religious studies. I usually teach classes on the Bible and I focus especially on the part of the Hebrew Bible that features laws, ritual instructions, sacrifice, and an urgent rhetoric of obedience. When I came to Syracuse University in 1999, I taught Ph.D. seminars for the first time. Syracuse's graduate program in religion draws students interested in philosophical and sociological theories about religion, in comparisons among religious traditions, and in the problem of how to define what is religious in distinction from what is secular. So I needed to develop seminars that would appeal to these students.

My first seminar was called, "The Idea of Scripture." We studied beliefs about scriptures and practices with scriptures in Judaism, Christianity and Islam. We discussed how scriptures are interpreted, how they have influenced politics and social life, and how their contents have changed over time. I was pleased that I seemed to have found a way of applying traditional ideas from biblical studies about interpretation and canonization to a wider range of traditions and time periods.

But one student questioned the way I had structured the course. Dorina Miller Parmenter pointed out that I had left out half the subjects that should be covered in a course about scriptures. She wanted to know why we weren't discussing the physical books of scriptures. Before joining Syracuse's graduate program in religion, Dori had studied studio art and her artistic medium is books. She is a book artist and so very attuned to the material nature and form of books. She wondered why I wasn't talking about that.

Of course, the reason I wasn't talking about material books is that the topic had never occurred to me. Like most literary scholars, historians, and philosophers, biblical scholar like me are trained to interpret texts. We deploy a wide variety of approaches and methods to explain what a text means, why it was written this way, what texts it depends on, and what its influence has been. Actually, biblical scholars do pay attention to the material form of ancient texts, that is, to early manuscripts like the Dead Sea Scrolls. We pay attention to their material and ink and handwriting because that helps us understand the history of biblical literature. But we pay little attention to the forms and functions of later bibles.

I decided Dori had a point. But when I went to the library to supplement the course bibliography with readings about the material forms and functions of scriptures, I was surprised to find almost nothing on the subject. A search of databases showed that there is very little published research that discusses the ritual and social functions of the material forms of sacred texts, or of books in general. There is a great deal of information about particular manuscripts and editions. There is a growing body of scholarship about the history of publishing and reading. But there is very little that describes and analyzes the social significance and religious symbolism of material books. A handful of scholars had discussed the symbolic importance of books of scriptures in particular cultures and time periods. However, there was virtually nothing that generalized about the phenomenon more broadly.

So Dori and I decided to launch a collaborative research effort, the Iconic Books Project.[1] We started by doing something very unusual among humanists: we collected data. Since there were few scholarly precedents, we decided we needed to collect raw data about physical books. We did not restrict our project to scriptures, because we wanted to find out how the forms and uses of religious books differ from secular books and not simply assume that they do. We did not restrict our project to any particular culture or time period, because we wanted to find out how the forms and uses of books differ across cultures and time.

Our database contained written descriptions of books and book rituals, but it consisted mostly of pictures. We scoured the internet for pictures of books and of people handling books. I recruited some Syracuse undergraduate students to help with our research by searching the library's collection of art books. I told them to scan and bring to me every picture they could find with a book in it. We carried cameras with us wherever we went to record images of books on signs, on buildings, and on gravestones. Then we catalogued the pictures into computer files that could be searched and browsed. This became the database of the Iconic Books Project.

The more we looked for them, the more we saw books and other forms of written texts almost everywhere we looked. They showed up frequently in news stories. That was especially the case in the United States between 2000 and 2005. Evangelical Christians were trying to make the U.S. look more Christian by placing monuments to the Ten Commandments in courthouses and schools around the country. Here was an iconic text whose form and display carried obvious political implications. So my first attempt to write about iconic books focused on these monuments (see Chapter 7).

---

1. See the Iconic Books Project at http://iconicbooks.net.

An iconic book is a text revered primarily as an object of value and power rather than just as a container for words of instruction, information, or insight. Categorizing this phenomenon under the label "iconic books" points out its functional similarity to the icons of Eastern Orthodox Christian traditions, a topic that became the focus of Dori's early research.[1] Our study of iconic books and texts draws especially on comparative scriptures studies and icon theory to develop frameworks for understanding the ritual manipulation, display, production, and disposal of material texts (see Chapter 2).

When I taught the seminar on the Idea of Scripture again, the work of the Iconic Books Project influenced its outline and contents. Material books play obvious roles in religious rituals in many traditions, but so does reading the book aloud and interpreting its contents. I began to think of all of these activities as kinds of rituals. By the third rendition of the course, I organized the semester around the three dimensions in which texts can be ritualized: the iconic dimension in which physical books can be decorated, illuminated, given distinctive forms and shapes, and manipulated in various ways; the expressive (or performative) dimension in which their texts can be read, recited and sung aloud as well as acted out theatrically or illustrated artistically; and the semantic dimension of ritualized interpretation, preaching, commentary, and debate. The course went over well with my students, many of whom produced creative research on the ritualization of scriptures in one or another of these dimensions. At the end of the semester, I decided to write out these ideas in "The Three Dimensions of Scriptures" (revised as Chapter 1 below), which was published along with the papers of six students in my seminars, including Dori Parmenter's, in a thematic double issue of *Postscripts: The Journal of Sacred Texts & Contemporary Worlds.*[2]

The Iconic Books Database began to show some interesting patterns. I noticed, for example, that most art featuring texts shows not just texts or groups of texts by themselves but people holding, reading or writing books or other kinds of texts. Some Renaissance and Baroque period still-life paintings broke from this pattern, as did heraldic symbols from all periods. But from around 1870 on, art increasingly featured books by themselves, though the earlier motifs did not disappear. Recent art has seen that trend manifest itself in the book as a medium of art, "book art," that develops and mutates the form of the book into all kinds of constructions. Recent digi-

---

1. Dorina Miller Parmenter, "The Iconic Book: The Image of the Bible in early Christian Rituals," in *Iconic Books and Texts* (ed. J. W. Watts, Sheffield: Equinox, 2013), 63–92, first published in *Postscripts* 2 (2006/2008): 160–189; idem, "The Bible as Icon: Myths of the Divine Origins of Scripture," in *Jewish and Christian Scripture as Artifact and Canon* (ed. C. A. Evans and H. D. Zacharias; London: T. & T. Clark, 2009), 298–310.

2. Issue date 2006, though actually published in 2008.

tal technology also uses images of books as popular "icons" on many web sites. Along with these secular developments, recent media depictions of religious imagery has made the stereotypical form of scriptures, whether leather-bound bibles or Torah scrolls or geometrically designed Qur'an covers, widely recognized emblems of their respective religions.

Dori and I realized, however, that the database's breadth in time and culture made it difficult to handle. We were looking at many pictures from cultures and time periods with which we were unfamiliar. So we recruited an interdisciplinary group of researchers to discuss them with us at a series of symposia on Iconic Books hosted by Syracuse University in 2007 and 2010 and by nearby Hamilton College in 2009. We gathered together experts in diverse fields specializing in different periods of history and in a wide variety of cultures and religious traditions. Dori and I, together with S. Brent Plate, then founded the Society for Comparative Research on Iconic and Performative Texts (SCRIPT) in 2010 to continue this interdisciplinary collaboration.[3]

This book represents what I have learned from eighteen years spent working on the Iconic Books Project. It reflects the influence of my many colleagues, students and research collaborators in SCRIPT. I am very grateful to all of them. Its chapters were written at various points during this period, and have all been extensively revised and updated for inclusion together here.

---

3. SCRIPT's website can be found at www.script-site.net.

— 1 —

How Books Matter
The Three Dimensions of Scriptures

The use and abuse of scriptures was a frequent topic of news stories in 2003, 2004, and 2005. Courts and politicians in the United States led intense public debates over whether to display monuments of the Ten Commandments in public buildings. Tens of thousands of Muslims marched in streets around the world because American guards desecrated copies of the Qur'an at the prison in Guantánomo Bay, Cuba. These events and the media coverage that they generated showed that the scriptures of Muslims, Christians and Jews remain powerful symbols in contemporary culture.

These controversies did not revolve around interpretation of the meaning of these scriptures, nor even how they should be learned or obeyed. They focused instead on the physical display and manipulation of scriptures. At issue was not scriptures as texts or as verbal expressions, but rather scriptures as physical symbols of religions, cultures, and ideas, that is, scriptures as icons.

Scholars of religion and of scriptures were poorly prepared to discuss and evaluate these events. Modern research has focused on other aspects of the phenomenon of scripture. Scholars have devoted their time and publications to explaining the origins and meanings of scriptural texts. Take biblical studies as an example. Modern research has focused on describing the process by which the Bible was composed and the original meaning intended by its authors. Biblical scholars have also given considerable attention to the process by which the Bible became scripture. Such studies of "canonization," however, concentrate on the Bible's semantic form and contents, that is, on questions of when particular books became part of the Jewish and Christian scriptures and under what circumstances.

Wilfred Cantwell Smith, a historian of religion, criticized biblical scholars in the 1970s for their preoccupation with origins, which he described as studying the Bible before it was the Bible. He called for more historical and comparative studies of how the Bible *functions* as scripture.[1] In recent decades, many biblical scholars have in fact given more attention to the history of the Bible's interpretation. Some have even elevated subsequent meanings of biblical texts to the same level of importance as its original meaning to its authors. That begins to answer W. C. Smith's challenge, but he envisioned an approach focused on more than just the history of interpretation. He advocated study of the Bible's religious functions and effects in comparison with the scriptures of other religious traditions.

It was left to some of Smith's own students to develop that approach. William Graham, most prominently, argued that traditional scholarship on scriptures has ignored their *performative* function.[2] He pointed out that the most characteristic uses of scriptures in various religious traditions and cultures have to do with their reading, recitation, and memorization rather than with their interpretation. Graham argued that such textual performances are just as important as interpretation, often more important, for understanding the cultural significance of scriptures.

Graham's study of performance was not comprehensive enough to describe all the cultural functions of scriptures, or even all of their performative functions. His survey of the ways that texts are performed through reading, recitation, and memorization omitted or downplayed practices of performing the *contents* of scriptures. These take many forms, ranging from artistic depictions of scenes from scriptural narratives to the enactment of scriptural stories in dramas and, more recently, movies. Artistic and dramatic expressions of scriptural contents have played especially prominent roles in Hindu and Christian cultures.[3] In fact, it is without doubt the dominant mode of scriptural performance in contemporary Christianity because it has been reinforced by the invention of video technology in the twentieth century. But the changes wrought by new technology were not as innova-

1. Wilfred Cantwell Smith, "The Study of Religion and the Study of the Bible," *Journal of the American Academy of Religion* 39 (1971): 131–140; reprinted 1989 in *Rethinking Scripture: Essays from a Comparative Perspective,* ed. M. Levering, Albany, NY: SUNY Press, 18–28.

2. William A. Graham, *Beyond the Written Word: Oral Aspects of Scripture in the History of Religion.* Cambridge: Cambridge University Press, 1987.

3. Barbara A. Holdrege ("Beyond the Guild: Liberating Biblical Studies," in *African Americans and the Bible: Sacred Texts and Social Textures* [ed. Vincent L. Wimbush, New York: Continuum, 2003], 138–159 [144–146]) presented an account of scripture in the W.C. Smith/ William Graham tradition that recognizes the cultural importance for African Americans of performances of scriptural contents, as well as scripture's iconic role. Nevertheless, like almost all other interpreters, she found the most legitimate and legitimizing uses of scripture to involve the interpretation of their words: "It was the *content* of the Bible – not simply its status as a sacred object – that captivated the imagination of the slaves, catalyzing their devotion, nurturing their hopes, inspiring their visions, and fueling their rhetoric" (p. 147).

tive as you might imagine. Late nineteenth and early twentieth century culture, at least in America, was already infused with imaginary recreations of biblical landscapes and the extravagant staging of biblical epics.[4]

Omitting this aspect of scriptural expression leads to misrepresenting the last five centuries of Christian history. Graham argued that whereas previously most people's knowledge of scripture would have come through aural reception and oral recitation and memorization, such modes of oral expression have more recently been displaced by textual interpretation. That may have been true in some Protestant sub-cultures in some periods, but an exclusive focus on performances of the words of texts obscured the fact that contemporary Christian culture remains infused and informed by scriptural expressions. Anecdotal evidence suggests that most Christians' knowledge of the Bible is mediated by movies, music and art as much as by reading the text for themselves. Dramatic and artistic expressions of scriptural contents as well as public readings and musical performances of scriptural texts remain primary modes by which scripture influences people. If we include these more creative forms of scriptural performance alongside textual recitation, comparative and historical accounts of the use of scriptural expressions would give a more balanced assessment of contemporary culture.

Even with such an augmentation of the kinds of expressions included in the study of scriptures as advocated by Smith and Graham, however, we were still in no better position to explain news about protests over desecrations of the Qur'an or court battles over Ten Commandments monuments. These conflicts concern neither scriptural interpretation nor expression. Something was still missing in the scholarship on scriptures, namely research on its iconicity.

Scriptures are icons. They are not just texts to be interpreted and performed. They are material objects that convey religious significance by their production, display and ritual manipulation.

In 1980, Martin Marty called attention to the Bible's role as "America's Iconic Book."[5] He argued that, more than its contents, the book itself has become a dominant symbol in the nation's mental "carapace." Other scholars have noted the iconic function of scriptures in various periods and cultures. Karel van der Toorn pointed out that, in ancient Judaism, Torah scrolls functioned ritually in the same manner as divine images did

---

4. Burke Long, *Imagining the Holy Land: Maps, Models and Fantasy Travels,* Bloomington, IN: Indiana University Press, 2003.

5. Martin Marty, 1980 centennnial address to the Society of Biblical Literature, published as "America's Iconic Book," in *Humanizing America's Iconic Book* (ed. Gene M. Tucker and Douglas A. Knight, Chico, CA: Scholars Press, 1982), 1–23.

in Babylonian religions. Rather than being the aniconic religion of modern scholars' imaginations, he argued that Judaism simply focused its iconic attention on the scrolls themselves.[6] Jacob Kinnard has documented book veneration in medieval Indian Buddhism.[7] Its practice in contemporary Japan by the Buddhist Nichiren sect, Soka Gakkai, is well known. Michelle Brown described the devotional function of Christian manuscript illustration in medieval England.[8] A survey of African-Americans' use of the Bible documented that book's widespread iconic use along with interpreting its contents.[9] Until the twenty-first century, however, there was no comparative and historical research that gathered these diverse studies into a more comprehensive analysis of the nature and function of iconic books.

The Iconic Books Project set out to provide such a broader comparative and theoretical analysis. Starting from scripture's ritual manipulation and display in Christian traditions, Dorina Miller Parmenter described the parallel to Eastern Orthodox Christians' use of images of saints (icons) and scriptures.[10] Both icons and scriptures are handled in rituals and displayed prominently, both receive veneration, and both are believed to mediate divine presence. She also analyzed the history of myths of heavenly books—divine documents in heaven that determine human destinies and dictate religious practices. Such myths have their origins as early as the Babylonian and Egyptian cultures of four thousand years ago and remain pervasive today. Parmenter argued therefore that, like Orthodox icons, iconic scriptures are not only potent religious symbols. Many people believe that they participate in heavenly exemplars of which they are the earthly manifestations.[11]

Parmenter's research laid the basis for a better understanding of the scriptures in our news headlines. Iconic scriptures clearly remain power-

---

6. Karel van der Toorn, "The Iconic Book: Analogies Between the Babylonian Cult of Images and the Veneration of the Torah," in *The Image and the Book: Iconic Cults, Aniconism and the Rise of Book Religion in Israel and the Ancient Near East* (ed. K. van der Toorn, Louven: Peeters, 1997), 229–248.

7. Jacob N. Kinnard, *Imaging Wisdom: Seeing and Knowing in the Art of Indian Buddhism*, Surrey: Curzon, 1999; "On Buddhist 'Bibliolaters': Representing and Worshiping the Book in Medieval Indian Buddhism," *The Eastern Buddhist* 34/2 (2002): 94–116.

8. Michelle Brown, *The Lindisfarne Gospels: Society, Spirituality and the Scribe*, London: British Library, 2003.

9. James M. Shopshire, Ida Rousseau Mukenge, Victoria Erickson, and Hans a Baer, "The Bible and Contemporary African American Culture II: Report on a Preliminary Ethnographic Project," in *African Americans and the Bible: Sacred Texts and Social Textures* (ed. Vincent L. Wimbush, New York: Continuum, 2003), 66–80.

10. Parmenter, "The Iconic Book," 63–92.

11. Parmenter, "The Bible as Icon," 298–310. See also Marc Drogin, *Biblioclasm: The Mythical Origins, Magic Powers, and Perishability of the Written Word*, Savage, MD: Rowman & Littlefield, 1989.

ful motivators in contemporary cultures. New research into iconic books as a trans-cultural, trans-historical phenomenon sheds interesting light on current developments (see Chapter 2).

The iconic aspect of scriptures, however, also needs to be understood in relation to scriptures' other religious and cultural functions. We need an explanatory model of scriptures with the capacity to include all of their aspects and effects.

The history of comparative studies of scriptures cautions us that this enterprise can easily become a tool for inter-religious polemic and supercessionism, rather than for inter-cultural understanding. For example, the traditional Muslim recognition of the three "religions of the books" (Judaism and Christianity, in addition to Islam) creates a polemical hierarchy of religions that is a typical strategy in all three Western traditions. The idea of scripture has been used since antiquity as a religious yardstick to measure the distance of other cultures from the epitome of divine "truth" in the Torah, the New Testament, or the Qur'an.[12]

So theorizing about the nature of scriptures easily falls prey to self-serving value judgments and colonial exploitation. Early attempts to provide more balanced comparisons between religious traditions nevertheless tended to export the Western model. Thus Max Müller's massive series of books introduced nineteenth-century Europeans to "eastern" traditions by presenting them under the title, *The Sacred Books of the East*, to raise their status by analogy with Christian scriptures. Even W. C. Smith's comparative efforts to explore the functions of scriptures produced an evolutionary hierarchy of cultural development, with the Qur'an at the pinnacle: "The Islamic instance represents the notion par excellence of Scripture as a religious phenomenon," he argued, and though the processes of scriptural development continue a thousand years later in the Adi Granth of the Sikhs and in the nineteenth-century Book of Morman, Smith maintained that "none of these instances carry our development any further."[13] Graham repeated these sentiments and also reflected a distaste for popular iconic uses of scriptures: "Certain forms of Jewish and Christian treatment of their scriptures involve not only reverence for the physical text but even magical or quasi-magical uses of it that can only be termed bibliolatry," and he went on to cite examples in many religious traditions.[14] Historical judgments have

---

12. Graham, *Beyond the Written Word*, 47.

13. Wilfred Cantwell Smith, "Scripture as Form and Concept: Their Emergence for the Western World." In *Rethinking Scripture: Essays from a Comparative Perspective*, ed. M. Levering, Albany, NY: SUNY Press, 1989. 29–57 [31, 32].

14. Graham, *Beyond the Written Word*, 52-53, 61, 196 footnotes 17-18. He later provided a much more nuanced evaluation of textual iconicity in William A. Graham, "'Winged

thus often reinforced the traditional self-congratulations of scholarly traditions (see Chapter 8).

It is therefore understandable that many scholars suspect not only the methods but also the motives behind any comparative model of scriptures. Why compare the use of scriptures in different traditions at all when doing so runs such dangers? Why not study separately each community's use of scriptures in the context of only its own religious and cultural practices?

The importance of cultural context for understanding the functions of scriptures cannot be overstated. As Graham has emphasized, "scripture" is a relational concept that can only be understood in its relationship to a specific group: "The significant 'scriptural' characteristics of a text belong not only to the text itself but also to its role in a community and in individual lives."[15] The long history of textual studies within the Western religious traditions also shows, however, the limitations of a single-culture approach, as W. C. Smith pointed out.[16] A major value of comparative study is that it can bring attention to aspects of a culture that have been ignored, or consciously suppressed, by traditional scholarship. It is the fact that our deep traditions of scholarship on scriptures are nonplussed, not by newly discovered cultures or practices, but rather by scriptural practices such as those mentioned at the beginning of this chapter that appear in the heart of contemporary Western religious traditions, that illustrates the need for a broader, comparative study of the nature and functions of scriptures.

I believe that functional models of scriptures can be developed that address this need in a responsible and even-handed manner. The purpose of any such model should be to understand better those religious traditions that are self-consciously "scriptural" and to evaluate their claims about the role of scripture within their own tradition against historical and comparative evidence both within that tradition and outside it. In order to minimize the very real dangers that attend this enterprise, a successful model of scriptures should meet three criteria. First, it should provide several non-disparaging bases or scales for comparison within and between traditions to avoid the reduction of scriptural phenomenon to a single dichotomous scale easily susceptible to polemical manipulation. Second, it should also be capable of accommodating the full range of religious expressions and uses of scriptures and resist the temptation to focus on textual interpretation

---

Words': Scriptures and Classics as Iconic Texts," in *Iconic Books and Texts* (ed. J. W. Watts, Sheffield: Equinox, 2013), 33–46.

15. Graham, "Beyond the Written Word," 5–6.

16. The case for needing comparative studies of material textuality has also been made by anthropologist Webb Keane, "On Spirit Writing: Materialities of Language and the Religious Work of Transduction," *Journal of the Royal Anthropological Institute* 19 (2013), 1–17.

just because that is easier for scholarship to understand.[17] Third, it should be able to explain in a non-hierarchical manner the relationship and distinction between scriptures and other, non-scriptural, writings and between scriptures and other, unwritten, religious traditions.

Three Dimensions

To meet these criteria, I propose a three-dimensional model of textuality to explain books' cultural functions and religious significance. The religious adoption and use of scriptures should be understood as a form of ritual. Religious communities ritualize scriptures along three different dimensions: a semantic dimension, an expressive dimension, and an iconic dimension.

By describing these aspects as *dimensions*, I mean that all three are intrinsic to books and necessary to their nature and function. Books of scripture therefore have all three dimensions, but different religious groups and individuals ritualize the three dimensions to different degrees. The model thus provides a conceptual grid for comparing the ways that religious traditions regard and use their scriptures.

By describing the dimensions in terms of *ritualizing*, the model explains the similarities and differences between scriptures and other books and writings. All books and writings exhibit semantic, expressive and iconic dimensions at least to an incipient degree. Some secular texts (such as national constitutions and theatrical scripts) are also typically ritualized along one or two of their dimensions. What distinguishes scriptures, however, is that their religious communities ritualize all three dimensions.

In what follows, I will elaborate on these claims by describing each of the three dimensions of scriptures, then exploring the processes by which each dimension is ritualized before analyzing the claims to power made by ritualizing them.

---

17. Graham noted that understanding scriptures requires taking the affective aspects of religious life into account: "seeing, hearing, and touching ... A sacred text can be read laboriously in silent study, chanted or sung in unthinking repetition, copied or illuminated in loving devotion, imaginatively depicted in art or drama, solemnly processed in ritual pagentry, or devoutly touched in hope of luck and blessing. In each instance, in very diverse and not always predictable but still very real ways, such contact with scripture can elicit in reader, hearer, onlooker, or worshiper diverse responses: a surge of joy or sorrow; a feeling of belonging or even of alienation; a sense of guidance or consolation (or the want of either); or a feeling of intimacy with or awesome distance from the divine. These kinds of religious response are important to an adequate understanding of what it means to encounter a text as scripture. Such aspects are difficult, perhaps finally impossible, for the scholar to get at in any systematic way, but to ignore them entirely is to omit a substantial portion of their reality" (*Beyond the Written Word*, 6–7). He narrowed the focus of his own book, however, to analyzing only the performative function of scriptural texts.

The *semantic dimension* of scriptures has to do with the meaning of what is written, and thus includes all aspects of interpretation and commentary as well as appeals to the text's contents in preaching and other forms of persuasive rhetoric. This dimension has always received most if not all of the attention of scholars, for the very good reason that religious traditions themselves place great emphasis on scholarly expertise in scriptural interpretation. Most religious communities with written scriptures encourage many of their devotees to gain expertise in their interpretation, not only for personal devotion but also as a means for directing community behavior and for adjudicating conflicts. Insofar as the text is understood to be divine communication, its interpretation becomes a form of divination, usually the preferred if not the only legitimate means for determining the divine will. Religious leadership therefore depends, to a degree that varies from one tradition to another, on exegetical mastery of scripture's semantic meaning.

The *expressive dimension* of scriptures has to do with mental, oral, visual and theatrical presentations of what is written.[18] As I have already mentioned, scriptural presentations come in two major modes: expressions of the words of scriptures and expressions of the contents of scriptures. Expressions of scriptural *words* include many ritualized forms of public and private reading, as well as the memorization and recitation of texts. Often the words are sung in musical genres ranging from highly prescribed chants through choral oratorios to congregational hymns. Artistic displays of scriptural quotations, such as monumental calligraphy and inscriptions, should also be included under the category of expressions of scriptural words, though these artistic examples have iconic aspects as well.

Expressions of scriptural *contents* includes dramatizations of various sorts, including simple tableaus, street performances, staged dramas, and cinema. Artistic illustrations of scenes from scriptures also belong in this category. The two modes of expression often work in tandem to expose devotees to their tradition's scriptures. They hear the text read and sung, and also see it enacted in drama and art. Nevertheless, religious leaders are more likely to dictate precisely how scriptural words are to be recited than

---

18. In the original version of this essay and in my other publications up to now, I called this the "performative" dimension, and spoke of mental, oral, visual and theatrical "performances" of scriptural contents. The word "performance," however, is overly broad and easily confused with ritual performances more generally. "Performative" also engages a wide range of theoretical considerations that I did not presuppose (for an overview, see Hans Rudolf Velten, "Performativity and Performance," in *Travelling Concepts for the Study of Culture* [ed. Ansgar Nunning and Birgit Neumann; Berlin: de Gruyter, 2012], 249–266). I aim to indicate a more limited experience of presenting a written text mentally, orally, visually and theatrically as words and images. For that idea, the "expressive dimension" is a more appropriate label.

they are to control dramatic performances and artistic illustrations. Thus the first mode of expression tends to be regulated by religious traditions more than the second. As a result, drama and art often express creative appropriations of scriptures beyond the control of religious authorities.[19]

The *iconic dimension* of scriptures finds expression in the physical form, ritual manipulation, and artistic representation of scriptures. Scriptures often take special forms that distinguish them physically from other books: e.g. hand-written and "clothed" torah scrolls, jewel-encrusted gospel books, leather-bound bibles, bark sutras with lacquered covers, illustrated Sanskrit scrolls, etc. They are often displayed prominently on podiums or tables, hung on walls, or else hidden within special cases that call attention to them while simultaneously protecting them or even hiding them from casual view (e.g. synagogue arks). The Sikh scripture, the Guru Granth Sahib, must be given its own room if it is kept in a private house—a way of simultaneously hiding and displaying the sacred text. The text of scriptures may be presented with distinctive typographies (e.g. red-letter bibles) or elaborate calligraphy (e.g. many Qur'ans), or illustrated with expensive hand-drawn illuminations. When copies of scriptures look too much like other books, their owners often find ways to give them a distinctive form anyway, such as bible covers in leather or with distinctive decorations. In these ways and many others, scriptures are often distinguished physically from others books.

They are often treated differently than other books. They are carried in religious processions, displayed to congregations, and venerated through bowing and kissing. Many traditions have rules governing how scriptures should be handled, such as requiring that they never have other books placed on top of them or that a person be in a state of ritual purity before touching them. They are also manipulated in political ceremonies—displayed or touched as part of oath ceremonies and waved in political rallies and protests. Of course, what can be venerated can also be desecrated, so books of scriptures are defiled and destroyed as a means of attacking the religious traditions they represent.

---

19. To give just two examples: the depictions of the story of the binding of Isaac (the *Aquedah*, Genesis 22) in Jewish and Christian artwork developed independently and often at variance with the exegetical traditions, and have therefore often been criticized as incorrect (see Edward Kessler, *Bound By the Bible: Jews, Christians and the Sacrifice of Isaac* [Cambridge: Cambridge University Press, 2004], 173–174). Monica Jyotsna Melanchon provided another example: Dalit women in India use biblical role playing and story telling to "enable women to release themselves from androcentric interpretive processes. ... This process of acting out the text empowers Dalit women, whom society has trained not to act or to act in certain predefined ways" (Monica Jyotsna Melanchthon, "Dalits, Bible, and Method," *SBLForum* (December 2005), online at http://www.sbl-site.org/Article. aspx?ArticleId=459 (accessed August 15, 2006).

The distinctive forms and uses of scriptures makes them potent symbols in representational art. Saints and deities hold sacred texts in the artworks of many religious traditions. The artistic association of a deity with scripture legitimizes the scripture as authentic, and the association of a human with recognized scripture legitimizes the person's spiritual status. In recent (nineteenth and twentieth century) art, scriptures and other books have increasingly been depicted alone to represent various religious traditions or truth in general. Thus in the physical forms they take, in their ritual uses, and in their symbolic representations, scriptures function as icons.

Ritualizing Books

My thesis is that scriptures are produced by ritualizing their three dimensions—semantic, expressive and iconic—but these three dimensions are not unique to scriptures. All books and other texts participate in them. The use of any written document invokes the three dimensions at an incipient level. Most users of ordinary books, however, ignore the three dimensions of these writings as trivial.

Reading any book or other writing involves interpreting its meaning if it is to be understood. Understanding texts requires using their semantic dimension. That process of interpretation, however, usually occurs automatically and receives little attention when, for example, reading a newspaper or e-mail—or this book, for that matter. Only when you become aware of your lack of understanding do you pay attention to the process of interpretation, and then only until the problem is resolved.

The same thing can be said of the expressive dimension of books and other written texts. Writing is a visual code that must be translated into spoken or mental language. Any kind of reading involves expressing the text: it requires you to translate visual letter forms into words, at least in your own mind. Again, this process usually occurs automatically unless you become aware of difficulties, such as when the typeface or hand-writing is obscure. Otherwise, the expressive dimension of books and other writings remains an unremarkable feature of the reading process.

Before you can interpret a text's meaning, you have to translate visual shapes into words, and that requires recognizing this physical object as a text. The text's physical shape, whether in the codex form of modern books or as a scroll or as a letter in an envelope, and the look of its letters or signs represent to viewers the possibility of reading its contents. The iconic dimension of books and other writings represents at its most basic level an invitation to viewers to "read me." This too is a trivial prerequisite to any act of reading. These physical signs and shapes, however, also receive various other symbolic associations, such as of education, wisdom, and truth. As a result, books *per se* play iconic roles in very many cultures.

Though these three dimensions play intrinsic roles in the use of all books and other writings, they are easily ignored when their use is unproblematic. Drawing attention to them emphasizes seemingly trivial aspects of normal reading practices. By contrast, the ways in which religious traditions use scriptures draw attention to each of the three dimensions, giving spiritual importance to what is otherwise trivial.

Jonathan Z. Smith noted that this is precisely the function of ritual.[20] Building upon observations by Sigmund Freud and Claude Lévi-Strauss, he argued that ritual calls attention to and makes intentional the ordinary practices of everyday life. "Ritual relies for its power on the fact that it is concerned with quite ordinary activities placed within an extraordinary setting, that what it describes and displays is, in principle, possible for every occurrence of these acts."[21] Thus ritual turns every-day routines such as washing yourself, entering and leaving a room, and eating meals into deeply meaningful practices by focusing attention on them, formalizing them and, often, by prescribing precisely how they get done.[22]

Applying J. Z. Smith's definition of ritual to the three dimensions of scriptures illuminates the relationship between normal books and scriptures. Scriptures are books or writings whose use in all three dimensions has been ritualized. The otherwise trivial practices involved in reading a book are, in the case of scriptures, given sustained attention. Semantic interpretation is ritualized by commentary and preaching.[23] Reading and dramatization

---

20. Jonathan Z. Smith, "The Domestication of Sacrifice," in *Violent Origins* (ed. R. G. Hamerton-Kelly, Stanford, CA: Stanford University Press, 1987), 191–235.

21. Jonathan Z. Smith, *To Take Place: Toward Theory in Ritual* (Chicago, IL: University of Chicago Press, 1987), 109.

22. Similarly Catherine Bell, *Ritual Theory and Ritual Practice* (New York: Oxford University Press, 1992), 74, 92. For a broad survey of "ritual-like" activities under the categories of formalism, traditionalism, invariance, rule-governance, sacral symbolism, and performance, see Catherine Bell, *Ritual: Perspectives and Dimensions* (New York: Oxford University Press, 1997), 138–169.

23. Many scholars, in particular, are likely to resist the notion that textual interpretation should be considered a form of ritual. But J. Z. Smith's definition of ritual as detailed attention to ordinary activities describes rather well the practices of academic interpretation. Scholarly exegesis tends to be rule-bound and require explicit location within particular traditions of interpretation, and its expression in conference papers and journal articles tend to take the form of highly formalized performances—all characteristic features of ritualized activities as described by Bell. Despite these points, discomfort at imposing the label "ritual" on scholarship will likely continue because Western culture carries a deep-seated suspicion of ritual as empty and meaningless behavior. The burden of ritual theorists over the last three decades, including Smith, Bell and many others, has been to counter this bias and insist that rituals not only convey deep and important

both become ritual performances. The book's physical form is decorated, manipulated in public and private rituals, and highlighted in artistic representations. In each case, special attention is given to otherwise routine acts of reading. Religious traditions maintain the status of their scriptures by ritualizing normal features of books and other writings.

Of course, other kinds of texts may also be ritualized in one way or another. Nations ritualize the semantic dimension of their laws and constitutions by giving their interpretation prolonged attention through court decisions and legal commentaries, and their iconic dimension through public display and reproduction (see Chapter 7). Nor is the ritualization of these dimensions limited to physical texts. Non-textual symbols and oral textual traditions may also be ritualized in similar ways. Oral epics are performed ritually in many cultures, both by recitation and by dramatization. They may also be subject to ongoing interpretive scrutiny that ritualizes their semantic as well as their expressive dimensions. Oral epics, however, have no iconic dimension because they are not physical objects. Non-textual symbols, such as a cross or a flag, are subject to ritual manipulation and display in the iconic dimension. They lack a semantic dimension, of course, though they do generate many debates over their meaning. They also have no expressive dimension because they do not encode language.[24]

Therefore it is not primarily their semantic dimension that distinguishes scriptures from oral traditions and visual symbols. Scriptures differ from oral traditions because they are physical objects and so can be ritualized as icons. They differ from non-textual visual symbols because their words can both be interpreted and expressed in highly ritualized ways. Scriptures can unite epic and totem in one and the same thing.

Only a book or other form of writing can be ritualized in all three of these dimensions. That distinguishes scriptures from other kinds of religious symbols and traditions. It does not, however, distinguish scriptures from other books and texts which, as I have noted, may be ritualized as well. However, the *more* a book or text is ritualized in *all three* dimensions, the more likely it is to be regarded as a scripture. So the functional identification of scriptures depends not on a difference in kind from other books and writings, but on the *degree* to which a particular book or writing is ritualized as text *and* as expression *and* as icon.

---

significance to their participants, but also that human culture is saturated with ritualized behaviors. So by saying that scholarly exegesis in general, and scriptural exegesis in particular, is a ritual activity, I do not mean to disparage its significance in any way.

24. The origins of writing partly in pictographs (see Chapter 6) illustrates the vexed problem of distinguishing precisely the boundary between pictorial representation and writing, but this is not an issue that I can engage here.

Dimensional Variations

Religious traditions that utilize scriptures ritualize their three dimensions to different extents. They sometimes emphasize different dimensions in ritualizing different books. For example, though you can find tendencies towards ritualizing all three dimensions of the various scriptures in Hindu traditions, these cultures usually ritualize the expressive dimension more than the others. Recitation of the Vedic hymns from memory is so privileged that it has given rise to the belief that the fundamental characteristic of these scriptures is pure sound. This observation led Graham to state,

> The unique Hindu case offers the one unassailable example of a highly developed scriptural tradition in which the importance of the oral word has been so central as to dominate and largely even to exclude the written word altogether over most of its long history.[25]

Other Hindu scriptures, however, such as the Ramayana, tend to be presented through dramatic portrayals, sometimes lasting for days or weeks on end. This contrast in expressive modes is formalized in Hindu thought by classifying scriptures into two categories: *shruti* "what is heard" (the Vedas and other Sanskrit traditions) and *smriti* "what is remembered" (myths, epics, and laws, often in vernacular languages). Since mastery of the Sanskrit Vedas has traditionally been monopolized by male Brahmins, other Hindus have used and celebrated the vernacular epics especially as their scriptures, though also employing priests who know the Vedas for special ceremonies. Popular performances of the Ramayana have been so influential that not just marginalized groups but also various political parties have appropriated their social influence.[26]

Jewish tradition provides more examples of how the three dimensions can be ritualized in different ways for separate books. The elaborate rules that govern the creation, handling and storage of a Torah scroll emphasize its iconic dimension, while great stress is also placed on proper expression of the text in public Torah readings. However, the textual authority of the Talmuds and Midrash has often overshadowed that of the Torah, and the

---

25. Graham, *Beyond the Written Word*, 66.

26. For a historical summary and analysis of the power dynamics involved in the distinction between *shruti* and *smriti*, see Holdrege, "Beyond the Guild," 147–151. The contents of the two categories of Hindu scriptures suggests that the kinds of performance given a particular scripture may, to some extent, be directed by the dominant genre of its contents. This observation applies not only to Hindu traditions: narrative genres (e.g. the Ramayana, the Gospels) tend to evoke dramatic performances and artistic portrayals of their contents, while hymnic and hortatory genres (the Vedas, the Guru Granth, the Qur'an, much of the Torah) are more likely to find expression in performances of their words through recitation, memorization, calligraphy, and the like.

prayer book (*Siddur*) has often been almost as important for oral performance as the scroll of the Torah, though the kinds of performances they receive differ markedly from each other.

Muslims tend to ritualize all three dimensions of the Qur'an. The semantic dimension receives great emphasis through interpretation and commentary, though many interpreters of Muslim practice argue that oral performance of the words of the Qur'an by recitation eclipses all other uses in importance.[27] Elaborate calligraphy of the Qur'an's text and monumental displays of its codex form, however, also elevate its iconic dimension, as do purity rules for handling it.[28] Mass protests in 2005 over its desecration show how one dimension of a scripture may occasionally receive greater emphasis for circumstantial reasons (see Chapter 5).

Sikh tradition ritualizes all three dimensions of the Guru Granth Sahib to a very high degree. Temples serve as shrines to the scripture, which is treated with the utmost respect and veneration. Recitations of its words are a prominent feature of Sikh ceremonies, which occasionally include non-stop readings of the whole text over two days. Yet consultation of the meaning of particular scripture verses also plays a key role in providing spiritual direction to individuals and communities.[29]

Protestant Christians are famous for emphasizing the meaning of scripture, by which they mean proper interpretation of the Bible's semantic contents. Conflicts with liberals over biblical interpretation and theology led to the development of Christian fundamentalism in the early twentieth century. Christians of all denominations continue to ritualize the Bible's

---

27. Thus Daniel A. Madigan asserted that "Islam is also characterized by an almost entirely oral approach to its scripture. One finds no physical book at the center of Muslim worship; nothing at all reminiscent of the crowned Torah or the embellished lectionary. On the contrary, the simple ritual and the recitation of the Qur'an that forms part of it are carried out from memory" (Daniel A. Madigan, *The Qur'an's Self Image: Writing and Authority in Islam's Scripture* [Princeton, NJ: Princeton University Press, 2001], 3). See also W. C. Smith, "Scripture as Form and Concept," 32–35, and Graham, *Beyond the Written Word*, 88–115.

28. Mahmoud M. Ayoub and Vincent J. Cornell, "Qur'an: Its Role in Muslim Practice and Life," *Encyclopedia of Religion* (2nd ed., Farmington Hills, MI: Macmillan Reference, 2005), 11: 7570–7574; Seyyed Hossein Nasr, "The Spiritual Message of Islamic Calligraphy," in *Religion, Art, and Visual Culture* (ed. S. Brent Plate. New York, Palgrave, 2002), 112–117, excerpted from S. H. Nasr, *Islamic Art and Spirituality*, Albany: State University of New York Press, 1987; and Annemarie Schimmel, "Calligraphy and Islamic Culture," in *Religion, Art, and Visual Culture*, 106–111, excerpted from A. Schimmel, *Calligraphy and Islamic Culture*, New York: New York University Press, 1984.

29. Kristina Myrvold, "Engaging with the Guru: Sikh Beliefs and Practices of Guru Granth Sahib," in *Iconic Books and Texts*, ed. J. W. Watts, Sheffield: Equinox, 2013, 261-82; Eleanor Nesbitt, "Guru Granth Sahib," *Encyclopedia of Religion* (2nd ed.; Farmington Hills, MI: Macmillan Reference, 2005), 6: 3715–18.

semantic dimension through preaching, teaching (in churches and universities), scholarship, and a vast enterprise of popular and academic publishing. They also invest heavily in ritualizing the Bible's expressive dimension, most obviously in the ever-changing forms of Christian vocal music—much of it containing biblical texts and themes. As already mentioned, dramatic performances of various kinds also feature prominently in contemporary Christian culture and frequently evoke public controversies over the interpretive authenticity of particular films (such as surrounded the release of *The Last Temptation of Christ* in 1988 and *The Passion of the Christ* in 2004). Evangelicals also ritualize the Bible's iconicity in many ways, despite Protestantism's aniconic heritage (see Chapter 8) that tends to obscure the iconic dimension from their awareness. Worshippers carry bibles to church and often in secular settings as well. In their hands, they function as badges of Christian identity, a visual role enhanced by special book covers that distinguish the scripture from secular books. Ministers carry bibles as symbols of religious authority, especially while preaching and in portraits. Gifts of bibles mark rites of passage such as baptisms, confirmations, and weddings. In recent years, Evangelical Christians have become increasingly vocal in objecting to any public slights to the Bible's iconic status in secular society.

These brief descriptions of scriptures in various traditions are very broad and superficial, because ritualizing scripture within any religious tradition varies dramatically in kind and degree from time to time and place to place. Controversies over the proper use of scriptures often distinguish rival sects in doctrine and practice. Take Buddhism, for example: the training of Buddhist monks usually emphasizes rigorous study of scriptures to understand their meaning, thus ritualizing their semantic dimension. Lay people often sponsor recitations as a means of attaining merit, thus ritualizing the expressive dimension. Several sects in various periods have made one or another sutra the object of ritual veneration, thus ritualizing its iconic dimension. On the other hand, Zen schools typically downplay the significance of scriptures in any dimension. So the explanatory value of recognizing the three dimensions of scriptures does not depend on them being ritualized to the same degree in all times and places: they are not. It rather helps explain the religious tendency towards ritualizing scriptures in all three dimensions. It also provides a means for explaining the social effects of doing so.

The Social Power of Scriptures

Publicly ritualizing each dimension of scripture exerts different kinds of social power. Private ritualization produces various kinds of effects as well. So I conclude this chapter with some preliminary observations about the effects of ritualizing the three dimensions of scriptures on social position, on the persuasiveness of scriptures and their handlers, and on inner-religious conflict.

Ritualizing the semantic dimension of scriptures in public usually supports a claim to social *authority*. In disputes over doctrine or practice, the meaning of this or that scriptural text is cited to claim divine support for one or another position. Textual interpretation is used to justify opposing positions, and is also employed to arbitrate solutions. Those who, by persuasive skill or institutional position, wield the greatest exegetical influence in determining which text should apply to this situation and how it should be understood thereby gain authority to direct the community's beliefs and practices. As a result, in traditions with written scriptures, most internal controversy has an exegetical component. Communities privilege the ritualized interpretation of their scriptures' semantic dimension as the arena in which conflicts should be aired and settled. Hence the high premium placed by scriptural traditions on scholarly mastery of textual interpretation.

Ritualizing the expressive dimension of scripture exhibits and conveys a sense of *inspiration*. Though claims for divine inspiration of scriptures are common, it is in their expression that they have an inspiring effect on an audience and, often, on the performers themselves. Inspirational expressions in public may involve recitation or dramatic display, or lavish artistic reproduction of either the texts (calligraphy) or their contents (illustration) or both. Those who claim interpretive authority often display expressive mastery as well. Preaching, though based in textual interpretation and its authority, becomes inspiring to the degree that it also expresses the text, often through a virtuosic recital of a string of textual quotations and allusions. In this way, inspiring expressions are regularly used to buttress interpretive authority. But non-clerical actors and artists frequently present performances of the contents of scriptures that inspire audiences quite apart from, or even in conflict with, the concerns of institutionally authorized interpreters.

Ritualizing the iconic dimension of scripture serves purposes of *legitimation*. Elaborate decorations of scriptures and ritual manipulations of them legitimize religious ceremonies and institutions. Thus, for example, gospel books and bibles are paraded in church processions and placed in prominent positions on altars and pulpits to represent visually the legitimate source of the community's practices and beliefs. In portraiture, scriptures in the hands of rabbis, priests, monks, sages, ministers, imams, politicians, street protestors and soldiers all attempt to legitimize the person in that position or role. The most elaborate forms and ritual uses of iconic books are often created and displayed to legitimize the powers of governments (kings, courts, legislatures, and presidents). The legitimation conveyed by scriptures is most apparent in oath ceremonies by which public officials take office through the mediation of a book of scripture. Public monuments of the Qur'an or the Ten Commandments also evoke the image of scripture to legitimize the state. Conversely, those same monuments use the state's power, money, and influence to legitimize particular religious traditions, as do priceless jeweled bindings and elaborate calligraphies lavished on state-sponsored copies of scriptures. The display and manipulation of scriptures therefore legitimizes persons and institutions by ritually connecting them with a central symbol of the religious tradition.[30]

The terms "authority," "inspiration," and "legitimacy" are, of course, inexact and their connotations overlap, especially when used to describe scriptures. My purpose in distinguishing them here is not to claim strictly demarcated functions for ritualizing the three dimensions of scriptures, but only to indicate that ritualizing the different dimensions does exert different kinds of effects. Clearly, ritualizing all three dimensions reinforces each dimension's effects with that of the others to enhance the persuasive appeal of scriptures and their handlers.

Persuasive Scriptures

The persuasive function of scriptures is another neglected topic in scholarship. Despite widespread devotional claims to the decisive influence of one or another scripture on many people's beliefs and practices, academic study of scriptures has focused on their literary forms, historical development, and doctrinal influence rather than on their rhetorical impact. In part, this omission may be due to the fact that many scriptures do not appear persuasive to a casual reader. Their language is often difficult and archaic even in vernacular translation, their literary forms can be hard for moderns to understand, and their contents frequently outrage modern sensibilities. To readers outside the religious communities that treasure a particular

---

30. Roy A. Rappaport's theory of religion emphasized the *indexical* function of rituals to demonstrate the participants' acceptance of the religious tradition, which he called the *canon*. He noted that objects manipulated in ritual may index the performer, such as offerings, or may represent the canon, such as ancient temples and churches that demonstrate the endurance of the liturgical order. Some items, such as the crowns of kings, "seem to be intermediate .... Such objects are themselves parts of the canonical order, but their manipulation is in part self-referential" (Roy A. Rappaport, *Ritual and Religion in the Making of Humanity* [Cambridge: Cambridge University Press, 1999], 145). The iconic ritualization of scriptures provides another example of objects that reference both the "canonical order" (literally, in this case) as well as indexing those who hold, touch and read them in a self-referential manner (see James W. Watts, "Scripture's Indexical Touch," in *Sensing Sacred Texts* [ed. J. W. Watts, Sheffield: Equinox, 2018],173–184).

scripture, that scripture often appears anything but persuasive. The claims of devotees that they find their scriptures enormously persuasive need to be taken seriously, however, all the more so if outsiders find the claim puzzling. What accounts for the persuasiveness of these texts? Can recognizing the three dimensions of scriptures help us understand how scriptures exert persuasive influence?

Persuasion is the traditional subject of the study of rhetoric. So noting the persuasive effects of ritualizing scriptures suggests looking to rhetoric for some analytical tools for understanding these effects. As it happens, there is an ancient model of persuasion that matches the three dimensions of scriptures described here very well. Rhetorical theory has since Aristotle recognized three different circumstances that affect the persuasiveness of speeches: the persuasiveness of the arguments—*logos*; the credibility of the speaker—*ethos*; and the feelings of the audience—*pathos*.[31] Various strategies can be used to enhance a speech's effectiveness in each of these three modes. A speech must communicate a carefully reasoned argument clearly for it to be convincing (*logos*), and for this purpose Aristotle developed the enthymemic or rhetorical proof. The argument will be more appealing, however, if the speech evokes, for example, the audience's sympathy towards a victim or outrage against injustice or fear of foreign attack (*pathos*). Yet a carefully reasoned speech that appeals to the audience's emotions may still fail to be persuasive if the speaker lacks credibility. Therefore, speakers must buttress their *ethos* by presenting an appealing demeanor, by behaving in an appropriate and attractive manner and, if possible, by carrying with them a reputation for honesty and trustworthiness. In Aristotle's words, they must demonstrate "good sense, good moral character, and goodwill."[32]

Though scriptures are not public speakers, ritualizing each of the three dimensions of scriptures enhances their persuasiveness in one of these three rhetorical modes. Ritualizing the semantic dimension through detailed interpretation and commentary emphasizes the special importance of these words and their possible meanings. Much of the burden of commentary and preaching is to show that the archaic language and antiquated ideas contained in many scriptures in fact do address contemporary concerns with realistic and appropriate ideas, instructions, and models for behavior. The endless elaborations of the interpretive tradition that produce more and ever larger commentaries by growing numbers of specialists trained in esoteric cultures and long-extinct languages further enhances the worth of scriptures. They give the impression that only texts of extreme value could

---

31. Aristotle, *Rhetoric* II.1.1–30.
32. Aristotle, *Rhetoric* II.1.9.

possibly be worth the time and expense of such elaborate scholarly enterprises. The great religious authority credited to scriptures reflects long traditions of such enhancements of their *logos*.

Ritualizing the expressive dimension through recitations, dramatic
enactments, and the like prompts feelings of inspiration in those who hear
and see them, and often in the performers as well. Through long exposure
and communal reinforcement, people associate feelings of inspiration with
the sound of a scripture's words, with the melodies to which its lines are
sung, with the sight of its most famous verses, and with the dramatic and
artistic portrayals of its stories. Ritualizing the *pathos* of scriptures in these
ways promotes the idea that scriptures not only inspire but are themselves
the products of uniquely divine kinds of inspiration. Doctrines of scriptural
inspiration develop from such emotional experiences and tend to grow in
strength over time and in the uniqueness they ascribe to scriptures.

Just as speakers portray themselves to an audience as trustworthy by
their dress and behavior, ritualizing the iconic dimension of scriptures
through their decoration, ritual manipulation, and display demonstrates
visually their *ethos* as scripture. The expense of lavish decorations portrays
the great worth of the books. The scriptures' ritual display calls attention to
them as objects to be respected and obeyed. Their ritual veneration presents
them as material manifestations of divinity. All of these practices serve to
legitimize the scriptures and, by derivation, those people connected in some
way to them. Thus scriptures' iconic status enhances their own *ethos* and
grants legitimacy by association to those in contact with them.

The rhetorical effect of ritualizing the three dimensions of scriptures
is therefore to buttress claims for their persuasiveness. Devotees of various scriptural traditions commonly attest to the persuasive power of their
scriptures. They like to tell stories of immaculate conversions, in which
people adopted their religion only because of reading its scriptures. Belief
in the persuasive power of particular scriptures has therefore prompted
movements to expose as many people as possible to them by, for example,
placing bibles in hotel rooms and broadcasting Qur'anic recitations on radio
and television.

It may seem odd to suggest that a book can be described by categories
developed for public speakers. Yet ritual emphasis on the *logos, pathos,* and
ethos of scriptures has the effect of giving them personas more like people than like artifacts.[33] For example, devotees describe receiving comfort
from the physical presence of the scriptures and from the sounds of their

---

33. George Heyman, "Canon Law and the Canon of Scripture," *Postscripts* 2 (2006/2008):
    209–225.

words just as one might be comforted by the presence and conversation of a friend. Nor is this tendency to personify the scriptures restricted to private devotions. In a number of religious traditions, personification of scriptures has been formally expressed by close identification between the scriptures and the prophet who revealed them (e.g. Moses and the Torah, Mohammed and the Qur'an). Christians go further: the opening chapter of the Gospel of John equates the word (*logos*) of God metaphysically with Jesus Christ. As a result, it is common for Christians to describe both Christ and the Bible as "the Word of God." Some Buddhist traditions venerate the wisdom (*prajña*) that leads to enlightenment in the physical form of a book. The scriptures used for this purpose all employ the term *Prajñāpāramitā*, "wisdom perfected," as part of their titles. Medieval Mahayana sculptures often depicted *Prajñāpāramitā* as a goddess.[34] Though most interpreters have considered *Prajñāpāramitā* a real mother goddess, Kinnard argued that the sculptures reflect a more metaphorical understanding of wisdom as the "mother," that is, source, of enlightenment.[35] So the feeling of being persuaded by the scriptures has generated the sense that they are more than just texts. Their ritualization produces personal effects that lead to their identification with human prophets or supernatural personalities.[36]

Scriptures, however, do not keep their persuasive effects all to themselves. They share their ritualized enhancements of *logos, ethos,* and *pathos* with those who have special status as their interpreters, guardians, and performers. Religious leaders, scholars, and politicians find their own persuasive abilities enhanced by association with scriptures. Their words gain more authority by sharing the scriptural *logos*, their public performances become more inspiring by invoking scriptures' *pathos*, and the legitimacy of their positions of leadership is reinforced by the visible presence of scriptures' iconic *ethos*.

Conflicts Over Scriptures

Ritualizing the three different dimensions of scriptures provides to religious communities a large repertoire of strategies for responding to internal and external challenges. For example, historical study of the Bible has for two centuries challenged scripture's traditional interpretation in Judaism and

---

34. Jacob N. Kinnard, *Imaging Wisdom: Seeing and Knowing in the Art of Indian Buddhism* (Surrey: Curzon, 1999), 114–175.

35. Kinnard, *Imaging Wisdom*, 127–130.

36. See Kristina Myrvold, "Making the Scripture a Person: Reinventing Death Rituals of Guru Granth Sahib in Sikhism," in *The Death of Sacred Texts: Ritual Disposal and Renovation of Texts in World Religions* (ed. K. Myrvold, London: Ashgate, 2010), 125–146 [126–128, 141–143]; and Watts, "Scripture's Indexical Touch."

Christianity. Yet the Bible's religious status within these traditions seems largely unaffected, much to the amazement of many observers. Recognizing the roles of all three dimensions of Jewish and Christian scriptures permits a more complete and complex understanding of these modern developments. The debates over the claims of historical criticism remain restricted to the Bible's semantic dimension, which is the traditional forum for controversies over scriptural authority and meaning. In fact, sustained public arguments over the meaning and interpretation of scripture are themselves ritualized behaviors, calling attention to every detail of semantic interpretation. The very vehemence of these debates and the media publicity about them ironically reinforces the impression of the Bible's importance and authority even as they challenge various traditional understandings of it.[37]

At the same time, ritualizing other dimensions of the Bible continues and has arguably even increased over the past two centuries, unaffected by the controversy. Increased liturgical use of scriptures (in Reform Judaism including greater performance of the Hebrew text), campaigns to encourage memorization of key portions, and Hollywood movie enactments of biblical stories reinforce its performative ability to inspire. Even in the academy, some philosophers, theologians and cultural critics have begun advocating a return to ostensibly more authentic practices of scriptural expression, influenced in part by the works of W. C. Smith and Graham.[38] Given the usual tendency of religious orthodoxies to exert control over verbal performance, it is not surprising that this nostalgic appeal for pre-modern reading practices has reinforced conservative trends in several fields. At the same time, the mass-marketing of inexpensive bibles and media-savvy evangelis-

---

37. On the role of biblical scholarship in maintaining the cultural status of the Bible, see Elizabeth Schussler Fiorenza, *Rhetoric and Ethic: The Politics of Biblical Studies,* Minneapolis, MN: Augsburg Fortress, 1999; and Vincent L. Wimbush, "Introduction: Reading Darkness, Reading Scriptures," in *African Americans and the Bible: Sacred Texts and Social Textures* (ed. Vincent L. Wimbush, New York: Continuum, 2003), 7–22.

38. Thus Paul Griffiths (*Religious Reading: the Place of Reading in the Practice of Religion,* Oxford: Oxford University Press, 1999) excoriated the modern academy for "consumerist" practices of reading and wished for a return to the meditative uses of scriptures by medieval monastics, the *lectio divina,* Wesley Kort (*Take, Read: Scripture, Textuality and Cultural Practice.* College Park, PA: Pennsylvania State University Press, 1996) argued for retrieving the sixteenth century Reformers' use of scripture as a lens by which to view the rest of life, Catherine Pickstock (*After Writing: The Liturgical Consummation of Philosophy,* Oxford: Blackwell Publishers, 1998) maintained that medieval reading practices offer the only solution to the quandaries of post-modern epistemology, and Shlomo Bidderman (*Scripture and Knowledge: An Essay on Religious Epistemology,* Leiden: Brill, 1995) argued that the idea of scripture should itself function as a primary category of philosophical reflection. Diana Walsh Pasulka ("Premodern Scriptures in Postmodern Times," *Postscripts* 2 [2006/2008], 293–315) demonstrated that the programs of Griffiths, Kort, and Pickstock represent a nostalgic attempt to retrieve a lost heritage.

tic campaigns have made the Protestant Bible one of the most recognizable religious symbols of Western culture. These developments have reinforced the legitimacy of this iconic scripture and also its public power to legitimate those who hold it. They shift the emphasis from its problematic semantic dimension to the Bible's expressive and iconic dimensions. This shift illustrates how public ritualization of all three dimensions of scriptures makes them resilient to controversies around any one dimension.

Individual people also ritualize the dimensions of scriptures as part of their devotional practice, as do small communities. Such private or communal uses gain power by ritualizing scriptures as well, but the effects differ in kind and degree from the effects of more public ritualizations. Scriptural texts are widely used for personal divination through methods ranging from contextual interpretation to random selection. Frequently, they are searched for esoteric meanings unknown to others. Such secret knowledge can convey personal advantage spiritually or temporally, and can also be marketed for economic gain, such as Michael Droznin's *The Bible Code* which appeared on *The New York Times* bestseller list for thirteen weeks in 1997. As to the expressive dimension, individuals frequently memorize scripture for personal spiritual benefit. Scriptural texts may also be recited as proverbs for rhetorical advantage or as spells for achieving instrumental results. The iconic dimension is manifestly ritualized when people display physical scriptures or parts of scriptures in their homes, carry them as amulets, or manipulate them to gain blessings or merit for individuals and families. In these and other ways, personal religious practice in many cultures ritualizes the three dimensions of scriptures.

Religious authorities often discourage some private uses of scriptures while trying to control others. On the other hand, private use frequently circumvents, even challenges, the public ritualization of scriptures. These disputes can express conflicts between entrenched social elites and dissident individuals, minority religious groups, or other dis-empowered population groups.

Thus the iconic use of scriptures by individuals and minority groups can pose challenges to the larger religious and secular cultures. For example, many non-Muslims in both Africa and India carry and manipulate Qur'anic verses as protective amulets.[39] Such talismanic uses challenge the reli-

---

39. For examples from Africa, see Jack Goody, "The Impact of Islamic Writing on the Oral Cultures of West Africa," *Cahiers d'etudes africaines* 11 (1971): 455–466, and Michael A. Gomez, "The Preacher-Kings: W. E. B. Du Bois Revisited," in *African Americans and the Bible: Sacred Texts and Social Textures* (ed. Vincent L. Wimbush, New York: Continuum, 2003), 501–513. Information about examples from India comes from personal communication with my colleague, Ann Grodzins Gold.

gious boundaries maintained by religious and academic authorities alike. Hebrew Israelites preaching on New York City streets sometimes wear bibles strapped to their waists like swords wielded in opposition to a corrupt society.[40] In this case, the iconic books present an intentional challenge to the majority population of American society. Individuals and minority groups of various kinds can also employ the other dimensions of scriptures for self-empowerment in distinctive ways that clash with more broadly normative uses and applications.

The power dynamics surrounding books influence the politics and culture, and of course the religious practices, of very many societies in the twenty-first century. To take only my two original examples, many people wonder why the treatment of an inexpensive, mass-produced book in a military prison should prompt such outrage when the prisoners themselves live under great duress. Many also wonder why American politics and media can get fixated on the appropriate placement of a granite monument containing scriptural texts when so many more pressing issues seem to demand resolution. By appreciating how the iconic dimension of scriptures conveys legitimacy, we can better understand the religious passions and social forces aroused by such incidents (see Chapters 5 and 7).

The three dimensional model proposed here illuminates the stakes people have in these incidents, and in many other situations involving the semantic, expressive and iconic uses of books. This chapter only begins to unpack the implications of the three dimensional model for understanding how some books matter a great deal to very many people. The following chapters explore various facets of it in more detail. Nevertheless, the reality of religious practices and beliefs in the myriad of human communities that use sacred texts will always exceed the ability of any single conceptual tool to reduce it to a few principles. I advance this three dimensional model not to preclude other ways of analyzing the nature and functions of scriptures, but simply as one useful means for understanding their impact on history and contemporary affairs. The following chapters give particular attention to the effects of ritualizing the iconic dimension because it has received the least attention up to now.

---

40. Research by Marshall Mitchell is summarized by Velma Love, "The Bible and Contemporary African American Culture I," in *African Americans and the Bible: Sacred Texts and Social Textures* (ed. Vincent L. Wimbush, New York: Continuum, 2003), 49–65.

— 2 —

Iconic Books and Texts

> Having taken refuge in the Buddha, honour and respect even a tiny piece
> of broken statue representing him.... Having taken refuge in the Dharma,
> respect even a fragment of paper bearing a single syllable of the scriptures.
> Place it above your head and consider it to be the true Jewel of the Dharma.
> (Patrul Rinpoche)[1]

Reading is not the only thing people do with books. They carry, show, wave,
touch and kiss books and other texts in religious and secular rituals. Images
of books appear in works of art, commercial logos, and religious icons to
evoke connotations of learning, knowledge, wisdom and transcendence.
Such physical manipulations and visual displays ritualize books as icons.

The iconic dimension of books has not drawn much attention from scholars. In the second decade of the twenty-first century, however, there has
been a surge in published scholarship on the ritualization of iconic books
and other texts.[2] This chapter draws on these studies to describe the phenomenon of iconic books and texts. Most of these essays focused on scriptures and other sacred text which provide the most extreme examples of
iconic ritualization. As a group, these studies covered ritualized texts from
a wide range of the world's religious traditions. They also discussed the clas-
sification of such texts, the visual effects of their scripts and fonts, and the
social effects of their public and private ritualization.

---

1. Patrul Rinpoche, *The Words of My Perfect Teacher* (Padmakara Translation Group, San
   Francisco, CA: Harper Collins, 1994), 183; quoted by Cathy Cantwell, "Seeing, Touching,
   Holding, and Swallowing Tibetan Buddhist Texts," in *Sensing Sacred Texts* (ed. J. W. Watts;
   Sheffield: Equinox, 2017), note 8.

2. Twenty-two papers on the subject from three symposia and from a seminar appeared
   in the journal, *Postscripts* in 2008 and 2012, and were collected in *Iconic Books and Texts*
   (2013). Kristina Myrvold edited eight more essays in *The Death of Sacred Texts* (2010).
   Additional articles appeared in *Postscripts* in 2017 and 2018 and were reprinted as *Sensing
   Sacred Texts* (2018) and in *Miniature Books: Production, Print, and Practice*, edited by Kristina
   Myrvold and Dorina Miller Parmenter (2019).

This chapter begins by describing how texts get ritualized in the iconic dimension before summarizing current theoretical approaches to describing and categorizing iconic books. The rest of this survey describes two basic ways in which books can be ritually manipulated—by their production and reproduction and by their possession and redistribution—and the social effects of doing so.

Ritualizing Iconic Scriptures

Written texts get used to validate legal identity and economic exchanges in the form of passports, bank checks, and currency. Written texts in the form of books, journals, constitutions and creeds also legitimize universities, academic fields, nations and religions by being ritualized in one or more ways. Ritual manipulation and display calls attention to the text and to the ideas, traditions, values, institutions and people associated with it. Ritualizing the iconic dimension creates iconic books and texts.

Religious communities and individuals frequently venerate books of scripture. By "venerate," I mean they use them in rituals in exactly the same ways that they or other religious groups use non-verbal religious symbols and images. For example, scriptures get paraded as the first or central element in processions inside places of worship. During holy days, they frequently get paraded through the streets. It can be a special honor to carry the holy book in procession. People gather to observe the processions, some in the belief that by viewing the scripture, they gain a blessing for themselves. They frequently try to touch or kiss it as well. In situations of crisis due to drought or war, communities have paraded sacred books to try to bring about divine intervention in their favor. This behavior resembles exactly the ways in which communities throughout the world utilize other kinds of religious objects. Like anything else, a book or other written text can serve as the object of religious fervor and devotion.

And not just by communities. Individuals also use scriptures for personal devotion and to gain blessings. They frequently manipulate the physical book by collecting, displaying and venerating copies of scriptures in their homes, and also by carrying it or part of it on their persons. Some communities encourage individuals to use scriptural amulets, in which case people openly state the benefits they hope to gain by using them. For example, orthodox Jewish men pray with boxes (*tefillin*) bound to their foreheads and arms that contain parchment manuscripts of selected texts from the Torah, which also get placed in *mezuzahs* on the door posts of Jewish homes.[3] Other

---

3. Marianne Schleicher, "Accounts of a Dying Scroll: On Jewish Handling of Sacred Texts in Need of Restoration or Disposal," in *The Death of Sacred Texts: Ritual Disposal and Renovation of Texts in World Religions* (ed. K. Myrvold; London: Ashgate, 2010), 11–30 [17–18].

Figure 1.   Processing the Gospel in the Church of the Holy Sepulchre, Jerusalem.
Photo by Lyn Watts, used by permission.

traditions may frown on such use, yet many adherents continue to carry
scriptures with them, such as the Muslim taxi drivers who display copies of
the Qur'an on their dashboards.[4] The histories of many religious traditions
are replete with attempts to suppress the use of scriptures as amulets, histories which therefore also document the pervasiveness of these practices.
Brian Malley observed, for example, that Christians ask clergy for guidance in ritualizing the iconic dimension of scriptures only when the church
approves of such practices. Ecclesiastical disapproval, on the other hand,
leads people to use folk traditions or other professionals like charmers or
physicians to ritualize scriptures for themselves.[5] So aniconic criticism of
iconic book rituals may do little to suppress them, but drive them underground instead.

4. Natalia K. Suit, "*Muṣḥaf* and the Material Boundaries of the Qur'an," in *Iconic Books and
Texts* (ed. J. W. Watts; Sheffield: Equinox, 2013), 189–206 [203].

5. Brian Malley, "The Bible in British Folklore," in *Iconic Books and Texts* (ed. J. W. Watts;
Sheffield: Equinox, 2013), 315–347 [338].

Categorizing Icons and Books

Material scriptures thus get ritualized in recognizably similar ways in many religious traditions. What should we call this phenomenon? We could label it with nouns and adjectives related to "idol," "fetish," or "talisman." Though these terms have long and useful histories of critical development in several academic fields, they also carry pejorative connotations that reinscribe anti-ritualistic biases.[6] Modern thought is characterized by, among other things, the tendency to dismiss rituals as superfluous at best and as superstitious impediments to recognizing the truth at worst. The origins of anti-ritualism are frequently attributed to scientific or Protestant world-views. The tendency to juxtapose "empty" ritual with true belief has, however, marked Christian polemics against Jews and pagans since antiquity, just as criticisms of using texts as amulets also date back at least as early as the fourth century C.E. (Chapter 8). This attitude has been a major factor in impeding the study of iconic books and texts.

The term, "icon," also carries a very long history of polemical as well as analytical use. It is a Greek word that played an especially important role in Byzantine Christian debates over the use of images in churches (the "iconoclastic" controversies of the eighth-ninth centuries C.E.). It has reemerged in recent discussions of the culture of images. The issues that swirl around the terms "icon" and "iconic" seem more likely than these other labels to provoke insight and reflection into the social and religious function of physical texts.[7] Though the terms carry many Christian implications that have to be modified for other traditions and cultures, they name an important and understudied phenomenon that links research on "iconic" books and texts in different cultures together.

It turns out that the medieval iconoclastic controversies can provide a theoretical starting point for understanding the nature of iconic texts. In Orthodox Christian traditions, icons of Christian saints are considered material images of invisible realities. They show what cannot be seen. Dorina Miller Parmenter observed that

> How one perceives an icon depends on one's perception of the status of the material world and the efficacy of human practice in facilitating a relationship with the divine world. That is, the issue of icons is an issue of ritual.[8]

---

6. See further in Dorina Miller Parmenter, "Material Scripture," in *The Oxford Encyclopedia of the Bible and the Arts* (ed. T. Beal, Oxford: Oxford University Press, 2015), online.

7. See Bruno Latour, "What is Iconoclash?" in *Iconoclash: Beyond the Image Wars in Science, Religion, and Art* (ed. B. Latour and P. Weibel; Karlsruhe: Center for Art and Media, 2002), 16–40.

8. Parmenter, "The Iconic Book," 67.

Christians in Late Antiquity ritualized their sacred books, especially the Gospels, by displaying them on altars and processing them through churches. Their bindings frequently portrayed icons of Christ or of saints, especially the writers of the Gospels. The Gospels could be used in religious and judicial rituals just like icons to represent the presence of the living Christ.

The insight that texts like icons are material images that show invisible realities provides a starting point for theorizing iconic books.[9] Writing turns invisible and, for all practical purposes, immaterial speech into visual images on physical objects. Immaterial sounds and transcendent meanings become material things. Writing allows language to be displayed visually and manipulated physically for practical and ritual purposes.

These connotations associated with "iconic texts" have traction across multiple religions. Comparisons of texts with images as objects of veneration appear also in Buddhist and Jain traditions.[10] The leaders of religious communities have sometimes invoked the functional resemblance between religious texts and images to defend rituals involving one or the other. During the iconoclastic controversies in medieval Byzantium, defenders of icons argued that if the iconoclasts were consistent, they should destroy Gospel books as well as icons because both visually mediate an experience of the invisible Christ.[11] Polemics against book veneration among Jains were answered by arguments observing that texts are like images in that both are material objects that mediate karmic benefits.[12] These arguments from different cultures both depend on recognizing the functional resemblance between books and icons.

Cross-cultural comparisons nevertheless create a complex knot of methodological problems for anthropologists and scholars of religion. There is a long history in many imperial and colonial enterprises of categorizing religions by whether they employ scriptures (e.g. "religions of the book") or not, to the detriment of oral traditions (Chapter 1). Nevertheless, iconic books and texts present a common set of phenomena in various cultures and time periods. Juxtaposing these diverse cultural materials alongside their

---

9. Parmenter, "The Iconic Book," 87.

10. Jacob Kinnard, "It Is What It Is (Or Is It?): Further Reflections on the Buddhist Representation of Manuscripts," in *Iconic Books and Texts* (ed. by J. W. Watts; Sheffield: Equinox, 2013), 151–164 [154–157]; and Nalini Balbir, "Is a Manuscript an Object or a Living Being? Jain Views on the Life and Use of Sacred Texts," in *The Death of Sacred Texts: Ritual Disposal and Renovation of Texts in World Religions* (ed. K. Myrvold; London: Ashgate, 2010), 107–124 [117–122].

11. Parmenter, "The Iconic Book," 75–76.

12. Balbir, "Is a Manuscript an Object," 117–118, 122.

ritual, social and political contexts illuminates the significance of iconic books and texts across a wide swath of human experience.

The phrase, "iconic books," usually refers to a much broader group of texts whose authors, titles and contents are widely recognized in popular culture.[13] Timothy Beal therefore distinguished ritualized iconic scriptures from such "cultural icons," while also observing that the Bible exhibits considerable cultural as well as scriptural iconicity.[14] William Graham distinguished three categories of iconic texts: scriptures, religious classics and cultural classics.[15] He suggested that the difference between them depends on ritualization. Scriptures get ritualized by religious communities in all three textual dimensions (iconic, expressive, and semantic), while classics get ritualized in only one or two of them (see also Chapter 1). Graham argued that this functional distinction separates cultural icons from scriptures, even when describing the same book. For example, the Bible serves as a cultural icon or classic for many people who do not participate in Jewish or Christian ceremonies that ritualize this scripture in all three dimensions. The distinction between a classic and a scripture then involves how a person relates to a book, not the form or contents of the book itself, as Graham observed: "'Scripture' is not a literary genre but a religio-historical one."[16]

Many scholars distinguish only two kinds of textual uses. Marianne Schleicher distinguished hermeneutical use of scriptures from artifactual use, which for her includes physical manipulation and verbal recitation.[17] An important contribution of Schleicher's analysis is that, contrary to scholars' usual assumptions, she argued that most uses of scripture are artifactual in nature. Katharina Wilkens distinguished two literacy ideologies governing the use of sacred texts: "semantic-purist" or "somatic-iconic."[18] She observed that many people are able to switch between these views of texts easily, the way bilingual people can change languages. Wilkens' analysis

13. Deirdre C. Stam, "Talking about 'Iconic Books' in the Terminology of Book History," in *Iconic Books and Texts* (ed. J. W. Watts; Sheffield: Equinox, 2013), 47–60 [47–48].

14. Timothy Beal, "The End of the Word as We Know It: The Cultural Iconicity of the Bible in the Twilight of Print Culture," in *Iconic Books and Texts* (ed. J. W. Watts; Sheffield: Equinox, 2013), 207–224 [208–210, 222].

15. Graham, "'Winged Words'," 34–35, 44–45.

16. William A. Graham, "Scripture," *Encyclopedia of Religion*, 2nd ed. (New York: Macmillan, 2005), 12: 8194–8205 [8195].

17. Marianne Schleicher, "Artifactual and Hermeneutical Use of Scripture in Jewish Tradition," in *Jewish and Christian Scripture as Artifact and Canon* (ed. C. A. Evans and H. D. Zacharias; London: T. & T. Clark, 2009), 48–65 [49–51].

18. Katharina Wilkens, "Infusions and Fumigations—Literacy Ideologies and Therapeutic Aspects of the Qur'an," in *Sensing Sacred Texts* (ed. J. W. Watts, Sheffield: Equinox, 2018), 115–136.

provides helpful language for analyzing controversies over the material manipulation of texts, and also for understanding why many people seem unperturbed by them.

Schleicher and Wilkens have added important detail and nuance to theories of how people interact with books and other written texts. I continue to think that the iconic and expressive dimensions are sufficiently distinct both in normal reading and in their ritualization that distinguishing them adds analytical precision. Polemics about the proper use of books tend to draw sharp dichotomies, as Wilkens' analysis of literacy ideologies shows. Scholarly analysis that distinguishes three dimensions of textual ritualization is less likely to be drawn into such in-group conflicts.

Brent Plate suggested adding a fourth dimension to the analysis of written texts, an aesthetic dimension that evokes both human sense perception and art.[19] Plate noted that the iconic, expressive and semantic dimensions all involve sense perception too, but he argued that identifying an aesthetic dimension draws attention to the liminal role of the senses. Plate's aesthetic dimension then does not add a fourth step to the three-step analysis of the process of reading a text, each of which can be ritualized separately (Chapter 1), but rather calls attention to the role of aesthetic or sensory elements throughout the process of handling and reading texts.

Dorina Miller Parmenter has used affect theory to understand the feeling of protection that many people get from carrying scriptures.[20] Affect theory goes beyond sensation to consider how sensation and emotion constitute people's experiences. On that basis, Parmenter identified scriptures as "good objects" that are socially situated as powerfully effective objects.

The theories of Beal, Graham, Schleicher, Wilkens, Plate and Parmenter all point to the role of sacred texts in maintaining webs of social and ideological relationships based in sensation and affect. The rest of this chapter draws on their research and that of other participants in the Iconic Books Project to show how these relationships generate practices of reproducing and possessing books.

Claude Lévi-Strauss observed that rituals characteristically emphasize repetition and apportionment.[21] So ritualizing the expressive and semantic dimensions of texts takes the form of repeatedly reading and interpreting

---

19. S. Brent Plate, "What the Book Arts Can Teach Us About Sacred Texts: The Aesthetic Dimension of Scripture," in *Sensing Sacred Texts* (ed. J. W. Watts; Sheffield: Equinox, 2018), 5–26.

20. Dorina Miller Parmenter, "How the Bible Feels: The Christian Bible as Effective and Affective Object," in *Sensing Sacred Texts* (ed. J. W. Watts, Sheffield: Equinox, 2018), 27–38.

21. Claude Lévi-Strauss, *The Naked Man* (tr. J. and D. Weightman; New York: Harper and Row, 1981), 672.

the texts and encouraging others to take part in these activities. In ritualizing the iconic dimension of texts, repetition and apportionment take the form of reproducing texts and distributing them as prized possessions. I will summarize research on the reproduction of iconic texts and its tendency to emphasize textual transcendence before turning to the ritualized distribution and possession of books and its tendency to legitimize their owners.

Reproducing Iconic Books

Rituals can reproduce oral traditions into physical forms. For example, an oral or written text may be recited "into" other materials that are then regarded as manifestations of that scripture. Just as the Native American Haudenosaunee (Iroquois) speak their oral traditions of social relationships into beaded belts called *wampum*,[22] Sikhs and Hindus read scriptures over water that can then be drunk.[23] Some Muslims drink water into which the ink of Quranic verses has been mixed,[24] while Tibetan Buddhists eat the written texts of mantras.[25] In these material forms, adherents believe that the oral or written text can be consumed for beneficial effects, even by those who cannot read or do not understand its language.

More typically, books get reproduced by making written copies of them. Written texts, like other artifacts, can be reproduced as much as time, skill and resources allow. Some religious communities ritualize the reproduction of iconic books. Ancient rules require Jewish scribes to purify themselves and say prayers before copying a Torah scroll on the tanned skin (parchment) of a pure animal.[26] Sometimes, the scribes leave a few letters for members of the sponsoring congregation to complete so they can participate in creating the holiest object in Jewish tradition. The Dharmashastra and other texts by Shiva devotees in medieval India prescribed how to worship before and after copying texts that are intended as sacred donations.[27] Medieval

---

22. Philip R. Arnold, "Indigenous 'Texts' of Inhabiting the Land: George Washington's Wampum Belt and the Canandaigua Treaty," in *Iconic Books and Texts* (ed. J. W. Watts; Sheffield: Equinox, 2013), 361–372 [365].

23. Myrvold, "Engaging with the Guru," 270–271; Joanne Punzo Waghorne, "A Birthday Party for a Sacred Text: The Gita Jayanti and the Embodiment of God as the Book and the Book as God," in *Iconic Books and Texts* (ed. J. W. Watts, Sheffield: Equinox, 2013), 283–298 [291–293, 297]; Måns Broo, "Rites of Burial and Immersion: Hindu Ritual Practices on Disposing of Sacred Texts in Vrindavan," in *The Death of Sacred Texts: Ritual Disposal and Renovation of Texts in World Religions* (ed. K. Myrvold, London: Ashgate, 2010), 91–106 [103].

24. Wilkens, "Infusions and Fumigations," 116–121.

25. Cathy Cantwell, "Seeing, Touching, Holding, and Swallowing," 148–153.

26. Schleicher, "Accounts of a Dying Scroll," 14–15; Martin S. Jaffee, "Torah," *Encyclopedia of Religion* (2nd ed.; Farmington Hills, MI: Macmillan Reference, 2005), 13: 9230–9241.

27. Florinda De Simini, *Of Gods and Books: Ritual and Knowledge Transmission in the Manuscript*

Christian monks distinguished themselves as holy ascetics by producing elaborately decorated books of the Bible.[28] The same thing happened in China and Japan, where the calligraphic copying of Buddhist sutras continues to be a popular devotional activity today. Contemporary neo-pagan Wiccans feel obliged to write a personal Book of Shadows by hand to serve as their magic book.[29]

Manuscripts written with human blood collapse any distinction between bodily relics and books. This phenomenon has a long and deep history in Chinese Buddhism, where it was associated with gaining merit through ascetic practice.[30] Somewhat similar if secular motives prompted a Lebanese Art and Culture magazine, *Audio Kultur*, to use human blood donated by five Lebanese-Armenian artists to print its 2015 issue commemorating the anniversary of the Armenian genocide.[31] Though not written in real blood, a fifteenth-century devotional book contains rosaries and a litany written in red ink and also ten consecutive pages of painted blood drops, some showing the signs of wear due to devoted kissing of Christ's wounds.[32] The Iraqi dictator, Saddam Hussein, made an intentional effort to turn blood writing into a relic by sponsoring a Qur'an written in his own blood. *The Guardian* reported that "Over the course of two painstaking years in the late 1990s, Saddam Hussein had sat regularly with a nurse and an Islamic calligrapher; the former drawing 27 liters of his blood and the latter using it as a macabre ink to transcribe a Qur'an."[33] His opponents questioned whether it was really blood or, if blood, really from Hussein,[34] but questions about their authenticity typically surround relic cults. Once displayed in a Baghdad

Cultures of Premodern India (Berlin: De Gruyter, 2016), 81, 102–113.

28. Michelle Brown, "Images to Be Read and Words to Be Seen: The Iconic Role of the Early Medieval Book," in *Iconic Books and Texts* (ed. J. W. Watts; Sheffield: Equinox, 2013), 93–118 [103–107].

29. Shawn Loner, "Be-Witching Scripture: The Book of Shadows as Scripture within Wicca/Neo-Pagan Witchcraft," in *Iconic Books and Texts* (ed. J. W. Watts; Sheffield: Equinox, 2013), 239–258 [244–249].

30. John Kieschnick, "Blood Writing in Chinese Buddhism," *Journal of the International Association of Buddhist Studies* 23 (2000), 177–194.

31. *Audio Kultur* 12 (2015), online at http://audiokultur.com/still-here-still-bleeding/; also NPR, April 24, 2015: A Most Indelible Ink: A Magazine Printed Using Blood, by Martha Ann Overland.

32. British Library, MS Egerton 1821; see British Library, Treasures known and unknown in the British Library: Kissing Images, by John Lowden, online at http://www.bl.uk/catalogues/illuminatedmanuscripts/TourKnownC.asp (accessed January 17, 2017).

33. *Guardian*, December 19, 2010: Qur'an etched in Saddam Hussein's blood poses dilemma for Iraq leaders, by Martin Chulov.

34. *Telegraph*, July 29, 2001: Iraq builds 'Mother of all Battles' mosque in praise of Saddam, by Philip Smucker.

mosque, this Qur'an has been locked out of sight since Hussein's overthrow in 2003. This relic of a discredited regime which is also sacred scripture poses a quandary for subsequent governments of Iraq.

Scribes gain status by copying iconic texts. Medieval Buddhist and Christian monks dedicated themselves to inscribing, and often decorating, books of scripture as a form of ascetic ritual service. The beauty and fame of their books raised the prestige of their monasteries.[35] Modern publishers build and market reputations for producing quality books for particular religious traditions.[36] Of course, authors frequently assert the authority of their texts,[37] but copyists and publishers also legitimize themselves by reproducing prestigious books in authoritative form.

Fear of social and religious instability fuels many efforts to reproduce iconic text, just as it drives the formation of scriptural and cultural canons.[38] Japanese monks and laypeople in the eleventh and twelfth centuries copied and then buried elaborate sutras in the belief that Buddhist teaching (the Dharma) would be forgotten in the coming age.[39] Some professors in mid-twentieth century American universities, fearing the destruction of Western culture by totalitarian states, published the Great Books series and created college curricula based on it.[40]

More often than ritual reproduction, however, scriptures get reproduced just like any other book, distinguished only by heightened concerns for accuracy. Contrary to their reputation for cultural conservatism, religious communities have frequently welcomed technological innovations like printing and digitization because they promise greater accuracy and wider distribution of their scriptures. In the fifteenth century, Christians and Jews quickly applied Johannes Guttenberg's invention of the printing press with movable metal type to their scriptures, as did Guttenberg him-

---

35. D. Max Moerman, "The Death of the Dharma: Buddhist Sutra Burials in Early Medieval Japan," in *The Death of Sacred Texts: Ritual Disposal and Renovation of Texts in World Religions* (ed. K. Myrvold; London: Ashgate, 2010), 71–90 [77]; Brown, "Images to Be Read," 97, 104–107.

36. On Jewish publishers, see Jeremy Stolow, *Orthodox by Design: Judaism, Print Politics, and the ArtScroll Revolution*, Berkeley: University of California Press, 2010; on Wiccan, see Loner, "Be-Witching Scripture," 249.

37. For an ancient example, see Claudia V. Camp, "Possessing the Iconic Book: Ben Sira as Case Study," in *Iconic Books and Texts* (ed. J. W. Watts; Sheffield: Equinox, 2013), 389–406 [399–405].

38. Heyman, "Canon Law," 209–225.

39. Moerman, "Death of the Dharma," 79–90.

40. Karl Ivan Solibakke, "The Pride and Prejudice of the Western World: Canonic Memory, Great Books and Archive Fever," in *Iconic Books and Texts* (ed. J. W. Watts; Sheffield: Equinox, 2013), 347–360.

self. In the nineteenth century, Muslims and Sikhs embraced the invention of lithographic printing, which is better suited than metal type for reproducing the Arabic and Gurmukhi scripts of their scriptures. They established social institutions for producing standardized editions and for monitoring the work of printers.[41] In the twenty-first century, Jewish scribes check the accuracy of their manuscripts with the aid of digital scanners.[42]

Printing scriptures has a much older history in Buddhist cultures. Sutras were printed with carved wooden blocks already in eighth-century Tibet. Koreans built printing presses using movable metal type in the fourteenth century, one hundred years before Guttenberg. These examples show that other goals can motivate printing activities than just a wish for wider distribution of texts. In Buddhist tradition, reproducing a sacred text earns merit quite apart from reading it. So sutras have been inscribed or printed for patrons who cannot read them,[43] sometimes for immediate burial.[44] Some Tibetan monks printed sutras on water.[45] In fact, ceremonial display and deposit have motivated much text production almost since the origins of writing. Ancient Near Eastern kings sponsored the copying and deposit of myths in temples to commemorate their piety before the gods (Chapter 6). Ritual and social display also motivated many early modern European buyers of Bibles, despite the rhetoric of Christian reformers urging semantic study and comprehension of scripture.

Religious emphasis on reproducing scriptures has resulted in ever increasing numbers of copies. That was already the case in medieval manuscript cultures in Europe, in the Middle East, and in Asia.[46] It has accelerated with every advance in textual reproduction technology.[47] Scripture reproduction has been fueled by the participation of people who are not religious

---

41. Myrvold, "Making the Scripture a Person," 132–133; Suit, "*Muṣḥaf* and the Material Boundaries," 197–198; Jonas Svensson, "Relating, Revering, and Removing: Muslim Views on the Use, Power, and Disposal of Divine Words," in *The Death of Sacred Texts: Ritual Disposal and Renovation of Texts in World Religions* (ed. K. Myrvold; London: Ashgate, 2010), 31–54 [35].

42. Schleicher, "Accounts of a Dying Scroll," 19.

43. Miriam Levering, "Scripture and its Reception: A Buddhist Case," in *Rethinking Scripture: Essays from a Comparative Perspective* (ed. M. Levering; Albany: SUNY Press, 1989), 58–101 [74]; Yohan Yoo, "Possession and Repetition: Ways in which Korean Lay Buddhists Appropriate Scriptures," in *Iconic Books and Texts* (ed. J. W. Watts; Sheffield: Equinox, 2013), 299–313 [304–305].

44. Moerman, "The Death of the Dharma," 79–90.

45. Kurtis Schaeffer, *The Culture of the Book in Tibet* (New York: Columbia University Press, 2009), 147.

46. Brown, "Images to Be Read," 93–118; Moerman, "The Death of the Dharma," 79–90.

47. Beal, "The End of the Word as We Know It," 207–224.

professionals. Lay people sponsored the production of Jain manuscripts for the use of monks.[48] Wealthy Buddhists sponsored, and often copied themselves, sutras to bury so as to preserve the Dharma.[49] Christian businessmen in the nineteenth and twentieth centuries funded Bible Societies to publish and distribute inexpensive bibles.[50]

Efforts to represent iconicly the extreme value and distinctiveness of scriptures result in expensive copies distinguished by their elaborate script, decorations, materials and/or bindings.[51] If manuscript cultures excelled at producing scriptures with beautifully executed and decorated calligraphy, modern technological cultures excel at producing scriptures in exotic and expensive materials. The latter include Qur'ans inscribed in 24-carot gold plate and space-age amulets inscribed by lasers with the microscopic text of an entire Qur'an, Bible or Gita.[52]

In a few communities, the manuscript form of the scriptures continues in ritual use (e.g. Jewish scrolls) and distinguishes them materially and visually from mass-produced books. In most religious traditions, mechanical printing has replaced older methods for reproducing scriptures. To compensate, their fonts, page layouts, and bindings usually take distinctive forms that make them immediately recognizable as scripture—the double-column layouts and leather bindings of many bibles, the elaborate Arabic script and geometric cover decorations of many Qur'ans, the oblong lay-out and lacquered covers of many sutras, and so on.

In recent decades, however, American publishers have been producing bibles that look like other books and even like magazines. This commercial strategy for selling bibles in a saturated market may be undermining the Bible's status as a cultural icon of singular religious authority.[53] This trend manifests the ideals of modern typography which aims to make fonts so transparently readable as to become invisible, so that readers pay attention only to the semantic meaning of the text. Brent Plate noted that this ideal reproduces the modern tendency to dichotomize word and image, mind

---

48. Balbir, "Is a Manuscript an Object," 107–124.

49. Moerman, "The Death of the Dharma," 79–90.

50. Beal, "The End of the Word as We Know It," 207–224.

51. Brown, "Images to Be Read," 93–118; Parmenter, "The Iconic Book," 63–92; Moerman, "The Death of the Dharma," 79–90.

52. See the *Iconic Books Blog,* June 1, 2007: "Tiny Books," https://iconicbooks.blogspot.com/2007/06/tiny-books.html, and June 25, 2007: "Golden Qur'an at Pushkin Museum," https://iconicbooks.blogspot.com/2007/06/golden-quran-at-pushkin-museum.html.

53. Beal, "The End of the Word as We Know It," 211; idem, *The Rise and Fall of the Bible: The Unexpected History of an Accidental Book* (New York: Houghton Mifflin Harcourt, 2011), 129. Beal therefore pointed out that, contrary to common opinion, printing did not lead to greater standardization.

and body, and privilege the former in each case.[54] It builds on older roots in Protestant anti-ritualism.

Different social contexts play a role in shaping how iconic ritualization interacts with technological innovation. The religious pluralism of modern Korea, like sectarian American Protestantism, provides little effective resistance to corporate profiteering.[55] Arabic-speaking Muslims, by contrast, utilize mass production and distribution technologies to produce a standard edition of the Qur'an (the King Fu'ad edition) under the supervision of scholars from Al-Azhar University in Cairo.[56] Sikhs also established an organization that has, over the course of half a century, increasingly monopolized the production and distribution of the Guru Granth Sahib.[57] Christian societies have attempted such monopolies in the past: Oxford and Cambridge Universities and the "King's Printer" held exclusive licenses to publish bibles in England from the sixteenth to the eighteenth centuries. There has, then, been widespread concern that commercial publishing interests may undermine the iconicity of scripture.

Devotees of most religions try to distinguish the physical form of their scriptures. American Protestants, for example, continue to buy bibles in stereotypical leather bindings in large quantities. They also counter publishers' tendency to make bibles look like other books by putting them in decorative book covers to distinguish them. Even anti-ritualistic attempts to counter the iconicity of scriptures can end up reinforcing it instead: the functional expedient of repairing tattered bibles with duct tape has quickly turned the "duct-tape Bible" into a symbol of spiritual achievement.[58] Mass publishing has heightened concern about scripture disposal among religious groups that have not historically been worried about the issue.[59] So the ritual iconicity of scriptures can generate powerful resistance to the fragmenting effects of commodification.[60]

---

54. S. Brent Plate, "Looking at Words: the Iconicity of the Page," in *Iconic Books and Texts* (ed. J. W. Watts; Sheffield: Equinox, 2013), 119–133 [121].

55. Yoo, "Possession and Repetition," 299–313.

56. Suit, "*Muṣḥaf* and the Material Boundaries," 198.

57. Myrvold, "Making the Scripture a Person," 132–133.

58. Dorina Miller Parmenter, "Iconic Books from Below: The Christian Bible and the Discourse of Duct Tape," in *Iconic Books and Texts* (ed. J. W. Watts, Sheffield: Equinox, 2013), 225–238 [229].

59. On Muslims, see Svensson, "Relating, Revering, and Removing," 48; on Christians, see Dorina Miller Parmenter, "A Fitting Ceremony: Christian Concerns for Bible Disposal," in *The Death of Sacred Texts: Ritual Disposal and Renovation of Texts in World Religions* (ed. Kristina Myrvold; London: Ashgate, 2010), 55–70 [59–66].

60. Suit, "*Muṣḥaf* and the Material Boundaries," 201.

Transcendence by Textual Reproduction

Books are physical objects that appear to contain ideas, values and authority that we otherwise associate only with persons. Books encapsulate a human tendency to dichotomize mental vs. physical, mind vs. body, spirit vs. flesh, transcendent vs. immanent, subject vs. object—dichotomies that usually privilege the first element over the second. They also encourage conceptual slippage between the book and its author or authorizing authority on the one hand, and between the book and its conceptual contents on the other. For example, our minds conflate Shakespeare with his play and with his character, Hamlet, as the source of "To be or not to be, that is the question." In the case of scriptures, where doctrines of inspiration tend to conflate author and contents (e.g. the Bible is the Word of God in that God is believed to be both author and referent, so the subject in both senses of the word), the book of scripture becomes a tangible manifestation of deity—in some traditions, the holiest thing in the world.

The research on iconic books provides many examples of conceptual slippage between a book and a person or between a book and a transcendent ideal. The essays in *Death of Sacred Texts* show that concerns for "proper" disposal of worn-out scriptures almost always lead to treating books ritually like dead human bodies, and specifically like deceased saints. Like beliefs that mortal bodies contain immortal souls, devotees describe proper burial or cremation of scriptures as destroying the book's material form but not its message.[61] Books can also be treated like living persons. The Guru Granth Sahib is the "eternal guru" that succeeded to that office after ten Sikh gurus of the sixteenth and seventeenth centuries. Sikhs treat it with all the honors due a human guru.[62] Books can also be equated with transcendent ideals, often personified in divine figures. Ancient Jewish sages identified divine wisdom with the Torah.[63] Christians applied that motif to the incarnation of Christ with the result that Christ and Gospel, both "the Word of God," became identified in ritual and art as well as in theology.[64] Buddhist art shows sutras deified in the form of a goddess that represents the essence of the Dharma.[65] Despite the Hindu emphasis on oral recitation and teach-

---

61. Myrvold, "Making the Scripture a Person," 139; and Chapter 13 above.

62. Myrvold, "Engaging with the Guru," 263–265, 272.

63. Camp, "Possessing the Iconic Book," 401.

64. Parmenter, "The Iconic Book," 72–75; idem, "A Fitting Ceremony," 64–65; Brown, "Images to Be Read," 99, 101, 110–115; Jason T. Larson, "The Gospels as Imperialized Sites of Memory in Late Ancient Christianity," in *Iconic Books and Texts* (ed. J. W. Watts; Sheffield: Equinox, 2013), 373–388 [382].

65. Jacob N. Kinnard, "On Buddhist 'Bibliolaters': Representing and Worshiping the Book

ing, medieval documents already reflected the idea that gods also manifest themselves in sacred books.[66]

Books can be consulted almost like living persons. Individuals frequently manipulate the semantic text of scriptures in material ways for purposes of divination. The most common method of "bibliomancy" involves opening the book at random and taking the first sentence that one sees as indicative of one's fortune or of God's will. Sikhs present petitions to the Guru Granth Sahib and understand them to be answered in this way.[67] Brian Malley chronicled Christian "Bible dipping" in British folklore and among contemporary American evangelicals, which he contrasted with "normal" contextual reading.[68] But reading in literary context is not normal for traditional biblical interpretation. Religious authorities juxtapose verses from the entire scripture to establish an "orthodox" context of meaning. Bibliomancy differs simply by replacing trust in human experts with trust in supernatural intervention. Both approaches, however, constitute divination from literarily decontextualized verses of scripture.

Divine worship often revolves around a physical book as well as scripture reading and interpretation. Nineteenth-century Americans created home altars around large family bibles.[69] Korean marketers today recommend that the Golden Heart Sutra be enshrined as a household god.[70] Ancient Buddhist art depicts sutras being venerated on altars.[71] Recent years have witnessed increasing Hindu ritual devotion to the Bhagavad Gita as representing the god Krishna and as itself a goddess.[72]

Thus many religious communities understand their books of scripture as material manifestations of deity. For Jews, Sikhs and, arguably, many Protestant Christians, it is the only material object that regularly manifests God. Medieval Byzantine theologians maintained that both scriptures and

---

in Medieval Indian Buddhism," *The Eastern Buddhist* 34/2 (2002): 94–116; Kinnard, "It Is What It Is (Or Is It?)," 155–157.

66. C. MacKenzie Brown, "Purāṇa as Scripture: From Sound to Image of the Holy Word in the Hindu Tradition," *History of Religions* 26/1 (1986): 68–86 [81–82]; Broo "Rites of Burial and Immersion," 94; De Simini, *Of Gods and Books*, 215.

67. Myrvold, "Engaging with the Guru," 273–274.

68. Malley, "The Bible in British Folklore," 332–337; and idem, *How the Bible Works: An Anthropological Study of Evangelical Biblicism* (Walnut Creek, CA: AltaMira, 2004), 101–103.

69. Colleen McDannell, *The Christian Home in Victorian America, 1840-1900* (Bloomington: Indiana University Press, 1994), 83–85.

70. Yoo, "Possession and Repetition," 310.

71. Kinnard, "It Is What It Is (Or Is It?)," 157–161.

72. Waghorne, "Birthday Party for a Sacred Text," 284, 296–297.

icons provide visual mediation of invisible spiritual realities.[73] Sikhs regard the divine revelation that was originally embodied in human gurus being transferred into the book, the Guru Granth Sahib.[74] Since antiquity, some Christians and Jews have regarded giving up their gospels, bibles or torahs as tantamount to rejecting God and therefore as apostasy.[75]

This tendency to treat books of scripture as manifestations of deity takes intellectual form in myths about heavenly books. Ancient Mesopotamian and Egyptian literature already described the gods wielding tablets or scrolls that determine divine and human fates. Winning control of these texts grants the power to rule the universe.[76] Jewish tradition teaches that God first created the Torah and then created the universe on the basis of the Torah. God continues to study Torah every day.[77] Muslim and Hindu traditions emphasize that the sound of the recited Qur'an or Vedas express deity.[78] Mahayana Buddhist traditions explicitly equate scripture (the sutra) and its message (the Dharma) with its messenger (the Buddha) and deity.[79]

These myths of origin bring to mind stories of how religious icons were formed either by the gods or on the basis of models revealed by the gods.[80] Like holy images, myths of a book's divine origins often get reinforced by stories of the book's miraculous preservation. For example, medieval stories demonstrated the legitimacy of Christian doctrine by showing orthodox books miraculously unscathed by falling into fire or water.[81] Reproducing and protecting a sacred text then imitates God's creation and preservation of this holy object.

---

73. Parmenter, "The Iconic Book," 86–87; Brown, "Images to Be Read," 108–110.

74. Myrvold, "Engaging with the Guru," 272, 278.

75. Larson, "Gospels as Imperialized Sites of Memory," 382; 1 Maccabees 1:57, 63.

76. Parmenter, "The Bible as Icon," 63–92; and Chapter 6 below.

77. Zeev Elitzur, "Between the Textual and the Visual: Borderlines in Late Antique Book Iconicity," in *Iconic Books and Texts* (ed. J. W. Watts, Sheffield: Equinox, 2013), 135–150 [142]; Karel van der Toorn, "The Iconic Book: Analogies Between the Babylonian Cult of Images and the Veneration of the Torah," in *The Image and the Book: Iconic Cults, Aniconism and the Rise of Book Religion in Israel and the Ancient Near East* (ed. K. van der Toorn; Louven: Peeters, 1997), 229–248 [245–247].

78. Graham, "Winged Words," 41–43; Svensson, "Relating, Revering, and Removing," 33.

79. Kinnard, "It Is What It Is (Or Is It?)," 151–152; Graham, "Winged Words," 43.

80. Van der Toorn, "The Iconic Book," 247.

81. Claudia Rapp, "Holy Texts, Holy Men and Holy Scribes: Aspects of Scriptural Holiness in Late Antiquity," in *The Early Christian Book* (ed. W. E. Klingshirn, and Linda Safran; Washington: Catholic University of America Press, 2007), 194–222 [199–200]; Parmenter, "The Iconic Book," 83–84.

Possessing Iconic Books

Whether religious or secular, iconic books convey social legitimacy to their owners. Many people believe that simply having a scripture in one's possession conveys spiritual advantage and protection. Yohan Yoo documented how possession of sutras and sutra verses is as important as their oral or written repetition for many Buddhists. A Korean dynasty in the eleventh century sponsored the carving of the entire Buddhist canon, the Tripitaka, on 80,000 wooden print blocks. The goal was not to print paper copies, but rather to gain merit and divine protection by owning such a grand set of scriptures. Contemporary Koreans also try to gain merit by owning and gifting expensive sets of sutras or gilded sutras, and by carrying sutra verses engraved on their jewelry and clothing.[82] Malley assembled references in British folklore to bibles or bible verses being used to protect houses and babies, heal illnesses, banish ghosts and conduct exorcisms. In many cases, people used the physical presence of the book or written verse rather than its meaning to invoke protective power.[83] Sometimes, the reputation of a book's power becomes so great that access to it gets limited. A Jain manuscript was shown briefly to select individuals as an auspicious sight (*darshan*) that did not allow touching or reading.[84] Biblical books copied by venerated Irish saints were locked in sealed book shrines where no one could even see their elaborate decorations, much less read them.[85]

Some Christians have treated certain copies of scriptures like sacred relics. Saintly medieval scribes were buried with their books so both could be venerated in the tomb. Conversely, the books of certain scribes were believed to carry the same miraculous powers as relics of that saint's body.[86] Buddhists have taken the analogy between books and relics much further. The early Buddhist tradition of building sacred sites (stupas) around relics of the Buddha's body was transformed by Mahayana schools that built stupas around sacred texts (sutras) instead. They argued that the books embody the Buddha just as do bodily relics. In this way, new schools of thought gained legitimacy not only for new sacred sites but also for new books of scripture that extended and modified the Buddha's teachings.[87]

---

82. Yoo, "Possession and Repetition," 307, 310.

83. Malley, "The Bible in British Folklore," 317.

84. Balbir, "Is a Manuscript an Object," 117.

85. Brown, "Images to Be Read," 110–114; Parmenter, "The Iconic Books," 81–84.

86. Brown, "Images to Be Read," 110–114.

87. Kinnard, "It Is What It Is (Or Is It?)," 152; Will Tuladhar-Douglas, "Writing and the Rise of Mahayana Buddhism," in *Die Textualisierung der Religion* (ed. Joachim Schaper; Tübingen: Mohr Siebeck, 2009), 250–272 [259].

The belief that books of scripture are holy manifests itself frequently in efforts to protect them from pollution. Many people avoid putting a book of scripture on the ground or carrying it into the bathroom. They purify themselves before touching it. Concerns for preserving the purity of a book of scripture appear commonly among Muslims, Jews, Buddhists, Jains, and Hindus (though some Hindus regard the written text itself as polluting the pure form of the scripture which is oral).[88] Such concerns for scripture's purity can also be found among Christians, despite their tradition's ambivalence about purity rituals.[89]

Jews often show particular concern for any text that contains the name of God in Hebrew, because the divine name sanctifies the text containing it.[90] Early Christian manuscripts also abbreviated the divine names out of respect, and such *nomina sacra* became favorite subjects for elaborate illumination.[91] Christianity's unusual predilection for translating its scripture, however, has undermined the association of particular letter forms with sacrality. Nevertheless, a book of scriptures in all these traditions frequently "forces its user to be attentive to its tangible form," as Natalia Suit wrote of the Qur'an.[92]

The preservation and storage of books therefore ritualizes their iconic dimension just as much as reproducing them does. Books can become powerful sites of cultural memory. Jason Larson observed that when a book changes its place in collective memory, its "physical housing" changes too.[93] This change may involve its physical form, such as when the Christianizing Roman Empire assigned imperial scribes to produce the Bible in a single (pandect) volume with decorated covers.[94] It certainly involves its inclusion or exclusion from document archives that are built to preserve corporate memory and identity. Sometimes eschatology rather than politics fuels these concerns, such as among medieval Buddhists and Jains who feared that their teachings would be forgotten.[95] Libraries have therefore been characteristic features of monasteries and other religious buildings of many religious traditions across Eurasia since antiquity. Legendary stories of the

---

88. See Broo, "Rites of Burial and Immersion," 91, 98.

89. Parmenter, "A Fitting Ceremony," 55–70.

90. Schleicher, "Accounts of a Dying Scroll," 17–18; Watts, "Scripture's Indexical Touch," 179; cf. Parmenter, "A Fitting Ceremony," 64.

91. Brown, "Images to Be Read," 99.

92. Suit, "*Muṣḥaf* and the Material Boundaries," 202.

93. Larson, "Gospels as Imperialized Sites of Memory," 375.

94. Larson, "Gospels as Imperialized Sites of Memory," 383–384.

95. Moerman, "Death of the Dharma," 72–90; Balbir, "Is a Manuscript an Object," 108–111.

destruction of ancient Chinese and Egyptian libraries continue to fuel fears of losing the books that contain the heritage of religions and cultures.[96]

Legitimation from Possessing Iconic Books

Ritualized possession of an iconic book uses a text's prestige to legitimize its owner, whether that owner is an individual, a community, a tradition or an institution. Ritualizing a book's iconic dimension legitimizes the authority of its semantic contents, or at least the ideas that are believed to constitute its contents. Even an anti-hierarchical and individualistic tradition like Wicca has found the need to codify some rules and ideas in its iconic Book of Shadows.[97] Many other religious communities express antipathy against independent readers of a scripture who challenge its orthodox interpretation. For example, the Sikhs' ascription of highest authority to the "living" Guru Granth in the place of all human gurus creates resistance towards any religious leader who asserts independent authority.[98] In such cases, possessing the scripture has become more than physical ownership. By claiming a scripture as their own, communities and individuals assert the right to determine its meaning and on that basis to judge each other's orthodoxy.[99] Iconic books then come to "serve as icons of orthodoxy," in the words of Patrick Graham.[100] Carrying them on one's person and in portraits claims association with inspired authority and shows one's learning, piety, and orthodoxy.[101]

It is not surprising, therefore, that the stereotypical images of certain books have come to represent entire religious traditions as much as any other symbols. The Torah scroll, the black leather-bound Bible, the geometrically embossed Qur'an, and the lacquer-bound sutra all function as widely recognized religious symbols, especially in the era of the internet icon. This metonymic tendency to equate a religion with its book of scripture appeared already in internal and external depictions of Judaism in the second century B.C.E. and of Christianity by the third century C.E.[102] Ninth- and tenth-century C.E. sculptures employ scenes of book worship to

---

96. Solibakke, "Pride and Prejudice," 347–360; and see Chapter 10 below.

97. Loner, "Be-Witching Scripture," 247.

98. Myrvold, "Engaging with the Guru," 261–262, 279.

99. Camp, "Possessing the Iconic Book," 392–393.

100. M. Patrick Graham, "The Tell-Tale Iconic Book," in *Iconic Books and Texts* (ed. J. W. Watts; Sheffield: Equinox, 2013), 165–186 [172].

101. For Christian examples, see Graham, "The Tell-Tale Iconic Book," 177, 183, and Brown, "Images to Be Read," 101–102; for Hindu, see Broo, "Rites of Burial and Immersion," 94–95.

102. 1 Maccabees 1; Larson, "Gospels as Imperialized Sites of Memory," 382–383.

Figure 2. Rotating book case with which Buddhists can rotate many sutras at once. In the Museum of Buddhist Art, Seoul, Korea.

represent "the entire Buddhist tradition," as Jacob Kinnard observed.[103] The global dominance in recent centuries of Western culture and of media technology has encouraged this development even in traditions that emphasize oral traditions and performance. Thus Hindus increasingly identify the Gita as a unifying symbol of their religion.[104] A stereotypical magic book represents witches to Wiccans and to the wider culture.[105] Modern nations also employ iconic texts as emblems of national identity. For example, American political movements regularly reproduce "We the People" in the iconic calligraphy of the U.S. Constitution to assert the people's common interests. Conversely, monuments of the Ten Commandments get installed on U.S.

103. Kinnard, "It Is What It Is (Or Is It?)," 159.

104. Waghorne, "A Birthday Party for a Sacred Text," 286.

105. Loner, "Be-Witching Scripture," 252.

public lands and then removed by court order in a divisive contest to assert or deny the nation's religious identity as Judeo-Christian (Chapter 7).

Despite these uses of iconic texts by powerful institutions and parties, ritualizing their iconic dimension also offers individuals without expert training the opportunity to use scriptures for their own benefit. As Suit put it, the ready availability of printed copies of the Qur'an "makes a democracy of spiritual grace possible" to Muslims who display them in their cars or shop windows,[106] just like Christians who display bibles or bible verses to bless their families and their homes.[107] Those who cannot understand a scripture's words nevertheless receive its benefits by drinking water sanctified by Sikhs reading it aloud,[108] or by turning prayer wheels containing verses of Buddhist sutras,[109] or by buying expensive copies of sutras and displaying them in their homes.[110] Though modern prejudice associates such practices with traditional, even medieval, superstitions, modern printing technology has in fact made scriptures inexpensive and more readily available for such use. Sound recording technology has also distributed scriptural performances much more widely by, for example, making sutra recitations by Buddhist monks available cheaply.[111]

Like all rituals, ritualizing a scripture's iconic dimension frequently has different meanings to different participants. Sometimes, the same practices persist despite changes in doctrinal understandings, such as the contradictory motives and doctrinal drift in the history of Japanese sutra burials.[112] Sometimes conflicts between individuals and religious or secular authorities over the meaning of scripture possession, and therefore over who may possess an iconic text, burst into public disputes. Lawsuits have been filed over whether individuals or only synagogues may own Torah scrolls and to force private owners to yield ancient manuscripts to national museums and libraries (Chapter 3). Because lay people can most easily ritualize a scripture's iconic dimension, lay people tend to be most concerned about the misuse of material scriptures resulting in their accidental defilement or intentional desecration. The legitimacy they gain by possessing and venerating a scripture is threatened by its physical misuse (Chapter 5).

---

106. Suit, "*Muṣḥaf* and the Material Boundaries," 203.

107. Malley, "The Bible in British Folklore," 325–326; Parmenter, "The Iconic Book," 84.

108. Myrvold, "Engaging with the Guru," 271.

109. Tuladhar-Douglas, "Writing and the Rise Mahayana," 364–367.

110. Yoo, "Possession and Repetition," 309–310.

111. Yoo, "Possession and Repetition," 309.

112. Moerman, "Death of the Dharma," 86.

The Social Effects of Iconic Ritualization

Most of the essays referenced here focus on religious scriptures, which undoubtedly provide the most extreme examples of ritualizing books' iconic dimension. Many other books, however, also get ritualized iconicly (Chapter 10). Special editions of classics in collector bindings appeal to buyers who wish to display them. Digital technology enables wider access to the visual appearance of iconic books just as much as it facilitates access to their semantic contents (Chapter 4). Governments utilize their political and economic resources to gain or retain possession of nationalistic books and documents. They collect not only political documents, such as original or old copies of the Magna Carta and the Declaration of Independence, but also literary and religious works considered vital to national identity (Chapter 3). Mandates to preserve cultural heritage dictate the expensive collection and storage practices of academic and government libraries. Many people grow anxious at the prospect of trashing worn-out books of literary or intellectual significance, regardless of the availability of other copies. Public book burnings arouse horrified reactions imprinted by memories of twentieth-century totalitarianism.

Scholarly experts, by contrast, whether they be scribes, clergy, lawyers or professors, gain authority from ritualizing the semantic dimension of texts through interpretation, preaching, commentary, and debate. Their rhetoric therefore celebrates scribal achievements. Nevertheless, experts also benefit from the legitimacy generated by iconic ritualization. Not only does it legitimize them in their role as expert interpreters of iconic texts. Iconic ritualization can also generate new forms of semantic interpretation. For example, the increasing iconicity of the Torah in ancient Judaism led rabbis to develop interpretations on the basis of spelling conventions and the shapes of Hebrew letters.[113] Book myths that narrate the incarnation of a divine attribute in the material form of a book justify writing commentaries and paraphrases that domesticate the scripture as a scholar's possession.[114] They also motivate efforts to establish and enforce the canonical limits of scriptures and to standardize their texts.[115]

Ritualizing a scripture's iconic dimension can also impact its expressive dimension, and vice-versa. Suit observed old Qur'an manuscripts in archaic script being treated with remarkably little reverence by librarians in Cairo.

113. Elitzur, "Between the Textual and the Visual," 138–142.

114. Camp, "Possessing the Iconic Book," 399, 404.

115. In addition to the well-known Jewish, Christian, and Muslim histories of canonization, see Myrvold ("Engaging with the Guru," 264–265) for Sikh and Loner ("Be-Witching Scripture," 251) for Wiccan examples.

She wondered if the fact that they were no longer used to perform recitations led to them being regarded with less reverence.[116] A text's relic status can also be undermined by a lack of iconic veneration. Though libraries preserve books and so ritualize their material form in one way, librarians tend to be trained primarily to encourage reading. In modern secular cultures, iconic care and display is the function of museums. So old books do not receive as much aesthetic attention as old art.[117] Suit noted that the old manuscripts were later moved to a museum display where their artistry can be better appreciated, though they are less accessible to readers. Artists now draw attention to the aesthetics of books by creating various kinds of book art.[118]

Iconic ritualization frequently interferes with reading by making the text inaccessible to most people (in a synagogue ark, in a Gospel shrine, in a museum display where only a small part of a book can be shown at any one time) or by making its proper use so encumbered with rituals as to be impractical (because of purity restrictions or display requirements or the size and shape of the book itself). Some religious communities address this problem by producing scriptures in several different forms of greater and lesser sanctity. For example, Jewish scriptures get reproduced according to ancient rules as manuscript scrolls, of which the Torah scroll is the most sacred, which are stored in synagogue arks for use in community worship.[119] But the same biblical texts get printed in codex form together with commentaries and translations as the *Tanak*, or the Pentateuch alone as a *chumash*, which individuals can own and use for personal study. The Guru Granth Sahib printed in pandect form, often of massive size, gets venerated by Sikhs as the living and only guru of the community. But multi-volume editions, *sanchis*, have less sanctity and can be employed privately.[120] Traditionally, Hindus categorized their scriptures as either *sruti*, oral and restricted to Brahmins, or *smrti*, written and widely published.[121] Modern printing and scholarship has made the holiest vedas widely available, however, while raising some *smrti*, especially the Bhagavad Gita, to equal or even

---

116. Suit, "*Muṣḥaf* and the Material Boundaries," 194.

117. David Ganz, "Touching Books, Touching Art: Tactile Dimensions of Sacred Books in the Medieval West," in *Sensing Sacred Texts* (ed. J. W. Watts; Sheffield: Equinox, 2018), 84–86.

118. Plate, "What the Book Arts Can Teach Us," 5–26.

119. Schleicher, "Accounts of a Dying Scroll," 18–19; idem, "Engaging all the Senses: On Multi-sensory Stimulation in the Process of Making and Inaugurating a Torah Scroll," in *Sensing Sacred Texts* (ed. J. W. Watts; Sheffield: Equinox, 2018), 39–56.

120. Myrvold, "Engaging with the Guru," 268, 274–275.

121. Broo, "Rites of Burial and Immersion," 93.

higher status.[122] On the other hand, while Muslims and Christians may give some verses and chapters of their scriptures more attention than others, they do not distinguish particular forms of scripture as more sacred than other forms.

These studies and examples show that recognizing the iconic dimension of written texts and how it gets ritualized should play an essential part in describing the motives and methods for writing, publishing, marketing, buying, handling, displaying and storing books in any literate culture in the world. The physical form and visual appearance of written texts have been ritualized to create iconic books and texts for more than four thousand years. Writing continues to legitimize people, institutions, academic disciplines, nations and religions. Though the forms of ritualization change constantly due to cultural and technological developments, there is every reason to think that humans are continuing to utilize and ritualize the iconic dimension of books and other texts as much as they ever have before.

---

122. Waghorne, "Birthday Party for a Sacred Text," 293–294.

Relic Texts

An early Psalter written in Ireland, and long thought to be that written by St Columba's own hand ... gained its name, the Cathach of Columcille, from the fact that its hereditary keepers carried it, enshrined, before them into battle to ensure divine favour, as their Armenian precursors were wont to do and recalling the Byzantine practice of bearing the *palladium*, an icon of the Virgin, before their imperial hosts. The scriptural book itself had become one of the most powerful of intercessory icons.[1]

In Chapter 1, I argued that religious traditions typically ritualize their scriptures in three dimensions. They ritualize the interpretation of sacred texts (the semantic dimension) with preaching, teaching, commentary, and private study. They ritualize the performance of their sacred texts (the expressive dimension) with liturgical readings, dramatic performances, artistic illustrations and private meditation. They ritualize the physical form of their sacred texts (the iconic dimension) by their elaborate manufacture, stereotypical appearance, public display and ritual manipulation. Other kinds of texts may be ritualized in one or two dimensions, but the regular ritualization of a text in all three dimensions distinguishes it as a sacred text, a scripture.

However, there are some texts or, more accurately, some specific copies of texts, that tend to be ritualized only in the iconic dimension. Though highly venerated, people do not often read them and even more rarely interpret their meaning, nor do they perform most of them verbally or dramatically. That is, they are not ritualized in either the semantic or the expressive dimensions very much. Examples of such texts include most books on prominent display in museums, such as the earliest known manuscripts of the Bible and the Qur'an, Gutenberg Bibles, Shakespeare's first folio and any valuable first edition, the autographs of the Declaration of

---

1. Brown, "Images to be Read and Words to be Seen," 111.

Independence and U.S. Constitution, and so on. Old or unusual copies of scriptures feature prominently among them, but so do political documents and works of literature.

I call such books "relic texts." Relic texts are valued for being the *specific* objects that they are. They are rare, if not one-of-a-kind, and are in theory not reproducible. Relics, as known from Christian and Buddhist traditions and many other religions, are more appropriate models for how such books function than are icons. Both icons and relics are believed to mediate the sacred. But the value of icons is that they are reproducible, whereas the value of relics lies precisely in the fact that they are unique. Of course, because the demand for relics always outstrips the supply, the (re-)production of relics has long been the subject of scandal.

Many scholars studying iconic books have observed how some books function as relics. The most pervasive employment of these practices seems to be in Mahayana Buddhism where texts are frequently placed in the foundations of stupas in place of bodily relics of the Buddha.[2] Jacob Kinnard and Max Moerman followed Gregory Schopen to argue that early Mahayana Buddhists venerated sutras as superior objects to relics.[3] The extremely revered *Lotus Sutra*, for example, requires that in

> whatever place a roll of this scripture may occupy, in all those places one is
> to erect a stupa of seven jewels. ... There is no need to even lodge a Buddha
> relic in it. What is the reason? Within it there is already a whole body of the
> Buddha.[4]

Hinduism, by contrast, downplays the significance of material books in favor of the oral performance of Vedas from memory. Yet Måns Broo was able to draw attention to at least one example of a Hindu temple site surrounded by shrines (*samādhi*) for relics that includes a book *samādhi* as well. If one disposes of sacred texts by storing them, such storage sites can themselves attract worshipers as shrines, as has happened to a cave containing thousands of worn-out Qur'ans in Pakistan.[5] Parmenter described a ritual variation on this theme: in early Christian worship, the procession of the Gospel book to the altar containing holy relics imitated a funerary procession.[6]

---

2. Moerman, "Death of the Dharma," 71; Yoo, "Possession and Repetition," 299–300; Cantwell, "Seeing, Touching, Holding," 141, 145.

3. Kinnard, "It Is What It Is (Or Is It?)," 152–153; Gregory Schopen, "The Phrase '*sa prthivipradesas caityabhuto bhavet*' in the *Vajracchediku*: Notes on the Cult of the Book in Mahayana," *Indo-Iranian Journal* 17 (1975), 147–181 [168–169].

4. Leon Hurvitz, tr., *Scripture of the Lotus Blossom of the Fine Dharma (The Lotus Sutra)* (New York: Columbia University Press, 1976), 178.

5. *Time*, October 3, 2001. Keeper of the Koran, by Alexandra Boulat.

6. Parmenter, "The Iconic Book," 70.

Many traditions regularly display bodily relics for veneration rather than or in addition to burying them in shrines. In the same way, books associated with particular saints may be displayed as relics of that saint like their bodily remains. Broo described this kind of Hindu relic book which is displayed as a relic of the saintly person who wrote, copied or owned it.[7] Jonas Svensson pointed out that copies of the Qur'an associated with famous figures in the history of Islam also receive veneration as relics.[8]

Michelle Brown described the competition between the cults of saints in early medieval Britain using elaborately illuminated books, like the Lindisfarne Gospels and the Books of Durrow and Kells.[9] In medieval Ireland, Gospel books associated with venerated saints were encased in book shrines and also displayed for the veneration of Christian pilgrims.[10] David Ganz described the Vienna Coronation Gospels as a "contact relic": medieval emperors took their coronation oaths on this gospel book to connect with the founder of the dynasty, Charlesmagne, who sponsored the production of the book.[11] Christopher de Hamel proclaimed medieval illuminated manuscripts to be "the holy relics of our own time."[12] In Chapter 10, I will discuss how museums and libraries preserve books as the relics of modern secular cultures.

Relic texts can be distinguished from other books by how they are ritualized in the three dimensions. The iconic dimension of relic texts dominates and eclipses the other two dimensions. They are not read or interpreted very much because they share their semantic and expressive dimensions with other, non-relic copies of the same texts. Their social function therefore differs from other ritualized texts. Their authority is not invoked to settle disputes over doctrine nor do people usually look to them for help in achieving inspiration. Because relic texts are ritualized in the iconic dimension alone, their chief function is legitimation. Owning them legitimizes individuals and communities and conveys a sense of empowerment. Losing them threatens group identity.

These effects have appeared prominently in many news stories about how individuals, private institutions, and government agencies have gone to great efforts to gain and to keep particular relic texts for themselves. These

---

7. Broo, "Rites of Burial and Immersion," 102.

8. Svensson, "Relating, Revering, and Removing," 34–35.

9. Brown, *The Lindisfarne Gospels*, 9–11.

10. Brown, *The Lindisfarne Gospels*, 77.

11. Ganz, "Touching Books, Touching Art," 94–95.

12. *The Guardian*, 1 October 2016: Who owned this Canterbury Psalter? by Christopher de Hamel.

stories show the similar ways that owners use their relic texts to legitimize themselves, their institutions, their nations, and their religions.

Legitimizing Owners

Relic books convey the prestige of being the owner of a famous object. For individual and institutional collectors, that prestige can be valuable, as Nate Pederson observed:

> A tip to any public libraries struggling with declining patronage: go digging around in your vault! The public library in Windsor, Ontario discovered a Bible from 1585 languishing away in its vault earlier this year. Librarians promptly put the book on display and saw a 40 percent increase in visitors last month.[13]

The same motive drives many text digitization projects. Libraries and museums put high definition images online of their most iconic books in hopes of drawing more people through their doors to see the real thing. They also offer for sale physical mementos of the relic text, ranging from cheap postcards of individual pages to expensive facsimile reproductions of the entire book (see Chapter 4).

Jonathan Z. Smith noted the effects of reproduction on the status of iconic books when he distinguished "the sacred book as a sacred object, one that is always manufactured and all but infinitely reproducible, and, therefore, one to which there is almost never attached a claim of being 'original'" from reproductions that "become themselves the subjects of narratives, as is the case, for example, of the Lindisfarne Gospels, the Stonyhurst Gospel and the cult of St. Cuthbert."[14] Reproductions therefore seem to blur the distinctiveness of relic texts, producing what Zeev Elitzur termed "pseudo-relic books."[15] However, the tension between asserting the uniqueness of objects and producing many similar things for widespread distribution has been a characteristic feature of relic economies throughout history. In his study of the circulation of medieval bodily relics, Patrick Geary described their use to extend the influence of Popes:

> The most important donor of relics was, of course, the Pope, who had at his disposal the vast treasury of the Roman catacombs, containing the remains of the early Roman martyrs. Prior to the mid-eighth century popes stead-

---

13. *Fine Books & Collections*, October 4, 2011: Bishop's Bible Brings in the Visitors, by Nate Pederson, http://www.finebooksmagazine.com/fine_books_blog/2011/10/bishops-bible-brings-in-the-visitors.phtml.

14. Jonathan Z. Smith, "Canons, Catalogues and Classics," in *Canonization and Decanonization* (ed. A. van der Kooij and K. van der Toorn; Leiden: Brill, 1998), 295–311 [298].

15. *Iconic Books Blog*. September 29, 2009: Scholem's Mechanically Reproduced Relic Zohar, by Zeev Elitzur, http://iconicbooks.blogspot.com/2009/09/scholems-mechani-cally-reproduced-relic.html.

fastly refused to distribute these relics, preferring rather to distribute secondary relics or *brandia*, objects that had come into contact with the martyrs' tombs .... From the mid-eighth century on, however, the Roman pontiffs began to exploit their inexhaustible supply of relics in order to build closer relationships with the increasingly powerful Frankish church to the north.[16]

Thus belief in the uniqueness of relics led to producing secondary relics and eventually finding ways to increase the number of apparently genuine relics available for distribution. Relic texts participate in the same kind of relic economy. It is characteristic of the use of relic texts that owners try to combine ritualized display of these unique objects with attempts to profit from sales of their reproductions. People also try to create new relic texts by making a reproduction somehow unique: hence the continual efforts to make the world's largest Qur'an or Bible, or to cast a scripture in gold plates, and so on.[17] Private owners, by contrast, often want to hide relic texts and hoard their effects for themselves. Some people regard relic texts, like other kinds of relics, as having supernatural powers that benefit their owners.

Scholars frequently ridicule such beliefs. They find the public's veneration of a text's iconic dimension problematic and complain that people should focus on the text's semantic contents instead. That normative judgment stems from the scholars' success in controlling textual authority through their own meritocratic system of semantic interpretation (see Chapter 8). But in order to gain access to relic texts owned by private persons, scholars often seek allies in institutions and governments that want the legitimacy that comes from owning certain relic texts themselves.

The different interests of individual owners, scholars and public institutions create conflicts over relic texts. For example, an international effort to preserve centuries-old Indonesian manuscripts had difficulty gaining access to privately owned texts, according to the *Jakarta Globe*:

> The surviving manuscripts were written in various languages and scripts, including Arabic, Malay, Javanese, Sundanese, Sasak, Balinese and the Wolio language of Buton Island. ... "The problem is that there are many more important ancient manuscripts in private hands," [the coordinator for digitization] said. "The owners usually refuse us access to them because they consider them sacred relics that have been handed down for generations."[18]

16. Patrick Geary, "Sacred commodities: the circulation of medieval relics," in *The Social Life of Things: Commodities in Cultural Perspective* (ed. A. Appadurai; Cambridge: Cambridge University Press, 1986), 169–191 [182–183].

17. See, for example, entries in the *Iconic Books Blog* (http://iconicbooks.blogspot.com) for June 25, 2007 (Golden Qur'an at Pushkin Museum); August 11, 2009 (Giant Wooden Qur'an); and April 9, 2012 (Giant Afghan Qur'an).

18. "Digital Age Provides Hope For Ancient Manuscripts," *Jakarta Globe*, June 26, 2009.

The Indonesian scholars only wanted to make photographs and publish them digitally. The owners, however, seem to think this would desecrate the relic texts and weaken their potency.

Such conflicts do not just occur over religious texts. The same kind of issues swirl around secular relic books. A vivid example was provided by the publication of Carl Jung's *Red Book* for the first time in 2009.[19] The famous psychoanalyst wrote and illustrated the book by hand over a sixteen-year period starting in 1914. In it, he recorded his dreams, active imaginations and self-induced hallucinations. These experiences became the basis for much of his later theorizing about myths, dreams, and the unconscious. Jung never published the book and his family refused to do so or even let very many people see it, until recently.

The Red Book's relic status derives from its impressive physical appearance and one-of-a-kind nature. Sara Corbett described the book and its publication under the headline, "The Holy Grail of the Unconscious" for which she wrote a characteristic description of a relic book: "The Red Book had an undeniable beauty. Its colors seemed almost to pulse, its writing almost to crawl."[20] The reputation of the Red Book also depends on the story of its origins, what Parmenter calls the "legends of veracity" that surround relics and relic texts alike.[21] Part of this story is the fact that Jung himself recognized the iconic power of textuality and encouraged his patients in therapy to use it too:

> I should advise you to put it all down as beautifully as you can—in some beautifully bound book. It will seem as if you were making the visions banal—but then you need to do that—then you are freed from the power of them. ... Then when these things are in some precious book you can go to the book & turn over the pages & for you it will be your church — your cathedral—the silent places of your spirit where you will find renewal. If anyone tells you that it is morbid or neurotic and you listen to them—then you will lose your soul—for in that book is your soul.[22]

In the *Red Book*, therefore, Jung intentionally created a ritualized relic text, if only for his own use. For later Jungians, its ritualization in the iconic dimension as a relic text precedes and lays the basis for its inspirational reading (expression) and semantic significance: "[Jungian analyst Stephen Martin] added 'It gives me goose bumps just thinking about it'."

19. Carl Jung, *The Red Book: Liber Novus,* ed. Sonu Shamdasani; New York: W. W. Norton, 2009.

20. Sara Corbett, "The Holy Grail of the Unconscious, *The New York Times Magazine,* September 16, 2009.

21. Parmenter, "Bible as Icon," 299.

22. Sonu Shamdasani, "Introduction," in *The Red Book,* 216.

Corbett documented how the claims of the *Red Book's* private owners and public scholarship came into conflict, as they do with other relic books the world over.

> To talk to Jung's heirs is to understand that ... [they are] caught between the opposing forces of his admirers and critics and between their own filial loyalties and history's pressing tendency to judge and rejudge its own playmakers.

The tension led to conflicting claims of ownership that ran deeper than legal title or historical claim. The article quotes Martin about the quandary faced by Jung's family and by Jung's followers, among whom he counted himself: "They own it, but they haven't lived it," he said, describing Jung's legacy. "It's very consternating for them because we all feel like we own it."

Other news about conflicts over secular relic texts includes the report that a lost poem by P. B. Shelley was rediscovered in 2010, then immediately bought and sequestered by a private collector. Michael Rosen, speaking for the interests of literary scholars, argued in *The Guardian* that this should not be allowed. "We can easily envisage an owner owning a manuscript while we collectively own and know the piece of literature it contains."[23] He was also reacting to the ongoing legal battles over Franz Kafka's papers between the heirs of the publisher's secretary who possess them and the state of Israel's claims on them. An Israeli judge's order that the papers should be publicly inventoried was hailed as "a victory for the National Library of Israel and by Kafka scholars around the world."[24] This tendency of relic texts to bring individuals, institutions and nations into conflict with each other exemplifies a typical feature of relic economies, as Geary observed:

> High-prestige objects such as relics can play an important role in deeply divided communities. Disagreements and conflicts within society may be expressed and even conducted through disputes over the identity and value of such objects.[25]

Circulating the Pieces

Dealers often treat relic books like the relics of saints. Just as the bodies of dead saints were separated into small pieces to produce the maximum number of relics which were then displayed in elaborate and often framed reli-

---

23. Michael Rosen, "Owning manuscripts is one thing: owning the contents is quite another," *Guardian,* July 23, 2010.

24. Kate Connolly, "Franz Kafka papers should be made public, Israeli judge rules," *Guardian,* July 21, 2010.

25. Geary, "Sacred Commodities," 188, citing Peter Brown, "Relics and Social Status in the Age of Gregory of Tours," in *Society and the Holy in Late Antiquity* (Berkeley: University of California Press, 1982), 222–250.

quaries, so book sellers often tear apart relic books to sell individual pages to collectors, who frame them like artwork for public display.

This practice can lead to new conflicts over ownership, identity and proper display. For example, the Getty Museum fought a legal battle to retain ownership of eight illuminated pieces of parchment from the thirteenth-century Zeyt'um Gospels. The Armenian Church claimed that the pages were stolen during the genocide of 1916 and that the Getty did not hold legal title to them. This controversy involved debates not only over the ownership of the pages but also about the ethics of separating a manuscript into multiple parts. In its defense, the Getty cited common practice:

> Elizabeth Morrison, the Getty's acting senior curator of manuscripts, said that "well-regarded ... collections around the world" contain individual manuscript sheets. "The Getty in no way condones the practice of taking apart manuscripts, but we continue to collect individual leaves after careful examination proves that they have not recently been removed ... with motives of financial gain."[26]

Morrison's argument, then, is that there are legitimate motives for taking books apart, but the pursuit of profit is not one of them. She did not mention another common motive. Libraries and museums have often disassembled valuable codices in order to display more than two pages at one time, because display, not reading, is the typical way in which relic texts get used. Once disassembled, though, they are more easily sold in pieces on the antiquities market, and are probably more valuable that way. Both for display and for profit, then, private merchants and secular institutions frequently divide codices just like religious institutions have divided and distributed bodily relics.

The Armenian Church claimed that the pages belong with the rest of the manuscript. It received scholarly support from Columba Stewart, the executive director of the Hill Museum and Manuscript Library at St. John's University in Collegeville, Minnesota. He argued that the manuscript should be reunited for reasons of art, scholarship and religious devotion. The *LA Times* quoted Stewart as saying

> "It's better from an artistic perspective ... it can [then] be studied by scholars as a whole object." [Museums must avoid] "contributing to an improper fragmentation of a work." ... Beyond that, Stewart said, the Getty ... should consider that these works are still venerated: "Here's a living, breathing religious community, as opposed to classical antiquities."

This tendency to parcel out relic texts produces other conflicts between private owners and institutionalized scholars who are trying to unify the

---

26. Mike Boehm, "The Getty Museum is in a legal fight over Armenian Bible pages," *Los Angeles Times*, November 4, 2011.

pieces. For example, an Israeli museum has been trying to collect all the fragments of the oldest complete Hebrew Bible, the Aleppo Codex. But some owners have resisted parting with their pieces. One man always carried his small fragment with him for sixty years.

> He was convinced that thanks to the parchment, which he kept with him always in a transparent plastic container, he had been saved from riots in his hometown of Aleppo during Israel's War of Independence, and he had managed to immigrate from Syria to the United States in 1968 and start a new life in Brooklyn and make a living. The charm was with him when he underwent complicated surgery.[27]

Only when he died did the fragment become available to the scholars at the Yad Ben-Zvi research institute in Jerusalem. They, however, had their own iconic interest in asking for the fragments of the Aleppo Codex to be turned over to Israel. The head of Yad Ben-Zvi said, "This is the No. 1 asset of the Jewish people, and I believe the Jewish people would do a great deal to have it back."[28]

This situation illustrates a typical conflict over relic texts that pits the interests of scholars speaking for a reified collective (in this case, "the Jewish people") against the interests of individuals (some Jews from Aleppo). The relic text serves to legitimize the collective ("the No. 1 asset of the Jewish people"), but provides individual owners a sense of empowerment (a "good luck charm"). The Armenian Church was able, however, to mobilize at least some scholars to speak for a communal claim against that of a scholarly institution. Both cases invoke scholarship that is grounded in the authority of semantic interpretation to buttress attempts to control relic texts that legitimize institutional and communal identity through their ritualized possession and iconic display.

These cases illustrate clearly the contested values that swirl around relic texts, especially those that have been partitioned and parceled out, as people are prone to do with relics. Claims of historical title mix with communal identity claims, aesthetic arguments and the interests of scholarship to contest the ownership, location, and display of relic texts.

Nationalistic Relic Texts

The case of the Aleppo Codex also highlights the national interests in controlling the legitimacy conveyed by relic texts. Many countries make such efforts because sales of ancient texts frequently raise nationalistic concerns.

---

27. "Fragment of ancient parchment from Bible given to Jerusalem scholars," *Haaretz*, November 6, 2007.

28. "Ben-Zvi institute calls for return of centuries-old Aleppo Codex fragments," *Haaretz*, December 3, 2007.

Relic books are regarded as one-of-a-kind, so they often carry significant associations with particular places or countries. The massive and elaborately illuminated "Devil's Bible" was stolen from Prague by Swedish troops in the seventeenth century. Modern Czech governments have asked in vain for its return, but celebrated its display on temporary loan in 2005.[29] In 2007, the British government imposed an export ban on the Wardington Hours, a fifteenth-century illuminated Book of Hours. It acted in order to give the British Library time to raise the money to match a German buyer's offer.[30] Similarly, when the St. Cuthbert's Gospel was put up for sale by the Jesuits in 2012, the British Library raised £9 million to acquire what it called the world's "oldest intact book," because the original binding of this seventh-century manuscript of the Gospel of John has survived.[31] The British Library intends to digitize the book so that it is available to people "everywhere" online (see Chapter 4). But its campaign to raise the money emphasizes the urgency of keeping the Gospel "for the nation" because it is "a precious part of our heritage."[32]

The political symbolism carried by relic texts can bring governments into conflict with each other. In 2009, Jordan asked Canada to seize and hold some Dead Sea Scrolls manuscripts that were being displayed in Toronto.[33] Israel took control of the scrolls after the 1967 war when it conquered east Jerusalem. The Palestinian Authority has also laid claim to the scrolls. Canada refused to seize the scrolls, deferring the issue until territorial conflicts in the Middle East are settled. Very clear in the news coverage were the identity issues at stake for the Middle Eastern governments involved (Israel, Jordan, and the Palestinian Authority). Every side tried to employ the scrolls as relic texts to legitimize their own nation and contested the others' claims to them.

> Israeli officials released a statement saying the Jordanian claims are "completely ridiculous" and that the scrolls have little or no connection to Jordan's history. ... Palestinians have argued the scrolls, dating as far back as 250 BC, are an integral part of their heritage also.[34]

The same kinds of issues swirl around an Iraqi Jewish archive consisting of 3,000 documents and 1,700 antiquities. They were found in the flooded

---

29. "Return of Devil's Bible to Prague draws crowds," AP, November 19, 2005.
30. "British Library saves manuscript," BBC, June 27, 2007.
31. See Brown, "Images to Be Read," 111–112.
32. British Library, April 16, 2012. British Library acquires the St Cuthbert Gospel – the earliest intact European book (http://www.bl.uk/press-releases/2012/april/british-library-acquires-the-st-cuthbert-gospel--the-earliest-intact-european-book).
33. "Jordan asks Canada to seize Dead Sea scrolls," *Globe and Mail*, December 31, 2009.
34. "Canada refuses to seize Dead Sea scrolls," CBC News, January 3, 2010.

basement of the Iraqi intelligence building in Baghdad after the American invasion in 2003 and transferred to the United States for preservation. In 2010, Iraq asked for them back because, according to the Iraqi ambassador, "They represent part of our history and part of our identity. There was a Jewish community in Iraq for 2,500 years."[35] But the head of an Israeli museum dedicated to Iraqi Jews argued that the materials should be sent there: "The books belong to the majority of the Iraqi Jews, and they are not in Iraq. The books should be given to us, as the representatives of the Jews of Iraq."[36] Such efforts led to headlines in the Arab press proclaiming, "Israel suspected of seeking to 'steal' ancient Iraqi manuscripts."[37] Here an archive of historical interest became a relic when it was used to represent conflicting communal and national ownership claims.

Historic political documents can be even more central to nationalistic concerns. The legitimizing effect of ritual display plays a major role in the treatment of nationalistic relic texts, such as the manuscripts of the U.S. Constitution and Declaration of Independence. Since 1952, they have been enshrined in the Rotunda of the National Archives in Washington, D.C. All copies of the Constitution and Declaration are iconic in American political culture, but the manuscripts in the Rotunda are relics: they are not displayed so that visitors can analyze their meaning in depth or read them aloud in their entirety (the ink of the Declaration, at least, is much too faded to do either very well) but for their material, visual effect alone. Asked "Why is it important for people to come here to see the declaration firsthand?", Archives senior curator Stacey Bredhoff described the effect of viewing the Declaration of Independence this way:

> I think there is some kind of magic in standing in front of the original document. You're standing in front of the original Declaration of Independence, faded as it is, but still you can make out some of the signatures and you think, "Whoa, these people were real. This really happened."[38]

Walt Disney Studios capitalized on this mystique by making the Declaration of Independence the key to finding another treasure in its 2004 film, "National Treasure," that grossed $347.5 million worldwide.

The mystique of relic texts moves historians too. The *Philadelphia Inquirer* reported the re-discovery in 2010 of a draft of the U.S. Constitution in the

---

35. Glenn Kessler, "Iraq demands return of its Jewish archive," *Washington Post*, April 30, 2010.

36. "Iraq urges U.S. to give back Iraqi Jewish Archive," AP, January 16, 2010.

37. "Israel suspected of seeking to 'steal' ancient Iraqi manuscripts transferred to U.S.," Al-Arabiya, June 4, 2012.

38. William Risser, "Viewing Declaration of Independence can be almost magical," Gannett News Service, July 17, 2007.

archives of the Historical Society of Pennsylvania.[39] The researcher, Lorianne Updike Toler, reported the thrill of discovery in vivid language:

> "This was national scripture, a piece of our Constitution's history," she said of her find in November. "It was difficult to keep my hands from trembling." As other researchers "realized what was happening, there was a sort of hushed awe that settled over the reading room," Toler said. "One of them said the hair on her arms stood on end."

When texts become so iconic, the degree of authenticity required for relic status can be negotiable. The original Declaration of Independence was printed overnight after its adoption on July 4, 1776, and distributed by the hundreds of copies in Philadelphia and throughout the colonies. Only then was the well-known manuscript now displayed in the Rotunda written and signed by the delegates when they reassembled one month later.[40] Elitzur would therefore call the displayed document of the Declaration of Independence a "pseudo-relic".

Nevertheless, relic texts linked to national history or ideals prompt political and financial efforts to preserve national ownership even if they cannot plausibly claim to be "the original." The winning bidder for the 1297 Magna Carta auctioned by Sotheby's in 2007 was motivated by the desire to keep it in the USA.

> David Rubenstein, co-founder of the Carlyle Group private equity firm, paid $21.3m (£10.6m) for the document ... [He said] "I was concerned that the only copy that was in America would escape. I was convinced that it needed to stay here. This document stands the test of time. There is nothing more important than what it represents. ... This is a gift to the American people. It is important to me that it stays in the United States."[41]

However, lest the former colonies congratulate themselves too much, Oxford's Bodleian library then indulged in what the *Guardian* characterized as "scholarly one-upmanship" by displaying all four of its copies of the Magna Carta. Three date from 1217 and one from 1225, all older than the copy auctioned in New York. (The first charter was forced on King John in 1215. It is the 1297 version, however, that remains legally influential in England.) Attempts to keep a thirteenth-century copy of the Magna Carta in the United States date back to at least the 1930s, when the outbreak of World War II stranded Lincoln Cathedral's copy across the Atlantic. Rubenstein

---

39. Edward Colimore, "Early draft of the Constitution found in Philadelphia," *Philadelphia Inquirer,* February 2, 2010.

40. U.S. National Archives and Records Administration, "The Declaration of Independence: A History," online at https://www.archives.gov/founding-docs/declaration-history (accessed October 30, 2017).

41. "Magna Carta fetches £10m in New York auction," *Guardian*, December 19, 2007.

returned his copy to the National Archives in Washington, DC, which displays it near the U.S. founding documents in the Rotunda.

Efforts to control the Aleppo Codex, the Wardington Hours, and St. Cuthbert's Gospel show that governments do not limit their interest in relic texts to legal documents. Nations ritually index their identity and obligations through various kinds of relic texts just like individuals do.

Authenticity, Identity and Scholarship

As the above examples show, relic texts legitimize the person, institution or nation that owns and claims them, rather than providing the textualized authority and inspiration that humanistic scholarship usually addresses. They can also, however, be used to legitimize the textual tradition itself. Their antiquity and/or rarity can confirm the legitimacy of mass-produced copies of the same texts. Therefore relic texts can serve both scholarly and community or institutional stakes in particular textual traditions. Scholars consult relic books to authenticate details of the text, while public viewings of them serve to legitimize the prestige that the reproducible iconic text enjoys.

Owners involve scholars in ritualizing iconic texts and in disputes over ownership because the legitimizing effect of relic texts depends on belief in their authenticity. They must be as old and important as people say they are. The problem with relics has always been verifying their authenticity. Geary described this process for any relic: "The account of the relics' translation had to itself become part of the myth of production—the story of how they had come to their new community was itself part of the explanation of who they were and what their power was."[42] This is no less true of relic texts, which "become themselves the subject of narratives" as J. Z. Smith noted.[43] And, like other relics, these textual narratives can be falsified for profit.

In 2012, Rabbi Menachem Youlus pleaded guilty to selling fake Holocaust scrolls and was sentenced to four years in prison and ordered to pay almost $1 million in restitution.[44] Despite suspicions of fraud, however, buyers continue to be motivated by a desire for the legitimation of Jewish experience exemplified by Holocaust scrolls. For example, in 2010 when questions were raised about whether a particular Torah scroll from Youlus survived the Holocaust or not, the donor provided another scroll with a better attested Holocaust lineage. The donor explained that he had donated the Torah to the synagogue "so its congregants could have the sacred experience of

---

42. Geary, "Sacred Commodities," 186.

43. Smith, "Canons, Catalogues and Classics," 298; see also Parmenter, "Bible as Icon."

44. Martha Wexler and Jeff Lunden, "Maryland rabbi who peddled fake Holocaust Torahs sentenced to four years for fraud," *Washington Post*, October 11, 2012.

reading Scripture from a scroll that had survived the Holocaust. ... As one who has gone to the camps and assimilates into my being the horror of the Holocaust, this gives meaning to Jewish survival."[45] His goal was expressive as well as iconic ritualization.

As we have already seen, the Dead Sea Scrolls are another example of contested national and religious relics. They also illustrate the distinctive scholarly treatment accorded relic books. These manuscripts dating from the third to the first centuries B.C.E. were discovered in the mid-twentieth century C.E. One quarter of them contain texts of the Hebrew Bible, the earliest biblical texts now in existence. They have been the object of intense scholarly comparison with younger biblical manuscripts in order to legitimize and correct the biblical text. The other three-quarters of the scrolls contain non-biblical and previously unknown compositions. They also have received intense scrutiny as important sources for the history and religion of Judaism in the last centuries B.C.E.

Scholarly interest has focused on interpreting the semantic dimension of the non-biblical scrolls, while the biblical scrolls are ritualized more in the iconic dimension as relic books to legitimize the biblical text. So modern culture treats some of these ancient texts as relics (iconic dimension) while using others primarily for interpretive purposes (semantic dimension). The distinction is confirmed by the display of the scrolls in the aptly named "Shrine of the Book" at the Israel Museum in Jerusalem: a biblical scroll, Isaiah, receives pride of place in the central display. The dominance of its iconic dimension for both scholars and the public confirms its status as a relic text.

The scriptures of most religious traditions presuppose an original relic text that persists only in its iconic copies. The original has long since disappeared and in most cases never existed at all, at least in a textual form resembling its current manifestations.[46] The desire to nevertheless legitimize the tradition by means of a relic original generates beliefs in its existence in heaven.[47] Thus the Torah written by God before the creation of the world, or the Qur'an that stays with Allah, or the Golden Tablets of Mormon reclaimed by angels base religious traditions on heavenly relic texts that legitimize all their earthly copies. These relic texts cannot be viewed in a museum or place of worship, but belief in their existence still serves to legitimize these scriptural traditions.

---

45. James Barron, "Two Torahs, Two Holocaust Stories and One Big Question," *The New York Times*, April 13, 2010.

46. See Beal, *Rise and Fall of the Bible.*

47. Parmenter, "Bible as Icon."

Relic texts legitimize a story about a community. People use them to identify with and place themselves in that story. This is one of the most important social functions of ritual: to demonstrate publicly one's acceptance of a tradition and one's place in a community.[48] Relic texts frequently serve as important components of such rituals.

Relic texts are therefore an exception that proves the rule about ritualizing texts in three dimensions (Chapter 1). Though they are themselves not usually subject to semantic and expressive ritualization, they owe their exceptional iconicity to the fact that other, non-relic, copies of the same text are ritualized in all three dimensions. When particular books are readily available for semantic, expressive, and iconic ritualization, a few special exemplars can be set aside to serve purely iconic purposes as relic texts. The different effects of ritualizing books in each of the dimensions helps explain the popular appeal and social function of relic texts. Since ritualizing a text's iconic dimension bestows legitimacy, people will go to great lengths and spend large sums of money to own and display a relic text. They do so in hopes of legitimizing a nation, a religion, a public institution like a museum, library or university, or just themselves.

---

48. Rappaport, *Ritual and Religion*, 118–124.

— 4 —

Iconic Digital Texts
How Rituals Materialize Virtual Texts

A man asked a sheikh whether it was permitted to bring a mobile phone with the Qur'anic verses to the bathroom.

The sheikh answered, "It is permissible because the verses are in the memory of the phone."

The man asked again, "But sheikh, we are talking about the Qur'anic verses and the most beautiful names of Allah, and you are saying that it is permitted to take them to the bathroom?"

The sheikh replied, "Have you memorized any verses from the Qur'an?"

"Yes," said the man.

"Well then," retorted the sheikh, "when you go to the bathroom, leave your head by the door and then step in."[1]

A common observation in ritual studies is that rituals call attention to material bodies and objects.[2] For example, the ritual of the Catholic Eucharist focuses attention on the handling, consuming and storing of the bread and wine. University commencement processions emphasize the order and position of people of different academic ranks and achievements. Meditation exercises urge attention to bodily posture and the rhythm of breathing. Such examples of rituals that draw attention to material, location and posture can be multiplied endlessly. Ritual theory has therefore urged interpreters of religions to pay more attention to bodies and physical experience. This emphasis has coincided with a growing interest in material objects and bodies in various humanities disciplines. The new field of book studies brings this trend into textual studies as well.[3]

---

1. A popular anecdote recounted by Natalia Suit, "Enacting 'Electronic Qur'ans': Tradition Without a Precedent," *Material Religions* web blog, 18 November 18, 2015. (https://materialreligions.blogspot.com/2015/11/enacting-electronic-qurans-tradition.html)

2. Bell, *Ritual Theory and Ritual Practice*, 93, 96–101, 107–110.

3. For a survey, see Parmenter, "Material Scriptures."

Text rituals usually involve manipulating a physical book and its visual display. Books and other texts are displayed and manipulated in various kinds of rituals that draw attention to their appearance and material form.[4] So, the typical effects of ritualization apply to texts too: ritualizing texts usually draws attention to their material form and visual appearance.

However, descriptions of digital texts and images in popular culture celebrate their "virtual" nature in contrast to physical books, as the anecdote about the Sheik and the cellphone illustrates. The dichotomy of virtual versus material also shapes the marketing strategies of publishers (e-books), the choices of foundations funding humanistic research (the "digital humanities"), and the policy decisions of research libraries (online subscriptions versus print collections). In contrast to the increasing interest in bodies and materials in humanistic research, digital culture celebrates the fantasy that people (as avatars in virtual reality) and texts (as e-books) can escape their material constraints.

I call the notion of virtual texts a fantasy because of my experience studying iconic books. Iconic books and texts have also been digitized. In fact, some of them (e.g. bibles) were among the very first texts to be widely distributed and profitably marketed in digital form. This was already the case in the mid-1990s when specialty software companies successfully marketed digital biblical texts, dictionaries and biblical commentaries.[5] Despite the apparent contrast between digital texts and iconic books, the iconic status of some texts increases the market for their digital equivalents.

Furthermore, digitization provides users of iconic texts opportunities to ritualize them in new ways in both the iconic and expressive dimensions. Most of the discussion of digitization and sacred texts has focused instead on how digitization may be changing the semantic dimension of interpretation with consequences ranging from further ignorance of literary context to deconstructing canons.[6] Ritualizing the iconic dimension especially draws attention to the material form of digital texts. The more a digital text is ritualized, the more physical and less virtual it appears. Ritualization thus demonstrates the fictional nature of "virtual" reality: every written text consists of writing on some material substrate, even if it is just light on a screen. Ritual, by drawing sustained attention to practices with texts,

---

4. E.g. Parmenter, "The Iconic Book," 160–189.

5. Logos Bible Software for DOS/Windows, founded in 1992, and Accordance for Mac/iOS, founded in 1994, still dominate this market.

6. For example, see Jeffrey S. Siker, *Liquid Scripture: The Bible in the Digital World* (Minneapolis: Fortress, 2017), and Bryan Bibb, "Readers and their E-Bibles: the Shape and Authority of the Hypertext Canon," in *The Bible in American Life* (ed. P. Goff *et al.*; New York: Oxford University Press, 2017), 256–265.

inevitably draws attention to their material forms. In doing so, it destroys the illusion that digital texts are "virtual."

I will demonstrate this thesis by examining two kinds of ritualized digital texts: those whose digitization has been used to expand or restrict the ritual uses of digitized texts and those whose digitization has permitted new ways of seeing and manipulating their original material form. These examples draw attention either to the physical nature and location of digital devices or to the physical form of the material texts that digital images reproduce.

Virtual Book Rituals

Religious communities have used digital copies of their scriptures to modify how traditional ritual actions apply to scriptures. Digital technology has also raised their interest in experimenting with new forms of textual rituals. In the process, ritualized digital texts draw people's attention to the physical media that contain the text. For example, ritual use of the iconic digital texts may lead them to draw a distinction between the screen that displays a sacred text and the hard drive that stores it, or to highlight the rotation speed of a hard drive, or to point out the electrons that power all digital devices.

Traditional rules require users to be "pure" in order to touch many sacred texts. Thus the digital reproduction of Qur'ans and Torahs on tablets and cell phones draws attention to the physical location and position of the digital devices that contain them. Muslim scholars debate whether Quranic texts on screen can be desecrated, and Orthodox Jewish rabbis debate the sanctity of digital Torahs.[7] In each case, digitized ritual texts, like physical ritual texts, raise concerns about overuse and misuse.

Natalia Suit has described the daily routines necessary to keep copies of the Qur'an and Qur'anic verses separate from human pollutions. She also observed the differences created by digital texts, for which different rules apply. Suit concluded that the different material forms of the text interact with each other in an ever-evolving way.

> The transition from print to digital has ... engendered a critical change in the ways practitioners perceive Quranic text as an integral part of the *muṣḥaf* [a physical copy of the Qur'an]. The "electronic Quran" is not a book in the ordinary sense of this word at all. It is a text mediated by the screen of a computer, an electronic device, or a mobile phone, where it shares memory space with other texts and images. An electronic device can hardly be called a *muṣḥaf*. For that reason, opinions regarding how to act towards an electronic copy of the text are considerably at odds among the practitioners and scholars alike.[8]

---

7. Brad Anderson, "Scriptures, Materiality, and the Digital Turn: The Iconicity of Sacred Texts in a Liminal Age," *Postscripts*, forthcoming.
8. Suit, "Enacting 'Electronic Qur'ans': Tradition Without a Precedent."

She then quoted the anecdote that appears at the beginning of this chapter. Its exemption of digital texts from purity concerns by comparing computer or phone memory with human memory reproduces a very old tendency to compare the contents of books with the minds of human beings. Both books and people have physical exteriors and immaterial interiors that, according to very many religious traditions, are not confined to their particular physical containers (Chapter 8). Digitization drives this analogy even further into the heavens—or, at least, into "the cloud."

Suit observed that conceiving of digital Qur'anic texts as virtual rather than material has allowed some freedom from social restrictions imposed by traditional purity rules:

> The doctrinal confusion created by the use of new technology has been successfully deployed by menstruating women to read the Quranic text in spite of having their period. For that reason, it is not uncommon among the Egyptian women to read the Quranic text from a mobile phone during that time, following the opinion that an electronic device constitutes a carrier and a barrier of the text at the same time. It is a safe barrier as it cannot be crossed -- one cannot directly touch the digital letters. In this case menstruation has no effect on the practical use of the Quranic text.[9]

Digital media is widely celebrated for making information more widely accessible. In this case, digitization allows greater access to reading the Qur'an across the ritual barriers imposed by purity practices.

Yohan Yoo collected examples that show the various ways in which contemporary Koreans appropriate the power and inspiration of a Buddhist sutra by manipulating its material and, frequently, its digital form. Buddhist temples, for example, sponsor websites that offer viewers the ability to copy sutras with their computer mice, and so earn merit over the internet.[10] Similarly, some sites popularizing Tibetan Buddhism suggest turning a computer into a "digital prayer wheel" that allows the owner to "pray with electrons you already have around the house."

> Once downloaded, your hard disk drive will spin the mantra for you. Nowadays hard disk drives spin their disks somewhere between 3600 and 7200 revolutions per minute, with a typical rate of 5400 rpm. Given those rotation speeds, you'll soon be purifying loads of negative karma.[11]

---

9. Suit, "Enacting 'Electronic Qur'ans': Tradition Without a Precedent."

10. Yoo, "Possession and Repetition," 407–418. Another kind of digital prayer wheel, manufactured by Tibet Tech, allows one to manually rotate eight stacked CD ROMs containing "84 billion prayers" (see Tibet Tech Hand-held Prayer Wheel at https://www.amazon.com/Tibet-Tech-Hand-held-Prayer-Wheel/dp/B0055ALG26, accessed April 22, 2019).

11. Deb Platt, "Click Here for Good Karma." Quoted on "Digital Prayer Wheel." http://www.dharma-haven.org/tibetan/digital-wheels.htm, accessed May 5, 2011.

This writer publicized a technical detail of computer engineering, the rotation speed of hard drives, because of its ritual significance when put to use in a traditional devotional practice.

On the other hand, the fact that digital texts reify even further the distinction between the contents of scriptures and their material forms can make people feel that digitized scriptures lack ritual meaning. Brad Anderson observed that while digitization is changing practices of reading and interpreting the semantic dimension of scriptures, ritualizing the iconic dimension continues to emphasize material texts. While some oath ceremonies have begun to use e-book readers, most oath ceremonies still use material, and often old, scriptures. News media stories about the intentional desecration of scriptures or their miraculous survival through floods or fires continue to focus on material books, not digital devices. Dorina Miller Parmenter pointed out that an American Presbyterian denomination recommends that its churches revive the practice of reading scripture during worship services from large pulpit bibles: "Using a large and dignified looking Bible more adequately conveys the weight and significance of God's Word in Christian life."[12] So Anderson concluded that while digitization has transformed the semantic study of scriptures, their iconic and expressive ritualization continues to focus on codex books.[13] Similarly, Katja Rathkow noted that Evangelical Christians often use digital texts for bible study while venerating codex bibles for commemorative and ritual purposes, often simultaneously.[14]

The same distinction is emerging in people's use of secular books. For example, *The New York Times*' tech columnist, Nick Bilton, complained after his mother's death: "Now that she was gone, all I cared about were her physical books."

> Yes, as a technology columnist, I have become acutely aware of technology's built-in expiration date. ... Technology is about the future, not the past. ... As VHS tapes turned to DVDs and later streaming services, I didn't think twice about the lost physical objects — rather, I rejoiced in their disappearance.
>
> But books, I now understand, are entirely different. ... I want her physical books. I want to be able to smell the paper, to see her handwriting inside, to know that she flipped those pages and that a piece of her lives on through them.[15]

---

12. Parmenter, "Material Scriptures," quoting David Gambrell, "Reading Scripture in Public Worship," online at https://www.presbyterianmission.org/wp-content/uploads/readingscriptureinpublicworship.pdf, accessed November 2, 2017.

13. Anderson, "Scriptures, Materiality, and the Digital Turn."

14. Katja Rakow, "The Bible in the Digital Age: Negotiating the Limits of 'Bibleness' of Different Bible Media," in *Christianity and the Limits of Materiality* (ed. Minna Opas and Anna Haapalainen; London: Bloomsbury, 2017), 101–121.

15. Nick Bilton, "In a Mother's Library, Bound in Spirit and in Print," *The New York Times*, May 13, 2015.

Bilton pointed out the close connection between sensation—the touch, smell, and sight of books—and our memories. All of these examples illustrate how digital texts are drawing renewed interest and attention to the more traditional material forms of books.

The vast physical infrastructure of the internet increasingly calls attention to itself by the amount of electrical energy it consumes, and the pollution produced by generating it.[16] The materiality of digitized texts also draws attention when it accidentally breaks down. The proliferation of digitized library collections has unintentionally called attention to the physical media of the internet by falling victim to quickly changing software and hardware technology. For example, the British Library's pioneering Turning the Pages software was first conceived in 1996 for displaying some of the collection's outstanding treasurers.[17] But the rapid churning of digital technologies made some of its books load very slowly, if at all. The software, now marketed by a private firm, was reissued in 2007 and had to be completely recoded again in 2013 to produce Version 3.0.[18] Costly investments in digitization projects thus have to be repeated every decade at least, or else the materials grow increasingly difficult to access over the internet. For example, the digitized pages of the illuminated Hunterian Psalter at the Glasgow University Library carried this warning in 2017: "Please note that these pages are from our old (pre-2010) website; the presentation of these pages may now appear outdated and may not always comply with current accessibility guidelines."[19] Digitized texts that are not supported by steady funding streams often disappear after only a few years on the internet.[20]

One of the oldest forms of textualized ritual involves the preservation of the text. Ancient inscriptions were frequently created to be buried and saved for reading by humans or deities in the future (Chapter 10). The rapidly changing internet has raised concerns that modern digital culture will quickly be lost and forgotten. The Internet Archive was founded in 1996 to build an Internet library to permanently preserve digital collections for

---

16. James Glanz, "Power, Pollution and the Internet," *The New York Times*, September 22, 2012.

17. British Library Online Gallery, http://www.bl.uk/onlinegallery/virtualbooks/viewall/index.html, accessed October 31, 2017.

18. Turning the Pages, "History," http://ttp.onlineculture.co.uk/history/, accessed October 31, 2017.

19. Glasgow University Library, http://special.lib.gla.ac.uk/exhibns/psalter/psalterindex.html, accessed October 31, 2017.

20. See note 23 below. The elaborate graphics required to digitize iconic texts often undermine efforts to archive old internet pages. Thus the Internet Archive's Wayback Machine produces only a blank page for Vasser's Papyrus of Ani.

researchers, historians, and scholars. But in 2011 it announced that it was also creating a physical archive to back-up its digital collection.

> As the Internet Archive has digitized collections and placed them on our computer disks, we have found that the digital versions have more and more in common with physical versions. The computer hard disks, while holding digital data, are still physical objects. As such we archive them as they retire after their 3–5 year lifetime. Similarly, we also archive microfilm, which was a previous generation's access format. So hard drives are just another physical format that stores information. This connection showed us that physical archiving is still an important function in a digital era.[21]

They have therefore created a facility that can keep up to ten million items in long term storage. The age-old problem of textual preservation destroys the illusion of "virtual" texts.

Virtual Book Displays

The digitization of iconic books can also draw increased attention to the look and material form of the original text. Many libraries and museums digitize the most iconic texts in their collections to present them to the wider public. Digitization in these cases allows museums to display their relic texts more fully than ever before. I do not mean just that more people may see these texts by accessing the museum's web sites. I also mean that these texts can be displayed more fully because digitization overcomes restrictions on public display imposed by the physical form of the texts themselves.

Codex books are notoriously difficult for museums and libraries to display because, by the nature of their material form, you can only show the covers or one pair of pages at any one time. Codices were designed to be held by hands and their pages to be turned by hands, and scrolls were also designed to be continuously unrolled and rolled as they are read. Neither form is well-suited for display in museum cases, and codices especially so. This creates a puzzle for how to display relic texts that are too rare or valuable to allow the public to handle them.

Digital technology provides museums and libraries with ways to overcome these restrictions on display that are imposed by the physical form of relic texts. The British Library, for example, developed its "Turning the Pages" software that allows visitors to its building or its website to "virtually" flip the pages of a variety of its "treasures," such as the ninth century

---

21. Jeff Kaplan, "Why Preserve Books? The New Physical Archive of the Internet Archive," posted on June 6, 2011 on the *Internet Archive Blog*, http://blog.archive.org/2011/06/06/why-preserve-books-the-new-physical-archive-of-the-internet-archive/, accessed October 31, 2017.

Qur'an of Sultan Baybar.[22] The preference imposed by digital screens for "scrolling" a text can be utilized in an intuitively natural way to view relic scrolls, as in the case of the digitized version of the Papyrus of Ani, a beautiful Book of the Dead from ancient Egypt.[23]

One of the most publicized projects to digitize a relic text was the Codex Sinaiticus Project.[24] This project "virtually" reunited the scattered parts of an ancient manuscript and made it available for all to see on the internet. The Sinai Codex is a fourth-century manuscript that originally contained the entire Greek (Christian) Bible. It was discovered at St. Catherine's Monastery on Mount Sinai in the nineteenth century by a German scholar, Constantin von Tischendorff. He brought back to Europe most of its pages, which preserve text of the entire New Testament and roughly half of an ancient Greek translation (the Septuagint) of the Jewish scriptures. Its readings that vary from other Greek manuscripts were collated and became important evidence for reconstructing the original text of the Greek Bible, especially the New Testament. These readings of Sinaiticus, signified by the Hebrew letter *alef* (א), have therefore been a familiar and much-cited part of the text-critical apparatus of published Greek bibles throughout the twentieth century. Though the manuscript was published in facsimile in 1911 and again later in the century, there is little need for most scholars to consult images of the text.[25] Its collation with thousands of other New Testament manuscripts provides the essential database for text-critical reconstructions. So, for more than a century and for the vast majority of modern biblical scholars, the readings of the Sinai Codex have been decontextualized, dematerialized data that does not require much direct knowledge of the appearance of the manuscript itself.

I was therefore bemused by the media hype surrounding the digital reproduction and publication of the Sinai Codex in 2009. Parts of the manuscript currently reside in four different libraries, so its digitization required a joint project between the British Library in London, the National Library of Russia in St. Petersburg, the Leipzig University Library in Germany, and St. Catherine's Monastery in Egypt. The project was funded by major government and private foundations in Britain, Germany, and Greece at a cost

---

22. British Library. Online Gallery: Most Viewed Virtual Books. http://www.bl.uk/onlinegallery/virtualbooks/viewmostviewed/index.html, accessed January 17, 2017.

23. The Papyrus of Ani. 2009. http://projects.vassar.edu/bookofthedead/, accessed October 22, 2010, unavailable after May 2, 2011.

24. Codex Sinaiticus Project. http://www.codexsinaiticus.com/en/, accessed January 17, 2017.

25. Kirsopp Lake, ed., *Codex Sinaiticus Petropolitanus: The New Testament, The Epistle of Barnabas and the Shepherd of Hermas*, Oxford: Clarendon Press, 1911. http://www.biblefacts.org/church/pdf/Codex%20Sinaiticus.pdf, accessed May 2, 2011.

of £680,000 or one million dollars.[26]

As is typical with major text digitization projects, this one described its motivation as providing unlimited accessibility to the manuscript:

> The Codex Sinaiticus Project is an international collaboration to reunite the entire manuscript in digital form and make it accessible to a *global audience* for the first time. Drawing on the *expertise* of leading scholars, conservators and curators, the Project gives *everyone* the opportunity to connect directly with this famous manuscript.[27]

Publicity about the project emphasized the value of digitization for traditional textual scholarship, but also the benefit of seeing and studying the physical form of the text:

> By bringing together the digitized pages online, the project will enable scholars worldwide to research in depth *the Greek text*, which is fully transcribed and cross-referenced, including the transcription of numerous revisions and corrections. It will also allow researchers into *the history of the book as a physical object* to examine in detail aspects of its fabric and manufacture: pages can be viewed either with standard light or with raking light which, by illuminating each page at an angle, highlights the physical texture and features of the parchment.[28]

This emphasis on the physical manuscript is illustrated by one of the most commonly reproduced images from the project, a close-up view of a page showing scar tissue from the animal whose skin was turned to parchment to receive the scriptural text.

Digitization has therefore brought new attention to the physical form and material of the Sinai Codex. In fact, it has probably brought more attention, certainly from more people, to the manuscript's physical form than it has ever received before. That is understandable in the context of this project's emphasis on public access as its primary purpose. After all, that public is for the most part not able to read Greek, especially the unpunctuated uncial Greek letters of a fourth-century imperial manuscript. Since most of them cannot read the manuscript, members of this "global audience" must instead "connect directly" with it simply by viewing it. They can admire the regularity of its lettering, note the frequency with which the text has been corrected above or below the line or in the margins, and marvel at the translucence of its parchment, which is the remaining trace of the animal

---

26. British Library, March 11, 2005. "World's oldest Bible goes global: Historic international digitisation project announced." http://pressandpolicy.bl.uk/Press-Releases/World-s-oldest-Bible-goes-global-Historic-international-digitisation-project-announced-3f4.aspx, accessed May 19, 2011.

27. Codex Sinaiticus Project, italics added.

28. "The World's Oldest Bible," PRWeb UK, July 6, 2009. Italics added.

that was slaughtered to produce the medium. In other words, Sinaiticus functions as a relic. Its digital reproduction allows it to be viewed as a relic by far more people than ever before.

A focus on the book's physical form is a typical consequence of the ritual display of a text. The look and feel of a book or parchment page constitutes its iconic dimension. It is ritualized by displaying and manipulating the book in ritual contexts, such as worship services and holiday parades. But museums and libraries also provide contexts for the ritual display of books. Book displays draw sustained attention to books in the form of ritual viewings. They present certain "treasures" to public view as relics and, like other kinds of relics, iconic books provide both viewers and institutions a degree of legitimation. They legitimize the textual tradition, which in the case of Sinaiticus is the Bible, by serving as physical evidence of its antiquity. They legitimize the institution that displays them by illustrating the great value of its collection. Such legitimation reinforces the appeal of the tradition and the institution, which explains why expensive enterprises like the Codex Sinaiticus Project receive funding.

Digitizing iconic texts magnifies the effects of textual ritualization already at work in museum displays of books. The focus on the material book is magnified as well. These digital texts do not compete with their physical exemplars—quite the opposite, they draw more visitors to the museums and libraries to see these and other relic texts in person, or at least these institutions hope so. They also provide publicity for marketing an array of material reproductions of the texts, from expensive facsimiles of the entire codex to postcards of a single page. Digitizing relic texts therefore serve to extend the scope of the age-old relic economy that stimulates endless reproductions while insisting on the uniqueness of the original (Chapter 3).

Written texts lend themselves to ritualizing as relics because they embody ideas and values in material form. Texts are material objects that nevertheless contain something immaterial—the words, the composition, the work—that may be contained equally well in many similar objects. There has, therefore, always been something "virtual" about a text because it can be copied from one object to another and can exist simultaneously in many objects. We therefore speak regularly about texts like "Hamlet" or "the Bible" with little or no attention to the confusing variety of material forms that these texts can take (see Chapter 8).[29]

Ritualizing the iconic dimension of a text draws sustained attention to its particular physical form—such as the look and feel of *this* Bible that was produced in *this* way by *this* person and given to *this* church by *this* family

---

29. Beal, "The End of the Word as We Know It," 207–224.

on the occasion of *this* event. The narration of such a history serves to further ritualize the text that now becomes a singular object to be viewed and admired, as much as to be read. Digitizing such a relic text does not change this dynamic, but simply deepens and extends it to more people in more places. Digital ritualization continues to encourage and deepen reverence for the relic text by displaying its physical form in as much detail as possible.

Conclusion

My point here is that ritualizing digital texts draws attention to the nature of the physical medium. The text may be digital, but it is hardly "virtual"; in fact, ritualization draws devotees' attention to the fact that it never was. On the other hand, because digital texts exaggerate our consciousness of the immateriality of texts apart from their material forms, digitization also permits further loosening of any ritual restrictions that constrain contact with their material exemplars. You can carry digitized sacred texts into places that would desecrate material books. You can examine rare manuscripts more closely online than in a museum or library.

The ironic effect of digitally ritualizing iconic texts, then, is that it dispels the myth of virtual reality that surrounds digital texts. Digital texts simply provide new material containers for words, thus reproducing once again the original genius of writing—the representation of oral language by visual signs on material objects. However, they also strengthen the fantasy of virtual reality that has always grown up around written texts—the fantasy that the "work" exists somehow beyond and apart from its material media and oral memory. This fantasy, produced by the fact that texts can be replicated, has been extended by the almost effortless and seemingly endless replicability of digital media. While ritualizing digital texts brings recognition of their physical reality, as ritualization usually does, digitizing ritualized texts extends people's ability to read and see them anytime and anywhere. Ritualizing digital texts thus brings a digital text's material form to conscious awareness at the same time that it loosens ritual restrictions by taking a different material form than its non-digital exemplar.

Desecrating Scriptures and the News Media

Florida pastor Terry Jones riveted world media attention in 2010 when he threatened to burn a Qur'an on the ninth anniversary of the 9/11 attacks.[1] His threat prompted wide-spread protests in Muslim countries and appeals to cancel the event by American officials, from President Barack Obama on down. In the end, he did.[2] But then Jones burned a Qur'an the following March in his church sanctuary, prompting protests in Afghanistan and attacks on United Nations aid workers and U.S. soldiers that cost the lives of twenty-four people and injured more than one hundred.[3] He also burned Qur'ans in 2012 and 2014 but drew less publicity and, therefore, less protest.[4] Jones' stunts vividly demonstrated how someone can draw intense media coverage and galvanize religious and political outrage by desecrating scriptures.

Desecrations of books of scriptures actually appear regularly in news about religious and political conflicts. Twenty-first-century news media have reported scripture desecrations in various Western, Middle Eastern, African and South Asian countries.[5] Though the desecration of sacred sites, objects

---

1. Brian Stelter, "Coverage of Koran Case Stirs Questions on Media Role," *The New York Times*, September 9, 2010.

2. Damien Cave, "Pastor Cancels Burning of Koran," *The New York Times*, September 11, 2010.

3. Taimoor Shah and Rod Nordland, "Afghans Protest Koran Burning for Third Day," *The New York Times*, April 3, 2011.

4. For collections and syntheses of media stories about Jones and these events, see "Terry Jones (pastor)" on *Wikipedia* at https://en.wikipedia.org/wiki/Terry_Jones_(pastor) and "Dove World Outreach Center Quran-burning controversy" on *Wikipedia* at https://en.wikipedia.org/wiki/Dove_World_Outreach_Center_Quran-burning_controversy (accessed February 24, 2017).

5. The prominence in recent news media should not lead one to think that intentional text destruction and scripture desecration are new phenomena; they are age-old. For the ancient world, see Natalie N. May, ed., *Iconoclasm and Text Destruction in the Ancient Near*

and persons also raise political tensions, books of scripture have emerged as particularly potent objects of contestation. That is because scriptures encapsulate the religious experiences of many people who are used to handling the physical books with veneration. News of their desecration inverts the common religious experience of scripture veneration. This reversal can arouse strong and widespread reactions. Describing the effects of ritualizing books of scriptures in the iconic dimension (see Chapters 1, 2 and 3) explains the political furors aroused by media coverage of particular incidents.

The iconic dimension of scriptures can be manipulated by anyone who gains access to a copy of the book. Therefore the iconic dimension is the most accessible of the three dimensions of scriptures. Very many people own copies of scriptures and even more have access to copies, at least in recent centuries when mechanized printing has made scriptures inexpensive and readily available. People frequently see scriptures and they often hold, touch and carry them, even if they do not have the education to read and interpret their words or even understand the language they are written in. As a result, clerical hierarchies tend to have less control over how their iconic dimension gets ritualized. The iconic dimension of scriptures provides lay people access to a material manifestation of divinity that they can use for their own spiritual benefit. Ease of access also means that the iconic dimension is most easily attacked by deliberately mishandling the scripture. Such ritual abuse is called "desecration."

The legitimizing function of the iconic dimension of scripture explains not only religious communities' investment in ritualizing it, but also the explosive social power of desecrating scriptures. Insofar as the scripture has become identified with the religion to the point that the tradition's legitimacy is conveyed by manipulating the material book, its ritual abuse can feel like an attempt to delegitimize the whole religious tradition. That threat to the tradition may be felt most strongly by lay people who cannot perform the more specialized ritualizations of oral performance and scholarly interpretation but who are accustomed to ritualizing the iconic dimension for themselves. They have the most personal experience and stake in ritualizing the iconic dimension of scriptures, so they take its ritual abuse most seriously.

Scripture Desecration in the Twenty-First Century

Some stories of intentional desecration of Qur'ans have received widespread media coverage, often resulting in severe political consequences. Other accounts of scripture desecrations of Qur'ans, as well as of Jewish, Christian

---

East and Beyond, Chicago: Oriental Institute, 2012; and Nathaniel B. Levtow, "Text Production and Destruction in Ancient Israel: Ritual and Political Dimensions," in *Social Theory and the Study of Israelite Religion* (ed. Saul M. Olyan; Atlanta, GA: SBL, 2011), 111–139.

and Sikh scriptures, seem to have had more limited impacts. Comparison of the different treatments accorded to similar incidents shows the common features and important variables surrounding the phenomenon, including differences in religious tradition, political context and media coverage.

Qur'ans and the American Military

The most infamous report of scripture desecration so far in the twenty-first century appeared in 2005.[6] In a one-paragraph article dated May 2, *Newsweek* reported that guards at the U.S. detention facility in Guantánamo Bay, Cuba, had desecrated a Qur'an by flushing it down a toilet. It based this claim on a draft of an official government report that an anonymous source claimed to have read. One week later, the story was publicized in a news conference by a well-known member of the Pakistani parliament, Imran Khan, and widely reported by other media sources. Street protests then erupted around the world. In many places, protestors carried and waved copies of the Qur'an as they bitterly denounced its desecration. In Afghanistan, the protests turned violent, resulting in the deaths of seventeen people.[7]

In its May 16 issue, *Newsweek* retracted the story because its source was unable to confirm where he had seen the information.[8] But the lead reporter, Michael Isikoff, admitted to *The New York Times* that the magazine was also surprised by the political fallout: "The big point that leaps out is the cultural one. Neither Newsweek nor the Pentagon foresaw that a reference to the desecration of the Koran was going to create the kind of response that it did. ... They were as caught off guard by the furor as we were. We obviously blame ourselves for not understanding the potential ramifications."[9]

Other people anticipated that a charge of Qur'an desecration by the U.S. guards at Guantánamo would evoke a visceral response in the Muslim world. Muqtedar Khan, a political scientist at Adrian College in Michigan, told the Associated Press: "I think there is clearly a political dimension of what's happening there. ... It is very easy to mobilize Muslims on this issue. By the end of the month, there is going to be a global protest."[10] Sure enough, two weeks later, the AP reported that "Thousands of Muslims marched Friday in Islamic countries from Asia to the Middle East, burning symbols of America

---

6. See the helpful summary, "Qur'an desecration controversy of 2005," in *Wikipedia* (accessed October 25, 2008).

7. Hendrik Hertzberg, "Big News Week," *The New Yorker*, May 30, 2005; see also "Afghan anti-US violence escalates," BBC, May 12, 2005,

8. "Newsweek Statement On Qur'an Story," *Newsweek*, May 16, 2005.

9. Charles McGrath, "Reporter on Retracted Newsweek Article Put Monica on the Map," *The New York Times*, May 17, 2005.

10. Rachel Zoll, "For Muslims, desecrating Quran dishonors God," by AP, May 17, 2005.

to protest the alleged desecration of the Quran by military personnel at a U.S. prison in Guantánamo Bay, Cuba."[11]

These events focused critical attention on the U.S. Government and its practices at Guantánamo and other detention facilities. The Pentagon released a report by the end of May, 2005, that admitted five instances of guards misusing Qur'ans. It claimed that all occurred prior to 2003, when standard operating procedures were issued for the Guantánamo detention facility regarding "the handling and inspecting of detainee Korans." The intent of the procedures was

> to ensure the safety of the detainees and MPs while respecting the cultural dignity of the Korans thereby reducing the friction over the searching of the Korans. ... personnel directly working with detainees will avoid handling or touching the detainee's Koran whenever possible. When military necessity does require the Koran to be searched, the subsequent procedures will be followed.[12]

However, complaints about mistreatment of Qur'ans at Guantánamo continued to emerge in reports from the Red Cross, the FBI, and others in the following months, fueling ongoing media discussion of the investigations. The continuing cycle of charges and denials did not leave much time for verbal apologies, much less any form of ritual rectification.

There were other occasions when the U.S. military was accused of desecrating copies of the Qur'an. Complaints about damage to mosques from military operations frequently focused on the Qur'ans contained in those mosques. For example, already in 1998 the BBC reported that after a missile attack on Al Quaida camps in Afganistan that resulted only in light damage, "local people were nevertheless angry that mosques had been hit, and copies of the Koran destroyed in the resulting fires."[13] In Iraq in the aftermath of the Second Iraq War, such accusations could bring together rival factions. Iraqi Shiites marched and waved copies of the Qur'an in Fallujah in 2004 to protest a raid by U.S. troops on the main Sunni Mosque that resulted in the destruction of some copies of the Qur'an.[14] After the withdrawal of most U.S. troops from Iraq in 2011, desecration charges often served to polarize rival Iraqi factions. Both Iraqi and American military sources accused ISIS (ISIL) of placing bombs in Qur'ans.[15]

---

11. Eric Talmadge, "Muslims Protest Alleged Quran Desecration," AP, May 27, 2005.

12. US Embassy, "Guantanamo Procedures on Handling Koran," May 25, 2005. http://tirana.usembassy.gov/press20050523.html (accessed December 2, 2008).

13. "Taliban grants access to strike target," BBC, September 5, 1998.

14. "Shiites in Fallujah take to the streets; protest raid on Sunni mosque," AP, February 27, 2004.

15. "Daesh plants bombs in Qur'an copies in Fallujah," PressTV, June 9, 2016.

In May, 2008, on a firing range used by U.S. soldiers, Afghans discovered a Qur'an riddled with bullet holes, a target drawn on its cover and an expletive written inside. CNN reported that this discovery forced "the chief U.S. commander in Baghdad to issue a formal apology." A U.S. officer kissed a Qur'an and presented it to Afghan leaders during the ceremony. The offending soldier was transferred out of the country. This did not quell all expressions of outrage: "Sheikh Hamadi al-Qirtani, in a speech on behalf of all tribal sheiks of Radhwaniya, called the incident 'aggression against the entire Islamic world.' The Association of Muslim Scholars in Iraq also condemned the shooter's actions and the U.S. military's belated acknowledgment of the incident."[16] Unlike three years earlier, however, the complaints did not escalate into widespread international protests. This difference suggests that the fulsome and ceremonial apology seems to have calmed the outrage. Since desecrating scriptures involves ritual action, an apology works best if it takes ritual as well as verbal form, as in this case.

Apologies did not mitigate the reaction in Afghanistan after U.S. soldiers burned copies of the Qur'an in 2012.[17] The riots that followed led to the deaths of at least fourteen Afghans and two American soldiers.[18] While the military blamed its own poor training for the burning incident, the news sources do not show any reflection on whether a more ritualized apology would have made any difference to the violent reaction.

Interreligious and Intercommunal Conflicts

Though U.S. military activity in Iraq and Afghanistan has drawn attention to reports of Americans mistreating Qur'ans, the phenomenon of scripture desecration is more widespread and multifaceted than a simplistic Western-versus-Muslim dichotomy suggests. The following stories show the role of scripture desecrations in various interreligious and intercommunal conflicts over the past decades. In these cases, public ritual desecration of scriptures has been used intentionally to fuel conflicts between competing groups.

When the Taliban government of Afghanistan allowed giant ancient statues of the Buddha to be destroyed in March, 2001, mass protests erupted especially in India and south-east Asia. Some Hindu militants used the occasion to attack Islam by publicly burning copies of the Qur'an.[19] That action prompted a reaction in several parts of India, including Muslim-majority Kashmir: "The unrest began with a crowd of some 2,000 people staged a

---

16. "Iraq party: Punish U.S. soldier who shot at Quran," CNN, May 19, 2008.

17. Sangar Rahimi and Alissa J. Rubin, "Koran Burning in NATO Error Incites Afghans," *The New York Times*, February 21, 2012.

18. "Obama forced to apologise to Karzai for Koran burnings in Afghanistan," Agence France-Presse (AFP), *The Australian*, February 24, 2012.

19. "In pictures: Buddha statues protest," BBC, March 11, 2001.

procession to protest against copies of the Koran allegedly being burnt by Hindu hardliners. ... In the ensuing disturbances, a deserted Hindu temple was set on fire and more than two dozen government and private vehicles were damaged."[20] The tit-for-tat attacks on statues, then scriptures, then temples shows that their equivalent status as sacred objects was recognized by all sides in this conflict.

Accusations of and even calls for desecrating physical copies of scriptures have become highly publicized features of inter-religious conflict. In tribal areas of Orissa, India, anti-Christian attacks are likely to target bibles, among others things. Active missionizing of indigenous tribal peoples by both Christians and Hindus over the last half century has turned inter-tribal conflicts into inter-religious ones. Six weeks of violence in 2008 included many reports of Christians being forced to convert in ceremonies that included burning "their Bibles, hymnals and ... images of Christ."[21]

Resentment against Christian missionary activity also produced attacks on New Testaments in Israel. In May, 2008, the deputy mayor of Or-Yehuda in Israel collected several hundred New Testaments that had been distributed by missionaries. They were then burned by Yeshiva students. Leaders of Messianic (Christian) Jewish groups asked for prosecution under Israeli laws forbidding "desecration of any religious icon or item that a group holds sacred."[22]

Attempts to suppress religious movements often target all of their literature. Christian news organizations called attention to legal actions to suppress religious literature in several countries of Central Asia in 2012 and 2013. Russian authorities ordered the destruction of modern books touting the views of Muslims, Hare Krishnas, and Seventh Day Adventist. Protestants and their libraries were targeted by courts in Uzbekistan and Kazakhstan.[23] Christian media sources explained the repression as a reaction to successful Christian revivals in Central Asia in the preceding several years.[24]

Vandalism of Jewish synagogues often targets their Torah scrolls. In 2008 alone, scrolls were damaged or stolen during the vandalism of synagogues

---

20. "Koran burning provokes protests," BBC, March 24, 2001.

21. "Hindu Threat to Christians: Convert or Flee," *The New York Times*, October 12, 2008.

22. "Hundreds of New Testaments torched in Israel," CNN, May 22, 2008.

23. Felix Corley, "RUSSIA: 'I've never encountered the practice of destroying religious literature before'," Forum 18 News Service, March 21, 2012; Mushfig Bayram, "UZBEKISTAN: Raids, criminal charges and Christmas Bible destruction," Forum 18 News Service, January 31, 2013; Felix Corley, "KAZAKHSTAN: Court-ordered religious book burning a first?" Forum 18 News Service, March 14, 2013.

24. Melissa Steffan, "Bible Burning Spreads to Another Former Soviet State," *Christianity Today*, March 28, 2013.

in Jerusalem, Miami Beach, and Yorktown, New York.[25] In Hebron, Israel, Jewish settler groups claimed that Muslims had urinated near a Torah Ark in the shrine of the Cave of the Patriarchs, though local police could find no evidence to substantiate the charge.[26] The nature and number of these incidents was typical for prior and subsequent years.[27]

Children sometimes imitate the public scripture desecrations they hear publicized in news media. In December, 2006, three Muslim boys were expelled from an Islamic school in Melbourne, Australia, for urinating on and burning a Christian Bible. The Australian media reported that "The explosive incident has forced the East Preston Islamic College to call in a senior imam to tell its 650 Muslim students that the Bible and Christianity must be respected."[28]

When acts of scripture desecration feature frequently in religious and communal conflicts, charges of fresh incidents find a ready audience. The charge of desecrating the Qur'an was extended to the erasure or overwriting by "scribbled lines" of a few Qur'anic verses on the wall of a nursing school in Pakistan in 2007. As a result, "dozens of female students of a hardline Islamist seminary stormed the nursing hostel."[29] The school's principal and four Christian students were temporarily suspended pending a government investigation. The seminary students' actions were part of a larger campaign against "vice" in Islamabad that included occupying a government-run children's library. In 2009, one hundred Christian villagers were burned out of their homes in Gorja, Pakistan, and eight were killed by mobs angry over rumors that Qur'ans had been desecrated.[30]

In Nigeria, charges of Qur'an desecration have produced deadly results. The BBC reported in March 2007:

> Secondary school pupils in north-eastern Nigeria have killed a teacher after apparently accusing her of desecrating the Koran, police say. The teacher, a Christian, was attacked after supervising an exam in Gombe city. It is not clear what she had done to anger the students. ... Last year, in Bauchi State, a rumour swept the city that a Christian teacher had also desecrated the

---

25. "Vandals trash Bnei Akiva branch in northern Jerusalem," *Jerusalem Post*, August 4, 2008; "Synagogue Burns In Miami Beach, Torah Missing," MSNBC, April 23, 2008; "Teens arrested for vandalizing Yorktown synagogue," WCBSTV, May 4, 2008.

26. "Muslims desecrate, urinate in Judaism's 2nd holiest site," *WorldNetDaily*, September 7, 2008; "Cave of Patriarchs not vandalized, police say," *Jerusalem Post*, September 9, 2008.

27. See, for example, earlier incidents in Paris ("Paris synagogue vandalized, Torah scroll, cash stolen," AP, May 24, 1995) and Brooklyn ("Five Torah Scrolls Burned by Vandals At Brooklyn Temple," *The New York Times*, September 18, 1988).

28. "Muslim boys urinated on Bible," *Australian*, December 6, 2006.

29. "Pakistan probes alleged sacrilege of Koran verses," AFP, June 3, 2007.

30. "Tragedy in Gojra," *Forbes*, August 5, 2009.

Koran, which prompted riots in which at least five people were killed. In fact, the teacher had confiscated the Koran from a pupil who was reading it in class. Religious differences have long been used to justify all kinds of violence in Nigeria, our reporter says. In reality it is often fueled by ethnic or political conflicts and competition for resources, which can be fierce, given that so many people live in poverty, he says.[31]

The frequency and geographic range of these stories show that the social power of scripture desecration—and of charges of scripture desecration—is widely recognized and sometimes utilized in many cultures around the world.

Intrareligious/Intracommunal Conflicts

Intentional acts of scripture desecration and charges in the media against others for desecrating scriptures do not just arise in conflicts between nations and religions. They also appear within various religious communities where they mediate individual and intracommunal conflicts.

In the Indian state of Punjab, a simmering conflict involving class, caste and claims of leadership within the Sikh community gets expressed occasionally in desecrations and charges of desecrating the Guru Granth Sahib. The conflict involves, among other things, debates over whether any living human can aspire to be a successor to the original ten gurus, and thus in competition with the Guru Granth, and whether other religious movements should be allowed to use Sikh symbols and scriptures.[32] *Frontline* magazine summarized one series of events this way:

> In 2001, Dalit godman Piara Singh Bhaniarawala set off riots by releasing the Bhavsagar Granth, a 2,704-page religious text suffused with sakhis, or miracle stories, extolling his spiritual powers. According to the godman, the Bhavsagar Granth was written after upper-caste Sikhs in a neighbouring home refused to allow the display of the gurdwara's Guru Granth Sahib in a Dalit home. When Sikh neoconservatives burned copies of the Bhavsagar Granth, Bhaniarawala's followers retaliated by setting alight Birs, or copies of the Guru Granth Sahib. SGPC President Jagdev Singh Talwandi insisted that Piara Singh be booked for murder, claiming that the Guru Granth Sahib is a 'living guru'. Punjab's government balked at this measure but did prosecute Bhaniarawala for inciting communal hatred.[33]

In another leadership fight, Sikh authorities in Rajasthan, India, tried to pass legislation that would grant legal monopolies for printing copies of the Guru Granth Sahib. This effort was ostensibly an attempt to guard the

---

31. "Nigeria teacher dies 'over Koran'," BBC, March 21, 2007.

32. For an analysis of the social as well as religious issues behind the conflict, see Myrvold, "Engaging with the Guru," 261–262, and Ajay Bharadwaj, "Challenging the Faith," DNA, May 24, 2007.

33. "Faiths at War," *Frontline*, June 2–15, 2007.

scripture from profanation or desecration, but it also aimed to disempower rivals who supported independent publishing houses.[34] Two months later, activists kidnapped and publicly humiliated two men working for an independent publisher.[35]

In Iran, an attempt to displace Vice-President Esfandyar Rahim Mashaie in 2008 included charges that "girls danced with the Koran during a ceremony staged by his ministry." Apparently, a traditional procession that brings the Qur'an on a tray to the reader at the beginning of a ceremony was, in this case, conducted by "a dozen dancing girls clad in traditional clothes."[36] The news report was quick to point out, however, that Mashaie had recently provoked controversy by advocating warming relations with Israel. The charge of "insulting the Qur'an" seems therefore to have been a tactical maneuver in an on-going struggle over government policy.

Pakistan's draconian blasphemy laws, enacted during the martial presidency of General Zia-ul-Haq (1978–1988), make the charge of desecrating a copy of the Qur'an particularly dangerous there.[37] In one case, a man in Lahore apparently framed another for burning a Qur'an in order to buy his property at half price.[38] In another case, a Christian man was jailed without bail for burning a Qur'an. He confessed, but claimed to have done it as a ritual act aimed at getting his estranged wife to come back to him. He also claimed insanity.[39] The seriousness of these charges is illustrated by stories about people beaten after speaking ill of Muhammed, Islam or the Qur'an, and then being arrested while their attackers go free. Some religious and political leaders have called for the death penalty for blasphemers, and mobs and jailors occasionally carry it out.[40] Many of these cases seem to have originated in marital or business disputes. The Human Rights Commission of Pakistan has been protesting these laws for many years, as have Pakistani Christians.[41]

---

34. "New Law Proposed for Maintaining Respect for Sri Guru Granth Sahib Jee," *Panthic Weekly*, August 1, 2007.

35. "Selling of Birs in Amritsar: Brothers detained in Akal Takht room," *Chandigarh Tribune*, October 6, 2007.

36. "Iranian VP under fire for 'insulting Koran'," AFP, November 16, 2008.

37. Kunwar Idris, "16 Lessons from Goja," *Dawn*, August 8, 2009.

38. "Bone of contention? Blasphemy accused sells property at half price," *Daily Times*, July 9, 2007.

39. "LHC dismisses bail application of alleged blasphemer," *Daily Times*, July 12, 2007.

40. " 'Blasphemer' killed by mob," *Daily Times*, April 21, 2005; "Blasphemy case against Younis Masih: Extremists demand immediate hanging of blasphemer," *Daily Times*, September 20, 2005; "Strike in Muzaffargarh against 'blasphemer'," *Daily Times*, March 16, 2006; "'I'd kill blasphemer'," *Daily Times*, June 22, 2007.

41. "HRCP seeks inquiry into alleged blasphemer's death," *Daily Times*, August 27, 2003;

However, the efforts of human rights organizations to change the law suffered setbacks in 2010 when a general strike to protest proposed changes to the blasphemy laws "brought Pakistan to a standstill." The *New York Times* reported that, by contrast, "Protest rallies [against the blasphemy laws] by rights activists have been ineffective and relatively small."[42] In 2011, the governor of Punjab was assassinated because he supported reforming the blasphemy laws.[43] A group of local clerics praised the assassin and prohibited their followers from mourning the governor.

In 2012, however, Pakistani police responded to accusations against a young Christian girl for burning a Qur'an by arresting her accuser, a local imam.[44] This action was supported by the Chairman of the All Pakistan Ulema Council, an influential group of Islamic clerics, who hailed the Christian girl as a "daughter of the nation" and stated that "our heads are bowed in shame" because of the imam's attempts to frame her.[45] The girl and her family nevertheless moved to Canada to escape the threats of vigilantes.[46] Those threats are very real, as mob attacks have continued against those accused of blasphemy against Islam, whether using Qur'ans or not.

These stories show that people at various levels of society sometimes wield charges of scripture desecration for personal or political gain. Charges of venerating the *wrong* scripture can also be employed in this way. For example, when Pope John Paul II in 1999 received a Qur'an as a gift from a delegation of Muslim clerics and kissed it in a conventional Christian act of veneration, traditionalist Catholics cited this event as proof that the pope had betrayed the Christian faith. The charge continued to be repeated years later on traditionalist blogs.[47]

"Death sentence for blasphemy: HRCP to help Younis Masih appeal," *Daily Times,* June 1, 2007; "Seventh anniversary of Bishop Joseph's suicide: Sacrifice a source of inspiration, says NCJP," *Daily Times,* May 6, 2005.

42. Salman Masood, "Pakistanis Rally in Support of Blasphemy Law," *The New York Times,* December, 31, 2010.

43. Karin Brulliard. "Salman Taseer assassination points to Pakistani extremists' mounting power," *Washington Post,* January 5, 2011.

44. Mark Memmott, "Christian Girl Accused Of Blasphemy Cleared By Pakistani Court," NPR, November 20, 2012.

45. Jon Boone, "Christian girl hailed as 'daughter of nation' by senior Pakistani cleric," *The Guardian,* September 3, 2012.

46. "Rimsha Masih, Pakistani girl accused of blasphemy, finds refuge in Canada," AP via *The Guardian,* June 30, 2013.

47. Today's Catholic World, December 2, 2005, www.todayscatholicworld.com/dec05tcw.htm (accessed December 13, 2008); Traditio, December 2006, www.traditio.com/comment/com0612.htm (accessed December 13, 2008).

Scripture Desecration in Western Cultures

As this last story shows, charges of scripture desecrations also crop up in Europe and the United States, though with notably less effect on public opinion. The motives behind such acts seem to range from media blunders to symbolic acts of political and religious protest. In Europe and North America, however, these incidents also tend to prompt heated debates over whether such acts qualify for legal protection under the right to freedom of speech.

The image of a burning Bible appeared multiple times on German TV in July, 2007, in a documentary about Christian fundamentalism. The German print media, led by a report headlined "TV-Skandal!" in a glossy magazine, drew attention to it by asking several political and church leaders if one is allowed to burn bibles. The responses were predictably critical. One commented on how much greater the negative reaction would be if it had been a Qur'an: "What would happen in Germany if the ARD network had shown a burning Qur'an?" Another wondered what Muslims must think of Westerners, whom they all regard as Christians, burning their own Bible.[48] Though the writers and producers insisted that they had intended the image to represent the fire of faith and of the Word, public pressure forced the network to withdraw the documentary.

Around the same time in the U.S.A., a former student was arrested on hate-crime charges for throwing two copies of the Qur'an in public toilets at Pace University. The story generated charges of hypocrisy from many quarters, because similar acts by artists using Christian symbols have been defended on free-speech grounds. In the end, the man pleaded guilty to a reduced charge of disorderly conduct and was sentenced to community service.[49]

Rather less attention was given to news that artist Charles Merrill burned a rare and valuable Qur'an. He had previously marked and cut up a Bible. He explained his deliberate desecrations of the scriptures of two different religions as symbolic acts of protest: "The purpose of editing and burning Abrahamic Holy Books is to eliminate homophobic hate."[50]

The countervailing influence of free-speech commitments over desecration concerns in the media coverage of these last two stories might seem to represent a secularizing influence. But free speech concerns are themselves deeply rooted in religious history. The Western ideal of free speech grew from harsh experience of its absence in the early modern wars of reli-

---

48. "TV-Skandal! ARD verbrennt Bibel," *Bild*, July 14, 2007.
49. "N.Y. Student who Dumped Qurans in Toilet Gets Community Service," AP, March 3, 2008.
50. "Gay Artist Burns Rare $60,000.00 Koran," *PRNewswire*, July 26, 2007.

gion in Europe and from the suppression of one Christian denomination by another in the American colonies. Thus both by emphasizing the semantic contents of books over their material form (Chapter 8) and the right to free expression, Western cultural values continue to reflect important themes in Christian religious history and theology.

The Social Power of Scripture Desecration Stories

These stories of conflicts within religions and communities show very clearly the social power involved in the use and abuse of an iconic book. From power struggles in the higher ranks of the Iranian government and of the Sikh religious hierarchy to marital disputes and conflicts over property ownership between Pakistani individuals, charges of insulting or desecrating a book of scripture can shift the balance of power, sometimes decisively. The stories reveal wide-spread awareness of that power among people in various societies and a willingness by some people to use it against co-religionists. It is very easy to level a charge of desecration or insult, but very difficult to disprove it.

These stories confirm how much harder it is for political or religious authorities to control the iconic dimension of scriptures than other dimensions. Scholars and clergy traditionally dominate interpretation of the textual dimension of the Qur'an, Torah, Guru Granth and Bible. Debates over doctrine and orthodoxy, the semantic dimension, therefore tend to remain under the control of a few rival elites, even if they recruit popular sentiment to their cause. A broader range of people tend to be involved in scriptural performances, but even then recitations and readings tend to follow traditions—and sometimes even strict rules—of performance. The iconic dimension, however, can be manipulated by whoever has access to a copy of the text, whether to honor a scripture or to desecrate it or to frame a rival or to gain economic advantage or, as in the case of the hapless husband mentioned above, to try to harness its iconic power for personal ends. That story, if accurate, shows private (esoteric) use of a book coming into conflict with the same text's public (exoteric) veneration. Rules for handling scriptures attempt to control the iconic dimension and mostly succeed in public worship settings. But the mass production of scriptures by modern print technology has made scriptures readily available to many people whose private use of them is not easily regulated by laws or social pressures.

The iconic dimension of scriptures produces a tension within religious traditions between protecting the physical scripture from desecration on the one hand, and distributing it widely for educational and missionary purposes on the other. These four religions have handled this tension in different ways. Due to strong missionary impulses, Muslims and Christians have generally preferred to distribute their scriptures widely despite the risks of mishandling. Sikhs also desire to spread knowledge of the Guru Granth, but the ritual requirements for handling the scripture have constrained its distribution. A Sikh layman confided to a friend of mine that he does not own a copy himself. "You have to do something several times a day with that book, which is entirely too much trouble." The Jewish Torah scroll is also restricted mostly to synagogues due to both ritual requirements and its high price. The Torah, however, can be bound separately as a *chumash* or as part of the larger Jewish Bible and in both Hebrew and vernacular translations. The Torah in codex form and the Sikh scriptures in multiple volumes are widely distributed. The two different forms taken by both the Torah and by the Guru Granth thus allow simultaneously for their ritual restriction and their widespread publication. The digitization of scriptures allows for further distinctions in ritual practice (Chapter 4).

Nevertheless, the consequence of ritualizing the iconic dimension of scripture is that whoever comes into contact with a copy of scripture has the power to venerate or desecrate it. The news stories summarized above show great awareness of this power among the people involved in these incidents. The fact that lay people have greater control over the iconic dimension of scriptures than over its other dimensions explains why many people have a great emotional stake in how the scripture is treated. Charges of scripture desecration appeal directly to popular sentiment based in personal experience. Though often voiced by members of religious and political hierarchies, the charges carry an inherently populist force because of the nature of scripture's iconic dimension. Unlike the subtleties of doctrine or performance that require considerable education and experience to understand, anyone can venerate or desecrate the scripture. Most people who venerate a scripture fear accidentally desecrating it instead. The charge of intentional scripture desecration therefore arouses a visceral response.

A book of scripture combines two qualities otherwise rarely found together in these four religious traditions: on the one hand, it is a readily available material object and, on the other hand, it offers incomparable access to divinity in one way or another. Scriptures therefore become focal objects of very many people's religious aspirations. They feel an attack on the scripture is an attack on themselves, on their religion, and on their god.

As a result, as Cordell Waldron observed, "violence against books is understood by all parties involved as being comparable to violence against people and/or ideas and ... violence against a book can quickly lead to other forms of conflict."[51] This analogy between books and people also directs

---

51. Cordell Waldron, "New Testaments Burned in Israel," *Iconic Books Blog*, May 28, 2008.

the action of scripture desecrators. As Jonas Svensson noted, desecrators who know little to nothing about the tradition that venerates a particular scripture nevertheless succeed in desecrating it by subjecting it to acts that would be humiliating and destructive to persons.[52] Their message is received loud and clear.

Iconic Scriptures in the News Media

All the accounts of scripture desecrations surveyed above share another common characteristic: they became news stories. They were publicized by broadcast and print media, and amplified by the world-wide reach of the internet. Though practices and charges of scripture desecration are age-old, the rapid dissemination of their stories by modern media often amplifies and changes their effects. In some cases, the acts of desecration and, in many cases, the charges of desecration aimed to generate media coverage from the start.

Scriptures are themselves a very old form of media. Newspaper, television and web stories about them involve an interaction between modern media and older practices, not just of print media but also of calligraphy, liturgy and oral performance. Scriptures' iconic dimension, however, presents an especially compelling image for the largest number of people who are not expert interpreters or performers of the scriptures.

Stories about scripture desecrations therefore offer news outlets an opportunity to tap into a pre-packaged set of images, sounds, associations, and feelings almost guaranteed to draw the attention of a many people. That opportunity raises the danger that journalistic opportunism motivates the high publicity that some of these stories have received. As a result, serious consideration has and should be given to the degree to which journalism itself becomes a contributing factor in these incidents and their consequences. The dramatic ramifications of the Guantánamo affair focused critical attention on *Newsweek* in particular but also on the role played by other news sources and by politicians' manipulations of news sources.[53] Terry Jones' threats again prompted media soul-searching after the fact. Laurie Patton pointed out the amplified effects of media through digital communication:

> The Gainesville event might be the final culmination of the age of hijackers, where a small group's manipulation of a powerful vehicle has far-reaching

http://iconicbooks.blogspot.com/2008/05/new-testaments-burned-in-israel.html.

52. For the psychology behind this behavior, see Jonas Svensson, "Hurting the Qur'an – Suggestions Concerning the Psychological Infrastructure of Desecration," *Temenos* 53/2 (2017), 243–264.

53. Hendrik Hertzberg, "Big News Week," *New Yorker*, May 30, 2005.

disastrous effects. Only in this case, the vehicle is the Qur'an, not an airplane. And the manipulation need only be virtual. Never has book burning been so effective without even occurring. Symbolic actions on the internet and their consequences in the real world now occur almost simultaneously. And the threat of a symbolic gesture and an actual one become one and the same.[54]

That lesson may be sinking in. It is noticeable that stories of scripture desecration have not been publicized so prominently by Western media in the second decade of the twenty-first century as in the first.

The broad (frequently, world-wide) reach of modern media raises the question of whether media coverage is changing the nature and significance of the iconic dimension of the scriptures itself. That is, does publicity about scripture desecration influence how communities and religious traditions regard their own scriptures? And does such publicity change how they regard the scriptures of other traditions? The answer to both questions seems to be, "yes."

Within many religious communities, a charge of scripture desecration has probably been a powerful weapon in inter-personal and political conflicts for a very long time. The stories about using the charge in marital and property conflicts in Pakistan and inter-communal conflicts in Nigeria reflect its potency for gathering a mob or for influencing legal authorities. In these cases, local "old media" was sufficient to bring about results. Wider broadcast of the situation does not seem to have strengthened the charges. If anything, sympathizers for the accused used media publicity to mobilize help for them.

In other cases, such as the Hindu militants burning Qur'ans in front of photographers, the charge against the Iranian Interior Ministry of insulting the Qur'an, and the books being burnt in the Punjabi Sikh power struggles, the actors clearly intended for news media to publicize their actions and their charges in order to sharpen their attacks and inflame public opinion. In such cases, modern news media's involvement may generate more public focus on scriptures' iconic dimension, because that is the dimension most easily manipulated to generate a broad popular response. The media then becomes complicit in these conflicts.

The fact that many news stories do reach people of a wide variety of religious traditions and cultures means, however, that coverage of one scripture may also influence attitudes towards others. The Western media's attention to Qur'an desecrations over the last decades has heightened some people's sensibilities about the Christian Bible. That was obviously true in the case

---

54. Laurie Patton, "Virtual Book Burning and its Consequences," *Religion Dispatches*, September 13, 2010.

of the burning Bible on German TV, which was an entirely media-generated event. It was a TV documentary that used the image in the first place, and it was print media sources that first raised the possibility of scandal. They then sought out Christian leaders to comment, many of whom drew comparisons with hypothetical media treatments of Qur'ans. The whole incident seems to have been created by news media in conscious comparison with stories of scripture desecration from other cultures and religious traditions.

Nevertheless, such comparisons get made easily in religiously pluralistic cultures. Not only the news media, but also governments try to apply one standard to the treatment of all kinds of scriptures. Thus laws in countries as different as Israel and India mandate respectful treatment of all religious scriptures. The absence of such legislation in Western "Christian" countries elicits surprise elsewhere. Few understand that the absence of such laws has more to do with the free-speech ideals generated by old inner-Christian conflicts and the distinctive characteristics of the Christian scripture as a translated text (Chapter 8) than with the secularism of Western societies.

Thus one consequence of the media coverage of scripture desecration stories has been to heighten concern for the iconic veneration of scriptures in various cultures and religious traditions, including those of Europe and the Americas. Attention to desecrations of one tradition's scriptures brings increased attention to similar acts in other traditions. That is not surprising: the iconic ritualization of a book of scripture is not static even within an ancient religious tradition, but constantly changes, just as ritualizations of its other dimensions do. The cultural saturation of modern news and social media means that iconic scriptures provide convenient tools for both giving offense and taking offense. Today's politics gives many people reasons to do both.

— 6 —

Ancient Iconic Texts

A seven-foot tall black monolith is a popular attraction in the Louvre in Paris. Columns of cuneiform signs cover all sides of its stone surface, except for the bas-relief on the top that depicts the King of Babylon, Hammurabi, standing before the sun god, Shamash. The text contains Hammurabi's famous laws, which were distributed throughout the second-millennium B.C.E. Middle East on clay tablets. But this diorite stele represented his laws and his reign in his capitol city and still does in the Western imagination of the history of its laws (Figure 3).

Hammurabi's stele is dramatically iconic, but every written text has an iconic dimension. The sight and touch of a written text constitute its iconic dimension. When communities and individuals ritualize this iconic dimension, they produce iconic books and texts.

Texts can be written on almost any material. Popular media have included clay, leaves, bark, leather, paper, and electronic screens. Written texts are therefore material objects that are subject to physical manipulation and visual display. They can be created, carried, collected, and destroyed. They can be displayed in public or hidden away in private libraries or buried in the ground.

The material and visual form of a written text distinguishes it from the oral and aural experience of speech. Like writing, speech can take a simple form in ordinary conversation or become an elaborate performance in public addresses, sermons, and theatrical plays—its expressive dimension. Like written texts, speech can be subject to considerable debate as to its exact meaning and proper interpretation—its semantic dimension. But oral traditions cannot be visually displayed or physically manipulated. Written texts can, and this iconic dimension allows them to be used in ways that speech cannot. In fact, this difference seems to have motivated the invention of writing.

Figure 3.   Stele of Hammarabi's laws from Babylon, ca. 1700 B.C.E. The relief
shows King Hammurabi standing before the god Shamash. The rest of
the front as well as the back and sides of the stele is covered with the
cuneiform text of the laws. In the Louvre, Paris.

In contrast to the rich lode of iconic textuality readily visible in contemporary cultures (Chapter 2), historical investigations of the subject must
struggle with gaps in the evidence that grow larger the further back we look.
We also risk imposing anachronistic models of textuality and iconicity on
people and practices for which they may be inappropriate. However, historical analysis can provide explanations for cultural features and functions
that studies of contemporary practices may miss. In the case of iconic books
and texts, a historical survey provides a promising avenue for explaining
the persistence of iconic textuality. This chapter traces the ritualization of
texts' iconic dimension back to the first cultures to adopt writing on a large
scale, the civilizations of the ancient Near East.

The Iconic Dimension in the Invention of Writing

The origins of writing can be studied best in lower Mesopotamia. There archeologists found clay tokens and envelopes that eventually evolved into cuneiform writing in ancient Sumer. The tokens took different shapes to represent different commodities—sheep, cattle, barley, and so on. A set of tokens sealed inside a clay envelope functioned as a receipt to record the quantities of commodities exchanged among traders in a barter economy. Tokens were pressed into the outside of the envelopes to show how many tokens were contained inside. Cylinder seals rolled across the wet clay provided pictorial signatures to vouch for the accuracy of the accounting. Sumerian writing began when the token impressions, and then just sketches of the tokens (triangles, circles, squares), replaced the tokens themselves and, supplemented by pictographs, began to represent the sounds of Sumerian words rather than just the objects to which they referred. Nevertheless, more than five hundred years passed before anyone used writing for anything but receipts and accounts.[1]

Writing, then, was not invented five thousand years ago to communicate information in place of speech. Nor was it invented to preserve information for a long period of time as a mnemonic device, as many ancient and modern scholars have maintained.[2] Writing was invented to record information about economic transactions that could easily be communicated orally, and it probably was. Writing was invented to validate information, as Denise Schmandt-Besserat observed: "The pictographic tablets provided the elite governing the first city-states with a device by which to establish economic control."[3] The invention of writing did not aim to replace oral communication. Information preservation and communication was a side-effect.

The invention of writing instead turned oral language into physical evidence. Written texts made it possible to separate language from its speaker by putting it in physical form. Writing turned language into physical objects that independently confirmed or disconfirmed an oral accounting. It provided a check against lies told to defraud the owners of commodities. Writing was invented as a check against fraud.[4]

---

1. See the summaries in Denise Schmandt-Besserat, "Record Keeping Before Writing," in *Civilizations of the Ancient Near East* (ed. Jack M. Sasson; Farmingham, MA: Scribner's, 1995), 2097–2106; Jack Goody, *The Logic of Writing and the Organization of Society* (Cambridge: Cambridge University Press, 1986), 45–86; and Andrew Robinson, *Writing and Script* (Oxford: Oxford University Press, 2009), 5–35.

2. E.g. Plato, *The Phaedrus*, 274b–277a, and Walter Ong, *Orality and Literacy* (London: Routledge, 1982), 85, 96, 99, among many others.

3. Schmandt-Besserat, "Record Keeping Before Writing" 2105.

4. Goody, *Logic of Writing*, 152–159; contra Ong, *Orality and Literacy*, 96–104, who discussed

Around 2600 B.C.E., writing technology began to be used for prayers, incantations, poems, and stories. Modern readers find these genres far more interesting than lists of commodities, so literary genres dominate anthologies of ancient texts as well as most modern reconstructions of the history of textual culture. But accounting lists of various kinds continued to outnumber other kinds of texts throughout the history of cuneiform literature.

In modern times, financial accounts along with their supporting memoranda and correspondence became increasingly systematized and technologized through efforts at bureaucratic control by corporations and governments.[5] Possession and exchange of receipts, currency, bank drafts, and various other written accounts continue to provide the evidentiary basis for economic transactions of all kinds. In addition, modern legal identity and political rights depend on official documentation. Possession of government documents such as passports, visas, and other forms of identification establish a person's legal standing. While wealth depends on controlling paper and electronic accounts, legal status lies in "having papers" that can be produced on demand. The inability to do so is the defining characteristic of people who are most vulnerable to legal, economic and even physical abuse. They are the "undocumented."

Though economic and legal documents can and do get read, even today they often do not convey much information that has not already been conveyed orally. The verbs that govern the use of such documents, in phrases such as "Do you have a visa?" "Show me your ID," and "Give me a receipt," involve possession, display, and exchange. Like the cuneiform receipts for which writing was invented in the first place, modern economic and legal documents serve as physical evidence to validate orally transmitted information. Reading remains, at most, implicit.

Even the expansion and systematization of paperwork by modern bureaucracies has not changed this dynamic. Cornelia Vismann observed from her study of modern filing systems that "Lists do not communicate; they control transfer operations."[6] The verbs of possession, display, and exchange show the social power of documents as physical objects and as evidence. Governments go to great expense and use the latest technology to prevent forgery of the most important identification and economic documents, such as passports and currency. Writing technology, now supplemented by technology for reproduc-

---

the "distancing" effect of writing but gave little attention to its original and continuing function in economics and law.

5. See Goody, *Logic of Writing*, 87–126; and Ben Kafka, "Paperwork: the State of the Discipline," *Book History* 12 (2009): 340–353.

6. Cornelia Vismann, *Files: Law and Media Technology* (Stanford: Stanford University Press, 2008), 6.

ing images and sounds, remains the major means by which modern societies try to protect themselves against the dangers of lying and fraud. Writing can be used this way because of its material and visual form, its iconic dimension.

Iconic Textuality in the Ancient Near East

The surviving artifacts and texts from ancient Egypt and Mesopotamia exhibit at least four forms of iconic textuality. The most obvious is the monumental royal inscription. Throughout the ancient Near East, rulers commemorated their victories and donations on stone, often of monumental size and expense. In Egypt, kings covered almost every temple wall with texts, most of which were brightly painted in chromatic colors. The primary purpose of monumental texts was not communication. The vast majority of people were illiterate, including most of the kings and aristocrats themselves. No doubt scribes made themselves readily available in temples and courts to read the monuments to interested parties, for a fee. But the politics motivating the massive expense of producing texts in this form and on this scale required no translation by experts: the look of the texts displayed power and wealth. Their production and display claimed political legitimacy for the king and his regime.[7]

A second obvious form of iconic textuality can be found in ancient art showing scribes plying their trade (Figure 4). Such scenes appear fairly often in tableaus of agricultural or military life. Egyptian funerary art also contains many prominent portraits of scribes, or at least the deceased portrayed as scribes. Here we find already a phenomenon common in later cultures: portraiture depicting people holding texts or surrounded by texts in order to characterize their educational achievements and their authority in transmitting and interpreting the literary tradition. The images of texts in their hands claim scholarly legitimacy for them, just as mounted displays of the faculty's books do in universities today.[8] When ancient kings could not plausibly claim scribal skills themselves, they could show themselves in the company of the scribes in their employ to lay claim to the same traditions of textual authority and legitimacy.

These two forms of iconic textuality are not limited to the ancient Near East or to cultures that have developed from it. For example, artifacts from the classical Maya of Central America also prominently feature monumental texts celebrating royal achievements and memorial sculptures of scribes plying their trade. Iconic ritualizations of texts in these unrelated agricultural societies probably fulfilled similar social and political functions.

7. Mario Liverani, "The Deeds of Ancient Mesopotamian Kings," in *Civilizations of the Ancient Near East* (ed. J. M. Sasson, New York: Scribners, 1995), 2353–2365.

8. Beal, "End of the Word as We Know It," 207–224.

Figure 4.   Painted limestone funerary sculpture of a scribe, Egyptian, ca. 2,500–
2,350 B.C.E. In the Louvre, Paris.

References to two more forms of iconic textuality have been preserved
in ancient Near Eastern literature and art. Kings and priests frequently
displayed and manipulated ritual texts to legitimize how rituals were performed.[9] Royal and temple commemorative inscriptions mention such practices while recording compliance with the instructions found in old texts.
When restoring temples, texts were often found buried in their foundations to preserve the "original" designs of the gods. In Egypt, responsibility
for ensuring compliance with ritual texts was delegated to specialists, the
priests "who hold the ritual." Ceremonial art regularly depicts them holding high the scroll in which the ritual instructions were written. They kept
these ritual texts in a temple library or archive, called by Egyptians the
"house of life," and strictly limited access to them. Later centuries increasingly credited authorship of such ritual and omen texts to gods of wisdom—Ea in Mesopotamia and Thoth in Egypt.[10] Egyptian scribal portraits
sometimes depict their subjects writing at the inspiration of Thoth. Thus in

9. James W. Watts, "Ritual Legitimacy and Scriptural Authority," *Journal of Biblical Literature* 124/3 (2005): 401–417.

10. Francesca Rothberg-Halton, "Canonicity in Cuneiform Texts," *Journal of Cuneiform Studies* 36 (1984): 127–144; Siegfried Schott,"Thoth als Verfasser heiliger Schriften," *Zeitschrift für Ägyptische Sprache und Altertumsurkunde* 99 (1972): 20–25.

ritual and in art, texts were displayed and manipulated to legitimize rituals and the priests who presided over them.

Mesopotamian mythic traditions showed a particular interest in another form of iconic text, namely heavenly texts. They conceived of the gods assembling annually on New Years Day to determine the fates for the coming year.[11] The scribal goddess, Nisaba, or god, Nabu, recorded their decisions with a silver stylus on tablets of blue lapis lazuli. In other words, they wrote with stars in the sky.[12] A huge corpus of Mesopotamian omen literature sprang from this conception of the stars and all of nature as a book in which the gods write their decisions regarding human fate.[13] The omen series occupied the peak of the educational curriculum, mastered only by the best and most privileged scribes. From omen texts they learned to *read nature like a text.* This conception of nature as text motivated the Mesopotamian's exhaustive records of the omens they observed. Subsequent cultures have continued to view nature as a text to be read, a metaphor that inspires much of modern empirical science.[14] It provides mythic legitimation for the enterprise of interpretation that underlies all academic disciplines.

But not all divine texts could or should be shared with humans. Several prominent myths depict the record of the gods' decisions not just in the sky or in nature but as a material text, though of course of a heavenly kind. It consists of tablets, often called "the Tablets of Destinies," whose possession grants supreme power and kingship among the gods. The Babylonian creation epic, *Enuma Elish*, features the tablets as a minor element in its plot.[15] The primordial mother goddess, Tiamat, bestows them on her choice to be king of the gods, but after defeating her, Marduk takes them away. His victory makes him king of the gods, with obvious political implications for Babylon, the city that he patronized. In the *Anzu* epic, the tablets play a more central role in the plot.[16] Here the traditional high god, Enlil, who usually wears the tablets on a string, is tricked into taking them off in order to bathe. The supernatural bird Anzu steals them and thereby gains power to thwart every attempt by any god to get them back. Ultimately, the young

11. Shalom Paul, "Heavenly Tablets and Books of Life," *Journal of the Ancient Near Eastern Society* 5 (1973): 343–353.

12. Parmenter, "Bible as Icon," 298–310.

13. Stephanie Dalley, *The Legacy of Mesopotamia* (Oxford: Oxford University Press, 1998), 166.

14. See, for example, Peter Kosso, *Reading the Book of Nature: An Introduction to the Philosophy of Science* (Cambridge: Cambridge University Press, 1992), 5–7

15. Benjamin R. Foster, *Before the Muses: An Anthology of Akkadian Literature* (3rd ed. Bethesda, MD: CDL, 2005), 436–486.

16. Foster, *Before the Muses*, 555–578.

deity Ninurta kills Anzu by trickery, but then refuses to return the tablets to Enlil. He claims them and kingship for himself.

Though many cylinder seals depict scenes from these myths, the Tablets of Destiny appear nowhere in extant Mesopotamian art. On reflection, that is not very surprising. The tablets are heavenly texts, never meant for human eyes. They are therefore the paradigmatic occult texts. To reproduce them in art would be to infringe on that supreme divine prerogative. (In fact, one thing that distinguishes images of texts from other images is that while an image of a person produces only a likeness, a realistically detailed image of a text reproduces at least part of the text itself.)

So these stories depict the Tablets of Destiny as magical devices that give their owners power over heaven and earth. It is tempting to characterize the function of these stories as mystifying omen texts, as perpetuating a misunderstanding of a text's nature. Omen texts *really* functioned as sources of information to the scribes who read them and who used that information to try to interpret the course of events around them. Though we may find their reasoning and conclusions flawed, we recognize the work of ancient scholars as similar to our own: they interpreted the semantic meaning of texts in search of information that they could use, just as we do. *We think* that reading alone transmits the text's influence and authority. Stories of magic tablets simply obscure the fact that limited access to literacy and education reinforces social stratification.

That is of course true, so far as it goes. But Vincent Wimbush and Philip Arnold point out that indigenous and colonized peoples recognized the iconic power of colonizing texts in ways that the conquerors who wielded them often did not.[17] I want to apply that observation to ancient ideas about heavenly texts. What cultural reality in the experiences of non-scholars did these myths address? Where in the experience of ancient Near Eastern peoples did texts ever function in the way that the Tablets of Destiny do in *Enuma Elish* and *Anzu*?

As it turns out, texts were frequently the prizes and/or victims of military conflict in the ancient Near East, just as they are in these myths. Conquerors erased or usurped the commemorative inscriptions of their enemies, captured and employed their scribes, and stole their libraries to augment their own. The latter practice is particularly interesting for illuminating the

17. Philip P. Arnold, "Paper Ties to Land: Indigenous and Colonial Material Orientations to the Valley of Mexico." *History of Religions* 35 (1995): 27–60; Philip P. Arnold, "Paper Rituals and the Mexican landscape," in *Representing Aztec Ritual: Performance, Text, and Image in the Work of Sahagún* (ed. Eloise Quiñones Keber, Boulder: University Press of Colorado, 2002), 227–250; Vincent L. Wimbush, *White Men's Magic: Scripturalization as Slavery* (Oxford: Oxford University Press, 2012), 48–73.

mythic theme. Its outstanding practitioner in antiquity was the Assyrian king, Asshurbanipal.

During Asshurbanipal's reign in the mid-seventh century B.C.E., the Assyrian empire was at its height, ruling most of the Near East including Egypt. The Assyrians have a well-deserved reputation for brutality, reinforced by the fact that they decorated their palaces with reliefs depicting their military victories in violent detail. Even a domestic scene of the king reclining at dinner shows the head of an enemy hanging from a nearby tree. But Asshurbanipal also had a literary side. He boasted that he could read and write well, which was apparently not a wide-spread skill among royals at the time. He ordered his scribes and his armies to collect texts for him wherever they went. Their number and contents are enumerated in booty lists totaling the yield of personnel and goods from his military campaigns. In his capital at Ninevah, he built libraries in his palace and in the temple of Nabu where texts were catalogued, collated and reproduced.[18] These collections were discovered by archeologists and are the sources of many of our best texts from ancient Mesopotamia, including the *Enuma Elish* epic summarized above.

In light of these political and military experiences, the myths about the Tablets of Destiny appear less mystifying. The idea that gods battled for control of powerful texts to establish supremacy simply projects the textual politics of earth onto heaven. It may be that for the very elite scribes who mastered the Mesopotamian omen series or the Egyptian ritual texts, a text's power lay in it semantic referents. For them the gods' wrote their decrees in nature and written texts only taught scribes what to look for or what to do. But to the less literate and illiterate royal elites as well as to commoners, texts were more obviously used by kings and temples to manifest power, wealth, and authority. They were clearly prizes in wars that legitimized the winner's right to rule. The notion that possession of such texts conveyed supremacy would seem obvious enough.

Indeed, it still seems obvious. Libraries and rare books and texts continue to be used as the spoils of war to establish or buttress claims of national identity and international supremacy. For those who study the cultures and religions of the ancient Middle East, as I do, the best place to go to see ancient texts and artifacts is not in the Middle East, but in London. The British Museum and the British Library seem to house fully half of all the manuscripts and

---

18. Stephen J. Lieberman, "Canonical and Official Cuneiform Texts: Towards an Understanding of Assurbanipal's Personal Tablet Collection," in *Lingering Over Words: Studies … in Honor of William J. Moran* (Harvard Semitic Monographs 37, ed. Tzvi Abusch *et al.*; Atlanta: Scholars Press, 1990), 305–336 [318].

artifacts that I and others in my field study on a regular basis. They include much of Asshurbanipal's library, which was excavated by British explorers and archeologists in the nineteenth century when the British Empire was at its height. Lawsuits by various countries to reclaim some of these materials from European and American museums emphasize the fact that these objects continue to convey political legitimacy and cultural prestige. Thus texts, art and other cultural artifacts remain prizes of war, just as they were three millennia ago. That is just as true for texts like the Rosetta Stone in the Louvre in Paris as for art objects like Nefertiti's Bust in a Berlin museum. Scholars protest that the needs of researchers, focusing on the semantic dimension of texts, should take priority over politics, represented most forcefully by the iconic dimension. But these texts still function as icons of cultural and political legitimacy whether we like it or not (Chapter 3).

The motives behind ancient and modern textual politics are not very different, despite the wide cultural gap between the stated goals of ancient and modern librarians and collectors. A colophon to some of the texts in Asshurbanipal's Nabu temple archive testifies:

> I, Assurbanipal, king of the universe, king of Assyria, on whom Nabu and Tashmetu have bestowed vast intelligence, who acquired penetrating acumen for the most recondite details of scholarly erudition, no predecessors of whom among kings having any comprehension of such matters, I wrote down on tablets Nabu's wisdom, the impressing of each and every cuneiform sign, and I checked and collated them. I placed them for the future in the library of the temple of my lord Nabu, the great lord, at Nineveh, for my life and for the well-being of my soul, to avoid disease, and to sustain the foundation of my royal throne. O Nabu, look joyfully and bless my kingship forever! Help me whenever I call upon you! As I traverse your house, keep constant watch over my footsteps. When this work is deposited in your house and placed in your presence, look upon it and remember me with favor![19]

Here Asshurbanipal boasts of his literacy as a mark of piety to gain personal favor with the gods. But he also gained political advantage from his reputation for wisdom and learning. This reputation provided him practical advantages over his rivals. The literate king found it useful to be able to arbitrate the advice of his omen-reading advisers by scanning their texts himself. This is attested by colophons of texts in his palace library that list their purpose "for my review in perusing" and "for my examining."[20] His mastery of the semantic dimension of texts gave him advantages over literate subordinates and illiterate rivals. He boasted that, along with military skills,

---

19. Translation by Foster, *Before the Muses*, 831.
20. Lieberman, "Canonical and Official Cuneiform Texts," 318-20, 326–328.

I mastered ... the hidden lore of all scribal knowledge. I am experienced with celestial and terrestrial omens, I have discussed them with the faculty of learned men. I have debated the work, "If a liver is an image of heaven" [haruspicy], with learned masters of divination, I have worked intricate mathematical calculations that had no solution.[21]

King Asshurbanipal therefore collected and controlled texts (especially the omen series) in order to extend and maintain his power. He had reason to think that controlling the semantic and iconic dimensions of texts in his possession grants power on earth as well as in heaven.

Iconic textuality, however, was also a potent defensive weapon against cultural imperialism. In the face of the onslaught of Hellenistic culture in the last few centuries B.C.E., Egyptian, Babylonian and Jewish temples became bastions of traditional culture and scribal training. Egyptians regarded a temple as the earthly realization of a heavenly book, both in its architectural plan and its inscriptions. The temple's design proclaimed the distinction between inner holiness and outer pollution.[22] The same can be said of Jerusalem's temple and purity regulations in this period. Within temple walls, priests learned to read and write in their native languages in deliberate resistance to the Hellenizing political and social forces outside.[23]

Out of these circumstances developed the practice of ritualizing the iconic, expressive and semantic dimensions of the Jewish Torah to produce the first scripture in Western religious traditions.[24] In the following centuries, Christians consolidated their identity against the Roman Empire by wielding their Gospel books, until Christian emperors transformed Gospels into monuments of the imperium itself, thus producing the second Western scripture.[25] Iconic textuality, whether in monumental or manuscript form, represented visually in each of these situations the reconstruction and preservation of a culture and its values that was also furthered by the oral performance and semantic interpretation of texts.

---

21. Translated by Benjamin R. Foster, *Akkadian Literature of the Late Period* (Münster: Ugarit-Verlag, 2007), 47.

22. Jan Assmann, *Das kulturelle Gedächtnis: Schrift, Erinnerung und politische Identität in frühen Hochkulturen* (Munich: Beck. 1997), 179–185.

23. David M. Carr, *Writing on the Tablet of the Heart: Origins of Scripture and Literature* (Oxford: Oxford University Press, 2005), 177–214.

24. James W. Watts, *Understanding the Pentateuch as a Scripture* (Hoboken, NJ: Wiley Blackwell, 2017), 10–18 and *passim*.

25. Larson, "Gospels as Imperialized Sites of Memory," 373–388.

Writing Iconic Texts

It would be natural to think that iconic veneration of scriptures is an after-effect of scripturalization, a secondary product of people believing in the sacred nature, or at least the supreme value, of specific books. You might think that these texts were first written just to communicate through the meaning of their words. Then, as those words became increasingly influential, the physical text itself began to be venerated, decorated, carried around, and monumentalized in the ways mentioned above. That is what people usually assume about the Bible, that biblical books became iconic secondarily after their semantic contents gained influence and prestige. It is tempting to relegate ritualization in general, and ritualization of the iconic dimension in particular, to the *history* of biblical interpretation and ritual, to argue that they had no role in how scriptures were written and canonized.[26]

This assumption is called into question by, first of all, the forms and functions of texts in the earliest literate cultures. As we have seen, many ancient Near Eastern texts were created for iconic use. Kings inscribed texts lauding their achievements on stone monuments and walls to exhibit their power and wealth not only by their rhetoric but also by their scale and expense, especially in ancient societies with very low literacy rates.[27] Texts were frequently created for iconic uses that interfered with reading them: commemorative texts were inscribed on precious materials to be deposited in the foundations and in the inner sancta of temples, curses were written on clay images of enemies and then shattered, blessings were recorded in tiny script to be carried perpetually in personal amulets. There is ample evidence that many texts were not only copied but also composed in the first place to serve such iconic functions.

Therefore, iconic ritualization is not necessarily a secondary consequence from venerating sacred texts. It can instead be a generator of textual veneration in the first place. A good example of this process can be found in the first scripture of Western religious history, the Torah or Pentateuch, which consists of the first five books of Jewish and Christian Bibles—Genesis, Exodus, Leviticus, Numbers, and Deuteronomy.[28] The first reason to think

---

26. Reception history has become a major trend in biblical scholarship over the past three decades. Its influence remains restricted, however, by the tendency to distinguish the text's original meaning in the minds of its authors from its later interpretation and use. Timothy Beal ("Reception History and Beyond: Toward the Cultural History of Scriptures," *Biblical Interpretation* 19 [2011]: 357–372) has argued for a broader approach to the "cultural history of the Bible" that would incorporate the history of media and usage from the text's origins up to the present day.

27. Mario Liverani, "The Deeds of Ancient Mesopotamian Kings," in *Civilizations of the Ancient Near East,* (ed. J. M. Sasson, New York: Scribners, 1995), 2353–2365.

28. See Christian Frevel, "On Instant Scripture and Proximal Texts: Some Insights into the

that the ritual manipulation of physical texts accompanied the formation of biblical literature is the fact that the Pentateuch commands its own ritualization in the iconic and expressive dimensions.

Moses, at the end of Deuteronomy, orders the Levitical priests to assemble all the Israelites—men, women, and children explicitly included—to hear the whole Torah read aloud: "Every seventh year, ... you shall read this Torah in the presence of all Israel" (Deuteronomy 31:11–12). The Torah, then, portrays itself as intended for public display and expression. Furthermore, stories in the Hebrew Bible about later events record at least three occasions when this command was fulfilled: by Moses's successor, Joshua (Joshua 8); six hundred year later by King Josiah (2 Kings 22–23); and two hundred years after that by Ezra, the priest and scribe: "Ezra opened the scroll in the sight of all the people ...; as he opened it, all the people stood up. ... The Levites explained the Torah to the people, while the people stood in their places" (Nehemiah 8:5, 7). By their focus on the ritualized assembly of the people, these texts show the Torah functioning as scripture not just by having its contents published for all to hear (the expressive dimension), but also by its public display to provide the physical evidence that legitimized the authority of these different leaders (the iconic dimension). The writers of Deuteronomy intended their text to be ritualized in these ways from the start.

Deuteronomy also requires Israelites to use Pentateuchal texts as personal amulets and public inscriptions: "Bind [these words] as a sign on your hand and let them serve as a symbol on your forehead; inscribe them on the doorposts of your house and on your gates" (Deuteronomy 6:8–9). This command can be interpreted metaphorically to refer to the memorization of the Torah's instructions, but traditional Judaism has also taken it literally. For at least the last two thousand years, miniature parchments inscribed with selections of Pentateuchal texts have been placed in phylacteries (*tefillin*) worn on forehead and arms during prayers, as well as placed in containers (*mezuzahs*) on doorposts and gateposts.[29] Again, Deuteronomy itself commands this iconic ritualization of its text.

The Pentateuch also describes the tablets that contain the Ten Commandments, the Decalogue, as intended to function as a relic text from the start: "[God] gave Moses the two tablets of the covenant, stone tablets inscribed by the finger of God" (Exodus 31:18). It is interesting that, in

---

Sensual Materiality of Texts and their Ritual Roles in the Hebrew Bible and Beyond," in *Sensing Sacred Texts* (ed. J. W. Watts, Sheffield: Equinox, 2018), 57–80, and Watts, *Understanding the Pentateuch*, 108–122.

29. Yehudah B. Cohn, *Tangled Up in Text: Tefillin and the Ancient World*, Providence: Brown University, 2008; Frevel, "On Instant Scripture," 62–67.

every biblical text that narrates this story, the oral proclamation of the Ten Commandments always precedes their inscription by God or Moses.[30] No text describes anyone ever reading the tablets after they have been written.

I call the Decalogue tablets a "relic text" because they are valued for being the specific objects that they are. Relic texts are rare, if not one-of-a-kind, and are in theory not reproducible (see Chapter 3 above). The Pentateuch portrays the Decalogue tablets as written to validate the covenant between God and Israel. The tablets serve as physical evidence of the treaty that turns God into Israel's king and that requires the people of Israel to remain loyal to their divine monarch.

Sacred relics generally require reliquaries. Reliquaries are containers ranging in size from small boxes to huge buildings that are designed to house and protect relics. The Pentateuch requires that the Decalogue tablets be deposited in such a reliquary chest, the Ark of the Covenant: "I will inscribe the commandments on the tablets … and you must deposit them in the ark" (Deuteronomy 10:2). Though Deuteronomy mentions only a simple wooden box, Exodus 29 describes a very richly gilded box with a solid gold cover, surmounted by golden cherubim similar to Egyptian sphinxes or medieval griffins. Examples of similar chests surmounted by the jackal god, Anubis, have been discovered in Egypt, most notably in King Tutankhamen's tomb. They contained ritual texts as well as embalming chemicals and ritual wands. The Pentateuch describes Israel's ark as also containing a jar of manna, the miraculous food that sustained the Israelites in the desert (Exodus 16:32–34), and Aaron's staff that miraculously bloomed to demonstrate the priest's God-given supremacy over Israel's rituals and teachings (Numbers 17:10). But the ark is defined by the relic texts that it contains, by the tablets of the covenant given by God to Moses. Deuteronomy 31:24–26 requires that a copy of the Torah scroll also be deposited in the sanctuary beside the Ark of the Covenant. Thus the public, exoteric text—the scroll—gets associated with the mystical, esoteric text—the tablets—that it describes. Once the ark and its tablets disappeared, probably during the Babylonian conquest of Judah in 586 B.C.E., the scroll of Torah remained the only physical evidence for the tablets, the commandments, and the Torah. The ark and its contents remain literarily available now in the pages of the Bible.[31]

The Torah was also ritualized as a monumental inscription early in Israel's history, according to the stories about Israel's conquest of the prom-

---

30. Compare Exodus 20:1-17 with Exodus 24: 4, 12, and 31:18; Exodus 34:10–26 with 34: 27–28; and Deuteronomy 5:6–21 with 9:10–11 and 10:1–5.

31. For a more detailed defense of this thesis, see James W. Watts, "From Ark of the Covenant to Torah Scroll: Ritualizing Israel's Iconic Texts," in *Ritual Innovation in the Hebrew Bible and Early Judaism* (ed. N. MacDonald, BZAW 468, Berlin: De Gruyter, 2016), 21–34.

ised land of Canaan. Joshua inscribed the Torah on a stone altar before leading the Israelites in reciting its contents: "Joshua built an altar . ... On the stones, he inscribed a copy of the Torah that Moses had written for the Israelites" (Joshua 8:30, 32). Monumental inscriptions were commonly used in the ancient Near East not only to commemorate people and events, but also to ratify treaties and laws. Joshua's inscription of the Torah inside the land of Israel ratified its application as the law of the Israelites in *this* land.[32]

The means of iconic ritualization of scriptures have stayed remarkably consistent over the millennia, in contrast to the means by which Jews and Christians ritualize their semantic and expressive dimensions. Though the Psalms still get used as texts for worship music and also for communal and individual meditation, uses for which the Psalter seems to have been designed, the semantic and expressive uses of many other biblical texts have been dramatically transformed from their original functions. That includes much of the Pentateuch. Leviticus 1–16, for example, was written to pre-scribe or at least legitimize ritual performances in ancient Israel's temples. After those temples were destroyed almost two thousand years ago, the ritualized reading and interpretation of Leviticus 1–16 replaced those temple rituals in Rabbinic Judaism, while Christian liturgies for the most part excluded these texts entirely. The contents of Leviticus have been allegorized for theological meanings by Jewish and Christian commentators alike.

By contrast, the ritual manipulation of physical texts of scriptures or other sacred texts has remained remarkably consistent over four thousand years. The deliberate display and physical manipulation of scrolls and codices of scriptures by modern priests, rabbis, and even Evangelical ministers is quite similar to the depictions of priests, scribes, and angels doing the same thing in the art of ancient Egypt, Greece, and Rome. And when it comes to monumental display, Decalogue tablets in monumental form are still being installed on public land in the United States to validate the religious origins of the nation's laws. Lawsuits try to deny the legitimacy of that claim by requiring the removal of the monuments (Chapter 7).

The function of iconic ritualization is to legitimize the texts, their contents, and those people and institutions associated with the texts as their owners and interpreters. Proving possession by displaying relic texts or their reliquaries provides people with prestige and legitimacy. Relic texts get ritualized in the iconic dimension alone, so their chief function is legitimation. People do not read them much. Instead, they value their possession: owning relic texts legitimizes individuals and communities and conveys a sense of empowerment, while losing them threatens their identity (Chapter 3).

---

32. Frevel, "On Instant Scripture," 58–61.

Who or what then did the writers of the Pentateuch wish to legitimize by requiring the iconic ritualization of Torah scrolls and Decalogue tablets? The obvious answer is Israel itself and its claims to the land promised by God. The Pentateuch's sanctions, however, make those claims contingent on obedience to the stipulations of the covenant, that is, to Torah (Leviticus 27, Deuteronomy 27–30). So ritualizing the Torah's iconic dimension legitimizes the laws and instructions contained within it. It also legitimizes those people whose job it was to enact those instructions in Israel's temples and to teach the people of Israel how to obey the Torah properly.

Leviticus grants that job to one family, the descendants of the first high priest, Aaron:

> The Lord spoke to Aaron: . . . This is a permanent mandate throughout your generations: to separate the holy from the secular and the polluted from the pure, and to teach the children of Israel all the mandates that the Lord spoke to them through Moses (Leviticus 10: 8–11).

Aaron's descendants have not wielded religious leadership in Jewish and Christian communities for almost two thousand years. They were replaced in Judaism by scholarly rabbis who claimed Moses' mantle as interpreters of Torah and in Christianity by priests and churches claiming authority from the Christ of the Gospels rather than the Moses of the Torah. The Torah nevertheless continues to legitimize the authority of Aaron's descendants over one religious tradition, that of the Samaritans who now number less than one thousand people. Their current high priest is Abed-El ben Matzliach, who claims descent from Aaron through his son, Ithamar.[33]

From the sixth century B.C.E. through the first century C.E., however, dynasties of Aaronide high priests governed both Jewish and Samaritan temples. As this period wore on, they also accumulated political power. It was the high priest who represented Jews to foreign emperors such as Alexander and the Romans. One of these priestly dynasties, called the Hasmoneans or Maccabees, succeeded in wresting Judean independence from imperial domination for eighty years in the second and first centuries B.C.E. Some of these rulers claimed the title "king" as well as "high priest."

It was during the rise of Aaronide high priests in Second Temple Judaism that the Torah began to function as scripture for Jews and Samaritans. Its contents first directed the ritual practices of their temples. Then over time its application spread beyond the temples to the behavior of Jews and

---

33. See "High Priests" on the Samaritan community's website at http://www.the-samaritans.com/high-priests/. For the ancient history of the Samaritans, see Gary N. Knoppers, *Jews and Samaritans: the Origins and History of their Early Relations*, Oxford: Oxford University Press, 2013.

Samaritans in their villages and homes. Thus, while Aaronide priests consolidated their religious authority and political power from their base in the temples, the law book that governed those temples spread its authority and influence over Jewish and Samaritan communities.[34] Priests and Torah rose to prominence together: the priests ritualized the Torah and the Torah legitimized the priests.

Iconic ritualization was therefore a key factor in creating the first Western scripture, the Torah. The Torah narrates the gift of divinely written tablets to Moses, tablets that are never read but instead enshrined in a reliquary for the stone texts, the Ark of the Covenant, that represents God's presence with Israel. Simultaneously, Moses writes scrolls of torah (law or instruction) to accompany the Ark of the Covenant, that report on the tablets' origins and contents, among other things, and that must be read aloud regularly to the entire people of Israel. Religious devotion soon came to regard the Torah, too, as written in heaven.[35] In this way, iconic display joined ritualized expression and semantic interpretation as engines for scripturalizing Torah, both in antiquity and in later periods when bibles incorporated the Pentateuch into larger collections of scriptures.

Ritualizing texts in the iconic dimension therefore played a fundamental role in how the Torah, and later the rest of the Jewish and Christian Bibles, came to be scripture. It still plays a major role in preserving the Torah's and Bible's status as scripture in Jewish, Samaritan, and Christian communities. It was the ancient writers of the Pentateuch who mandated their text's iconic ritualization in these ways, though they could not possibly have foreseen the remarkable success of this strategy.

---

34. See C. T. R. Hayward, "Scripture in the Jerusalem Temple," in *The New Cambridge History of the Bible: From the Beginnings to 600* (Cambridge: Cambridge University Press, 2013), 321–44; and James W. Watts, "The Political and Legal Uses of Scripture," in *The New Cambridge History of the Bible: From the Beginnings to 600*, 345–64.

35. Sirach 24: 23; Baruch 4: 1; Acts 7: 53; see Parmenter, "The Bible as Icon," 298–310.

Rival Iconic Texts
Ten Commandments Monuments and the U.S. Constitution

In 2001, the newly elected Chief Justice of Alabama, Roy Moore, installed a two-ton granite monument of the Ten Commandments in the rotunda of the State Judicial Building. In the summer of 2003 after a series of lawsuits, a federal court ordered the monument removed as an infringement on the constitutional separation between church and state. This order prompted an outpouring of support for the monument and for Judge Moore. Evangelical Christians protested and prayed beside the monument, then in front of the building after they were evicted from the premises. A Jewish rabbi promised Moore the support of two Orthodox Jewish organizations. Delays in implementing the court order extended the protests for several weeks until the monument was finally removed from view.[1]

These events were covered extensively by the news media, both in the U.S. and abroad. They prompted many debates about religion, law and the state, but also much bemusement over the emotional intensity that this monument aroused. No one should have been surprised. Events like this were occurring around the country. For example, protesters had to be dragged away from a plaque of the Ten Commandments in Chester County, Pennsylvania, in 2002, to allow it to be covered while a lawsuit over its display was appealed. Though one judge ordered the plaque removed, an appeals court overruled her, saying that it could be preserved because of the 83-years-old plaque's historical value.[2] Lawsuits against Ten Commandments monuments on public land have been filed in numerous communities.[3]

---

1. "Alabama Chief Justice Unveils Ten Commandments in State Supreme Court," AP, August 1, 2001; "Commandments fight turns to high court," AP, August 15, 2003; "Ten Commandments monument moved," CNN, November 14, 2003.

2. Jonathan Gelb, "Hundreds protest shrouding of Commandments," *Philadelphia Inquirer*, April 23, 2002.

3. For a summary and analysis of the legal issues and responses, see Claudia Setzer and

Figure 5.   The Ten Commandments on a monument on the grounds of the Texas State
Capitol in Austin, Texas. Image courtesy of Wikimedia.

Sometimes, protests have occurred *against* Ten Commandments monuments
and, in a few places, such monuments have been vandalized with graffiti
proclaiming them unconstitutional.[4]

Clearly, a plaque or monument of the Ten Commandments carries powerful symbolism in contemporary America. But why has this symbol become
such an object of devotion and conflict? As I watched and read the news
coverage of the Alabama commandments, I realized that my research on
iconic books can cast some light on this state of affairs.

David A . Shefferman, *The Bible in American Culture: A Sourcebook* (New York: Routledge,
2011), 85–90.

4. For example, a protest against a local Ten Commandments monument took place in
   Austin, Texas, on March 29, 2000 (Metroplex Atheists, "Respect Our Constitution Rally
   2000," http://www.metroplexatheists.org/%20roc0300.htm, accessed March 9, 2004).
   Graffiti proclaiming "Not on public land" defaced a monument in South Bend, Indiana,
   as reported by Nancy Bounds, "Ten Commandments monument defaced by vandals in
   South Bend," *Elkhart Truth* (Elkhart, IN), August 8, 2001.

Ten Commandments monuments in the United States function more as visual symbols than as texts to be read. They are in that way quite like ancient Israel's tablets of the commandments (Chapter 6), though much more visible. The legal battles over their placement on government property provide a prominent example of contemporary controversies about iconic texts.

The nation's founding documents, the Declaration of Independence, the U.S. Constitution, and the Bill of Rights, have also been turned into monumental icons on government property. The controversies over Ten Commandments monuments can therefore be understood as competition between iconic texts for symbolic supremacy. Like the placement of divine images in ancient Near Eastern temples, struggles over the public display of iconic national and religious texts involve claims for their ideological precedence in America today.

Iconic Books and Texts Today

Previous chapters have surveyed iconic books across different cultures and religions, from the invention of writing 5,000 ago up to digital texts today. This historical and cross-cultural analysis shows that iconic ritualization of books has not declined in modern times. If anything, it has increased over the nineteenth and twentieth centuries, and plays a central role in very many contemporary religions as well as in the politics of many countries.

One kind of evidence for this conclusion can be found in the portrayal of scriptures in visual art. Prior to the nineteenth century, books or other kinds of texts were usually depicted in the company of people: they symbolize that person's scholarship or religious orthodoxy or, in the case of divine figures, the source of the book's authority.[5] Traditional Jewish art was reticent to portray Torah scrolls and preferred to depict the ark that contains the scrolls. But in imagery from the last one hundred and fifty years, sacred books and scrolls have been freed of such contexts and have themselves become objects of artistic interest. Pictures of bibles or torah scrolls or copies of the Qur'an now appear frequently as the focus of attention in works of art and in popular media. In contemporary visual culture, they have become independent icons of religious truth and power.

The Alabama Ten Commandments was also this kind of iconic text. Of course, proponents of the Ten Commandments movement promote reading the commandments as well: one philanthropist promised $10 to every child in America who memorized them, until he had to suspend the program because so many took the challenge.[6] But the granite monument was

---

5. Watts, "Scripture's Indexical Touch," 181–183.

6. "Founder suspends project that paid U.S. youths to memorize the Ten Commandments," AP, April 10, 2003.

designed to be seen as much as read. Its massive bulk symbolized divine authority behind human law. Its public display in a court building laid claim to representing religion as a fundamental source of American government.[7]

So the controversy over the monument is one symptom of contemporary culture's fascination with iconic texts. Examining this debate in the historical context of two American movements to ritualize iconic texts will cast the politico-religious conflict over Ten Commandments monuments in a different light than does the usual legal and political commentary.

The Ten Commandments Movement

In 2000, the Associated Press reported that "With its message on yard signs, book covers and on the walls of courthouses and public classrooms, a Ten Commandments movement is pushing forward in Kentucky and nationwide."[8] The article mentioned efforts to post Ten Commandments in courts and schools in Kentucky, Pennsylvania, and California. Ten Commandments rallies took place across the country. Frank Flinn wrote that "This controversy is quickly replacing abortion as the litmus test for Christian values in the public forum. A complicated constitutional lawsuit over abortion is difficult to pay for and argue. Hanging the Decalogue in a public hallway is both cheap and easy."[9] The escalating battles over such monuments in the following years confirmed his assessment.

Roy Moore initially gained fame in 1995 as an Alabama circuit judge who refused a court order to remove the commandments hanging in his courtroom. The AP reported that he then spoke to Christian groups around the country, urging "school boards to post the Ten Commandments even if it means a costly lawsuit for the district."[10] Moore then campaigned for Chief Justice of the Alabama Supreme Court on the slogan "The Ten Commandments Judge" and won by a wide margin.

When Moore installed his granite monument of the Ten Commandments in the rotunda of the Alabama Judicial Building in 2001, he did so in the middle of the night without consulting the other justices of the court. But he did make sure his action would be noticed. "A Florida TV preacher who supports Moore, D. James Kennedy, had a crew from his Coral Ridge Ministries

---

7. See The Ten Commandments Defense Fund, "Defending the right to display the moral foundation of law," http://www.tencommandmentsdefense.org/ (accessed February 12, 2004).

8. "Alabama chief justice defends controversial monument," AP, October 16, 2002.

9. Frank K. Flinn, "Whose Commandments? Which Version?"Scripps-Howard News Service, 2000.

10. Associated Press, "Ten Commandments replacing abortion as key Christian issue, scholar says," January 7, 2000.

film the installation and offered videotapes of it for a donation of $19," the AP reported.[11] In the lawsuits that followed, Moore testified that he began planning to put a monument in the judicial building at his inauguration in January 2001. So Moore acted self-consciously to promote a national movement of Christian political action and to defy its opponents. His defense attorney called the suits against the monument part of a national movement "to censor God." The Ten Commandments had become a symbol of Evangelical political goals.

The ensuing lawsuits led to removing not only the monument from the Judicial Building but Roy Moore himself, who lost his position as Chief Justice in 2003. After campaigning unsuccessfully for governor twice, Moore was reelected Chief Justice 2013 and removed again in 2016, this time for refusing to allow same-sex marriage. In 2017, Moore won the Republican nomination for the U.S. Senate, showing the continuing popularity of his defense of Ten Commandments monuments, though a sex scandal cost him the general election.

However, other courthouse monuments of the Ten Commandments are products of earlier movements. In fact, the commandments have been a common motif in Western religious and legal art.

The tablets of the commandments emphasize the centrality of law in Jewish tradition, and are a common feature of synagogue architecture. The tablets alone or with lions rampant often decorate the synagogue ark that occupies the most prominent position in front of the congregation and contains the Torah scrolls. The fact that the tablets are frequently depicted as containing only the numerals one through ten, rather than the actual commandments, further emphasizes their symbolic role in Jewish and Christian cultures.

During the fifteenth-century Protestant Reformation, some European churches replaced their pictorial altar pieces with biblical texts, often the Ten Commandments, as part of an iconoclastic reaction against images in churches.[12] In England, "decalogue boards" appeared after the Reformation, not only to display standards of Christian behavior but also to justify the legal power of the state over the church. Few have survived the changing tides of English religious politics: many were painted over by seventeenth-century Puritans who opposed all visual displays, even textual ones; others were reinstalled by eighteenth-century Evangelicals, but then were disman-

---

11. Bob Johnson, "Alabama chief justice defends controversial monument," *Athens Banner Herald* (Athens, GA), October 16, 2002.

12. Joseph Koerner, "The Icon as Iconoclasm," in *Iconoclash: Beyond the Image Wars in Science, Religion, and Art* (ed. B. Latour and P. Weibel; Karlsruhe: ZKM, 2002), 204–209.

tled again by the nineteenth-century Anglo-Catholic Oxford Movement.[13] Their fate shows that the Ten Commandments have long been a potent symbol when religion and state clash over legal issues. It also shows that their symbolism may be wielded by the state against religious dissidents as much as by religious groups against state authority.

Art in other contexts usually portrays the commandments in the hands of Moses, a scene often reproduced in monumental sculpture decorating graveyards and memorials, and also in American law schools and court houses. The U.S. Supreme Court building was erected in 1934 in Washington D.C. It portrays Moses holding the tablets of the commandments as the central and largest figure on its east pediment.[14] U.S. Court rulings allow such displays if they are motivated by historical, rather than religious, intent. In this case, Confucius and Solon flank Moses so that the three represent historical antecedents of U.S. law in Chinese, Hebrew and Greek cultures. But Moses' central position and larger size nevertheless gives succor to the Ten Commandments movement. Proponents often cite it and other artwork depicting Moses and the commandments in Washington's government buildings as examples of the federal judiciary's hypocrisy in outlawing Ten Commandments displays on public land.[15]

Religious groups erected some Ten Commandments monuments on public sites in American cities as early as the 1920s.[16] After World War II, Minnesota Judge E. J. Ruegemer and the Fraternal Order of Eagles, a nationwide service club, pushed to have the Ten Commandments posted on the walls of schools and court rooms.[17] Ruegemer defended this action as non-

13. Suffolk Country Churches, "Decalogue, Royal Arms," http://www.suffolkchurches. co.uk/zdecalogue.htm (accessed May 28, 2015).

14. Office of the Curator, Supreme Court of the United States, "East Pediment Information Sheet," updated May 22, 2003, http://www.supremecourt.gov/about/eastpediment.pdf.

15. So, for example, Rev. Pat Robertson: "We could have won this thing if we had said, 'Listen, you have the Ten Commandments in your courtroom in Washington. You have the Ten Commandments over the Speaker's dais in the House of Representatives. And if we have to take it down in Alabama, you have to take it down out of your building up there in Washington.' Had [Moore] pitched it that way, he may have been successful" (CBN News, "Sekulow Weighs in on Ten Commandments Battles," August 27, 2003). The same point was made visually by Carrie Devorah with photo essays collecting together the religious art in Washington's government buildings ("Exclusive Photo Essay: God in the Temples of Government, Parts I and II," *The National Conservative Weekly*, November 24, 2003 and December 19, 2003).

16. For the significance of the Ten Commandments in American culture, see Jenna Weissman Joselit, *Set In Stone: America's Embrace of the Ten Commandments*, New York: Oxford University Press, 2017.

17. Emmet V. Mittlebeeler, "Ten Commandments," in *The Encyclopedia of American Religion and Politics* (ed. P. A. Djupe and L. R. Olson; New York: Facts on File, 2003), 434.

Figure 6.   Moses, Solon, and Confucius on the east pediment of the U.S. Supreme Court
building in Washington, DC.

sectarian, because "The Commandments are not just a religious rule, but
a good code of conduct which can be followed by everyone, regardless of
creed."[18] The trend gathered steam in the 1950s when the Eagles began
donating granite monuments of the Ten Commandments to court houses
across the country. This effort was supported by the Hollywood producer,
Cecil B. DeMille, whose movie "The Ten Commandments" was released in
1956.[19] Though published estimates of how many monuments the Eagles set
up reach as high as 4,000,[20] a count by independent researcher Sue Hoffman
has documented only around 150.[21] In the 1990s, Evangelical Christians reen-
ergized such efforts by mobilizing to defend existing monuments and to
install new ones.

Proponents have often repeated the claim that the commandments dis-
till a moral and spiritual code common to Judaism, Christianity, Islam, and

18. Jay Sekulow, "What's the Problem With Public Displays of the Ten Commandments?"
American Center for Law and Justice, http://aclj.org/10-commandments/what-s-the-
problem-with-public-displays-of-the-ten-commandments (accessed May 29, 2015).

19. The Fraternal Order of Eagles, "Commanding Presence: Judge E. J. Ruegemer," March
2002, http://www.foe.com/magazine/march2002/mar_07.pdf (accessed March 18,
2004).

20. Warren Wolfe, "Ten Commandments: Different state, different judge, different time,"
Minneapolis Star Tribune, August 30, 2003.

21. Sue Hoffman, personal correspondence, February 16, 2005.

other religions. The Eagles worked to synthesize the different wording and enumeration of the commandments in Jewish, Catholic and Protestant traditions to produce a version acceptable to all. The commandments monuments were therefore one more expression of the mid-twentieth-century effort to promote an American civil religion that also added the phrase "under God" to the Pledge of Allegiance.[22] It built on a tradition dating back to 1864, when "in God we trust" first appeared on U.S. coins. These moves during the Civil War and the Cold War tapped religious sentiment to reinforce American nationalism. The Ten Commandments monuments, by virtue of their monumental character, gave God a visible place in public space, which is what their sponsors intended. That is the function of any public monument, as Robert S. Nelson and Margaret Olin observed: "The Monument expresses the power and sense of the society that gives it meaning, and at the same time obscures competing claims for authority and meaning."[23]

Claims for the universalism of the commandments encountered more resistance at the beginning of the twenty-first century, however, when immigration had diversified the American religious landscape and Christian and Jewish communities found themselves split internally over many issues, including state display of the commandments on government property. For example, several groups representing Christian and Jewish denominations as well as interfaith organizations filed legal briefs opposing Roy Moore's posting of the Ten Commandments in his courtroom,[24] in direct opposition to the Christian and Jewish organizations that supported it. The commandments now became a symbol of conservative political and religious agendas in an era when sharp ideological differences divided religious and political institutions alike.

Some advocates used the decades-old tolerance for Ten Commandments monuments for openly divisive purposes. Rev. Fred Phelps proposed erecting monuments on public lands in cities in Wyoming, Idaho, and Kansas to commemorate Matthew Shephard, murdered in 1998 because he was gay. But Phelps intended to commemorate Shephard not as a victim of murder, but as an object lesson of someone who "entered hell" because of his homosexual behavior. In Pennsylvania, Phelps announced a similar effort to focus on a

---

22. The classic description of American civil religion was by Robert N. Bellah, "Civil Religion in America," *Dædalus* 96/1 (1967), 1–21.

23. Robert S. Nelson and Margaret Olin, "Introduction," in *Monuments and Memory, Made and Unmade* (ed. R. S. Nelson and M. Olin; Chicago: University of Chicago Press, 2003), 7.

24. Presbyterian Church (USA), amicus brief: "James v. American Civil Liberties Union of Alabama, *et al.*," May 8, 1997, http://oga.pcusa.org/media/uploads/oga/pdf/am17.pdf (accessed May 28, 2015). Similarly, Associated Press, "Court mulls Commandments displays; Jews split, Christians silent," February 21, 2005.

gay man who committed suicide in 1997. Phelps cited a ruling of the Tenth Circuit Court of Appeals that "any city that displays a Ten Commandments monument on public property must also allow monuments espousing the views of other religions or political groups on that same property."[25] The city council of Casper, Wyoming, frustrated Phelps' legal challenge by removing their Ten Commandments monument, donated by the Eagles in 1965, from the city park to a "historic monument plaza" which it shares with copies of the Declaration of Independence, the Preamble to the Constitution, the Mayflower Compact, the Bill of Rights and the Magna Carta.[26] In 2003, a small sect, Summum, sued the city of Pleasant Grove, Utah, to allow its monument of aphorisms to stand beside the Ten Commandments in the city park. This case was eventually decided by the U.S. Supreme Court, which ruled against Summum on the grounds that "The placement of a permanent monument in a public park is a form of government speech and is therefore not subject to scrutiny under the Free Speech Clause" of the U.S. Constitution.[27] Similarly, after a Ten Commandments monument was donated and installed on the grounds of the Oklahoma State Capitol in 2012, the Satanic Temple petitioned to install its statue of Baphomet there too.[28] The state legislature refused, but then was itself forced to remove the Ten Commandments monument after a successful suit by the ACLU on the separate legal grounds that the state was endorsing religious speech.[29] While the court cases dragged on, one man smashed the monument by hitting it with his truck.[30]

As controversy and court cases continue to swirl around when and under what circumstances decalogues can appear on public property in the U.S., many advocates of monuments to the Ten Commandments have moved or erected them on private property, often as a direct result of the controversies.[31] However, the conflict also continues to be fought on its original battleground, government property: a state senator sponsored and funded a

---

25. Associated Press, "Group seeks monument condemning gay victim," February 1, 2004.

26. "F.O.E. Ten Commandment Monuments in Wyoming (11)," Jefferson Madison Center for Religious Liberty, http://www.eaglesmonuments.com/states/Wyoming.html (accessed January 22, 2017).

27. Pleasant Grove City, Utah, *et al.* v. Summum, 555 U.S. 460 (2009), https://www.law.cornell.edu/supct/html/07-665.ZS.html.

28. Nash Jenkins, "Hundreds Gather for Unveiling of Satanic Statue in Detroit," *Time*, July 27, 2015.

29. Heide Brandes, "Oklahoma's Top Court Says State Must Remove Ten Commandments Monument," Reuters via the *Huffington Post*, July 27, 2015.

30. " 'Satanist' claims he destroyed Ten Commandments statue in Oklahoma," AP via *The Guardian*, October 26, 2014.

31. Bob Unruh, "Decalogues Everywhere, with Thanks to ACLU," *WorldNetDaily*, June 7, 2008.

monument installed on the Arkansas State Capitol's lawn in 2017, and the ACLU immediately planned a legal challenge.[32]

These developments illustrate not only the complicated legal problems posed by religious monuments, but also the iconic tendency of monuments to generate more monuments. When society enshrines some texts, it encourages the creation of more iconic texts and monuments. Opposing social groups tend to interpret the symbolic relationship between such texts differently: some see them as mutually supportive while others view them as contradictory. Since the relationship between iconic texts is symbolic, such disputes cannot be resolved by simply interpreting the contents of the texts.

The net effect of this history is that the Ten Commandments have become a symbol in America for the claim that U.S. law and government developed from religious roots and that they should remain true to them. However, the Ten Commandments are not alone in being displayed on public property as iconic texts. In fact, the Ten Commandments movement was playing catch-up with another movement in American society, namely, one to elevate the country's foundational documents as icons. That movement has developed in ways that parallel both the Ten Commandments movement and many of the other ways in which religious groups revere and popularize their sacred texts.

Iconic American National Texts

Since the late 1940s, another American service organization, the Exchange Club, has been placing "Freedom Shrines" in public schools, government buildings and courthouses throughout the U.S. The shrines contain twenty or thirty documents, including the Declaration of Independence, the U.S. Constitution and the Bill of Rights, as well as materials ranging in date from the Mayflower Compact of 1620 to Martin Luther King, Jr.'s "I have a dream" speech in 1963.[33] The National Exchange Club developed Freedom Shrines as part of its "Americanism" project to promote "pride in country, respect for the flag and appreciation of our freedoms."[34] The club claims to have placed more than 12,000 shrines nationwide. It distributes the shrines to its local clubs together with suggested rituals and speeches for dedication ceremonies.[35]

---

32. Laurel Wamsley, "Ten Commandments Installed At Arkansas State Capitol; ACLU Plans Lawsuit," NPR, June 27, 2017.

33. The National Exchange Club (NEC), "Freedom Shrine," https://www.nationalexchangeclub.org/the-freedom-shrine/ (accessed November 4, 2017).

34. The National Exchange Club (NEC), "Americanism," http://www.nationalexchangeclub.com/ProgramsService/a.htm (accessed February 12, 2004).

35. The National Exchange Club (NEC), "Exchange Marketplace," http://exchangemar-

Also in the middle of the twentieth century but on a grander scale, the founding documents of the United States were installed in the rotunda of the National Archives in Washington D.C. At the installation ceremony on December 13, 1952, President Harry S. Truman said:

> The Declaration of Independence, the Constitution, and the Bill of Rights are now assembled in one place for display and safekeeping.... We are engaged here today in a *symbolic* act. We are *enshrining* these documents for future ages.... This magnificent hall has been constructed to exhibit them, and the vault beneath, that we have built to protect them, is as safe from destruction as anything that the wit of modern man can devise. All this is an honorable effort, based upon *reverence* for the great past, and our generation can take just pride in it.[36]

After undergoing extensive renovations, the rotunda of the National Archives was reopened on September 18th, 2003. The National Archives promoted the event with rhetoric of not only national, but world renewal: "The Charters of Freedom: A New World is at Hand." Its description captured a sense of the rotunda's architectural effect:

> Placed in the center of the grand 75-foot high domed semi-circular Rotunda, the Charters are currently displayed in a raised marble case, flanked by two 35-foot murals depicting the presentation of the Declaration of Independence to John Hancock, president of the Continental Congress, on the left; and James Madison presenting George Washington with the final draft of the U.S. Constitution, on the right. The Declaration is mounted vertically on the wall above the Constitution and the Bill of Rights. Each night the Charters are lowered twenty feet into a steel and reinforced concrete vault beneath the display area.[37]

Truman rightly described the foundational documents as "enshrined." The architecture of the rotunda and its display cases evokes, consciously or unconsciously, the impression of a massive synagogue ark that protects and displays Torah scrolls.

The tendency to characterize the Constitution as incomparable was taken even further by the publicity for the new National Constitution Center which opened in Philadelphia on July 4, 2003. It promotes itself as a constitutional theme park:

> Just as the Constitution affects every facet of Americans' daily lives, so will the National Constitution Center (NCC) use a wide variety of media – inter-

---

ketplace.safeshopper.com/23/cat23.htm?580 (accessed February 12, 2004).

36. From the U.S. National Archives and Records Administration, http://www.archives.gov/ (accessed September 8, 2003, italics added).

37. From the U.S. National Archives and Records Administration, http://archives.gov/exhibits/charters/ (accessed September 8, 2003, italics added).

active and multi-media exhibits, live actors and interpreters, film, music, artifacts, television, text panels and labels, sculpture, and the Internet – to bring the document to life.[38]

This textual theme park invites comparison with Christian bible theme parks that have been popular in America since the mid-twentieth century. The Evangelical park, Heritage USA, in Fort Mill, South Carolina, attracted millions of people annually for a decade but closed in the late 1980s, as did the Catholic Holy Land USA in Waterbury Connecticut. But others continue to attract visitors: Holy Land Experience opened in Orlando, Florida, in 2000, and Field of the Woods in Murphy, North Carolina, which among other things advertises "the world's largest Ten Commandments," has been open to visitors continuously since 1945.[39]

Similarly, in Philadelphia's Constitution Center, the text of the Constitution is etched in 450 feet of illuminated glass encircling the main exhibit hall. At the center's opening, boosters proclaimed the universal importance of the Constitution in language that makes the claims of the Ten Commandments' movement look modest by comparison. "Through these elements, NCC visitors will discover the history behind the *world's most important document* as well as the depth and breadth to which it affects every single American today."[40]

This rhetoric begs the question of the Constitution's relationship to that other document venerated by many Americans as the most important text in the world, namely, the Bible.[41] There is an old tradition of American legal thinking that compares the interpretation of the U.S. Constitution with the interpretation of scripture.[42] Less well known is the long if irregular tradition of venerating the Declaration of Independence and the U.S. Constitution

38. The National Constitution Center, http://www.constitutioncenter.org/index.shtml, (accessed July 8, 2003).

39. For Heritage USA, see Wikipedia, "Heritage USA," at http://en.wikipedia.org/ wiki/Heritage_USA; for Holy Land USA, see Wikipedia, "Holy Land USA," at http:// en.wikipedia.org/wiki/Holy_Land_USA; see Holy Land Experience at http://www. holylandexperience.com/; for Field of the Woods, see RoadSide America, "World's Largest Ten Commandments," at http://www.roadsideamerica.com/story/2613; all sites accessed May 29, 2015.

40. Accessed July 8, 2003, italics added; for the current, somewhat less hyperbolic publicity, see The National Constitution Center at http://www.constitutioncenter.org/index. shtml.

41. My description here of iconic veneration of the U.S. Constitution draws on the research of my former student, Jason Lewis, used with his permission.

42. See Edward S. Corwin, "The Constitution as Instrument and Symbol," *The American Political Science Review* 30/6 (1936): 1071-1085; Max Lerner, "Constitution and Court as Symbols," *The Yale Law Journal* 46/8 (1937): 1290–1319; Thomas C. Grey, "The Constitution as Scripture," *Stanford Law Review* 37/1 (1984): 1–25; Sanford Levinson, *Constitu-

as iconic texts. The Declaration quickly became an icon of American independence. Its hand-written and signed text was widely reproduced and performed aloud in the 1780-90s and again in the 1820-30s, reinforced by celebrating the date on this document, July 4th, as *the* national holiday.[43] Abraham Lincoln drew on the Declaration regularly, especially its proclamation that "all men are created equal," to justify the Union cause during the Civil War.

In the judgment of Peter Gardella, the Constitution "has been less powerful as an icon than the Declaration, but more important as a text."[44] Within one year of the document's ratification, however, Benjamin Rush described the procession of the Constitution through the city of Philadelphia as

> truly sublime. The Constitution was carried by a great law officer [Chief Justice Thomas McKean of Pennsylvania], to denote the elevation of the government and of the law and justice above everything else in the United States.

Rush went on to say,

> I do not believe that the Constitution was the offspring of inspiration, but I am perfectly satisfied that the Union of the States, in its *form* and *adoption* [i.e. the Constitution], is as much the work of a Divine Providence as any of the miracles recorded in the Old and New Testament were the effects of a divine power.[45]

On the fiftieth anniversary of the drafting of the Constitution, President John Quincy Adams paraphrased a biblical reference to learning Torah (Deuteronomy 6: 7-9) to declare:

> Teach the [Constitution's] principles, teach them to your children, speak of them when sitting in your home, speak of them when walking by the way, when lying down and when rising up, write them down upon the doorplate of your home and upon your gates.[46]

Adams was the only U.S. President to take the oath of office on a bound corpus of Constitutional law rather than on a Bible.[47]

---

tional Faith, Princeton: Princeton University Press, 1988; Jaroslav Pelikan, *Interpreting the Bible and the Constitution* (New Haven, CT: Yale University Press, 2008).

43. Peter Gardella, *American Civil Religion: What Americans Hold Sacred* (Oxford: Oxford University Press, 2014), 101–103.

44. Gardella, *American Civil Religion*, 117.

45. Michael Kammen, *A Machine that Would Go of Itself: The Constitution in American Culture* (New York: Alfred A. Knopf, 1994), 45.

46. Levinson, *Constitutional Faith*, 12.

47. The Constitution itself (Article VI, clause 3) requires office holders in the federal and state governments to take oaths to support the U.S. Constitution, so ritualizing itself as

The famous manuscripts of the Declaration of Independence and the Constitution on display in the National Archives are "engrossed" copies, intentionally produced after their adoption for public display. The contents of both documents circulated immediately in printed form. Though the manuscripts were created from the beginning to serve as icons, they were neglected through much of the nineteenth century.[48] Only in the 1920s were they put on display in the Library of Congress. But after World War II, the Constitution and Declaration of Independence toured the United States on a "Freedom Train." The tour stopped in over three-hundred cities in all forty-eight states and was visited by over three million people. Attendees were encouraged to sign a "rededication scroll" that was then placed in the Library of Congress.[49]

The Constitution has also been ritualized in its expressive dimension. Pageants focusing on the Constitution began to be performed in 1935 in preparation for the upcoming Constitutional sesquicentennial, directed by a Pageantry and Drama Commission appointed by the U.S. Congress.[50] Many school children were required to memorize the Constitution's preamble. Public readings of the preamble now feature in annual celebrations on September 17th, which was officially designated Constitution Day in 2004. In 2011, a new Republican majority in the U.S. House of Representatives opened the legislative session by reading the Constitution aloud.[51] Art commemorating the Constitution's adoption, such as Howard Chandler Christy's painting, Scene at the Signing of the Constitution (1940) and Alton S. Tobey's More Perfect Union (1987), is widely reproduced and readily recognized in American today.

Nevertheless, the energy for expressive ritualization seems always to fade quickly, while iconic ritualization has grown steadily more prominent. Since the mid-twentieth century, the U.S. government and various private groups have been raising the iconic status of the Constitution and its associated documents by treating them as visual symbols of the nation's government and ideals. Of course, proponents also hope to encourage greater familiarity with them as texts by reading them. Like the Bible, writers often

the object of national loyalty. Gardella misinterpreted this oath in claiming that "With regard to the oaths taken by officeholders, the Constitution itself stood in the place of God" (American Civil Religion, 125). The Constitution instead puts itself in the place of the sovereign, that is, the king, to whom the former colonists had previously been required to swear loyalty.

48. Kammen, Machine, 72–73.

49. Jeffrey F. Meyer, Myths in Stone: Religious Dimensions of Washington DC, Berkley: University of California Press, 2001; Gardella, American Civil Religion, 107–108.

50. Kammen, Machine, 300–309.

51. Philip Rucker and Krissah Thompson, "Two new rules will give Constitution a starring role in GOP-controlled House," Washington Post December 30, 2010.

bemoan the fact that the Constitution is more venerated than read and remembered.[52] But the focus on the physical form of the U.S. Constitution and Declaration of Independence, whether the "original" documents (in the National Archives rotunda) or in reproduction (in the Constitution Center and in Freedom Shrines), encourages a symbolism and universalistic rhetoric otherwise associated with the sacred texts of various religious traditions.

The Rivalry of National Iconic Texts

The protestors at the Alabama courthouse would probably not have liked claims for the incomparability of the U.S. Constitution, though the Ten Commandments movement is not inherently anti-constitutional, far from it. Some Evangelical leaders hold a very high view of the Constitution as "the greatest document ever penned by human hands," an oft-repeated catch-phrase that exempts comparisons with divinely-inspired scripture.[53] The idea was first expressed by Supreme Court Justice William Johnson in 1823.[54] Mormons take the next step and proclaim the U.S. Constitution itself as divinely inspired, as also did 2008 presidential candidate Ron Paul.[55]

Most proponents of Ten Commandments monuments, however, want the Constitution and the federal courts that interpret it to acknowledge the higher authority of God and scripture. Some protestors in Alabama wore t-shirts that juxtaposed a cross over the American flag and waved their bibles as they burned copies of the federal court order to remove the monument from the rotunda.[56] This ritual concisely represented the conflict as one between iconic texts, one raised in honor while the other was destroyed. It also illustrated the fact that the texts that each side champions represent

---

52. Meyer, *Myths in Stone*, 85–86.

53. Used in this way by, for example, the conservative commentators Cal Thomas ("The Battle for the Constitution," Townhall.com, accessed June 4, 2003) and David Black ("Why Do Conservative Christians Uphold the Scriptures Yet Compromise on the Constitution?" August 7, 2003, http://www.daveblackonline.com/why_do_conserva-tive_christians_u.htm [accessed May 29, 2015]); Rev. Jerry Falwell preferred to restrict this accolade to the Declaration of Independence ("Founding Fathers," Liberty Alliance, August 10, 2000).

54. Corwin, "Constitution as Instrument and Symbol," 1075.

55. See *The Book of Mormon: The Doctrine and Covenants of the Church of Jesus Christ of Latter-Day Saints* 101: 80; cf. Frederick Gedicks, "American Civil Religion: an Idea Whose Time is Past," *George Washington International Law Review* 41 (2012), 891–908. In 2007, Ron Paul issued a "Statement of Faith" on his campaign website which in the second-to-last paragraph read: "I am running for president to restore the rule of law and to stand up for our divinely inspired Constitution" (originally posted at http://www.ronpaul2008.com/homeschoolers/statement-of-faith; later available at http://www.asianews.com/modules.php?name=News&file=article&sid=3177 [accessed May 27, 2015]). The line did not appear in the Statement of Faith distributed by his 2012 campaign.

56. Associated Press photo, August 31, 2003.

and, to some degree, camouflage other realities: Evangelicals use the Ten Commandments as a cipher for the whole Christian Bible, an iconic book that represents for them the sum of Evangelical beliefs about religion and politics. The Federal Courts use the Constitution as a cipher for their own authority over American law, and over every aspect of government and society that law governs. This sets the two texts, as icons, on a collision course for symbolic supremacy.

Some communities have compromised by combining the two movements. They have incorporated the Ten Commandments into a display of significant "historical" documents, since court rulings allow historical, but not religious, displays. An imitator of Roy Moore erected a short-lived monument in North Carolina in front of the Winston-Salem City Hall with the Ten Commandments on one side and the Bill of Rights on the other.[57] More enduring examples can be found in Charles County, North Carolina, the Georgia State Capitol, and the Garrard County Courthouse in Lancaster, Kentucky. The Christian Coalition sponsored the installation of such a display in the Alabama State Judicial Building after failing to save Moore's monument.[58] But Moore himself rejected this compromise: "To put things around the Ten Commandments and secularize it is to deny the greatness of God," he said.[59] "First, they hid the word of God in a closet; and now they tried to hide it among other historical documents. Neither is an acknowledgment of God."[60]

Moore's career exemplifies the fact that we live in a period of iconic struggle in which many of the most contested icons are books or texts. Analysis of this news from the perspective of comparative iconography allows us to see patterns of cultural development that the legal arguments obscure.

Some Evangelical observers have commented on the irony of advocating stone monuments of commandments whose contents forbid "carved images of anything in heaven, on earth, or under the earth."[61] Christian opponents of Roy Moore have bluntly labeled his efforts "idolatrous."[62] From this per-

57. "City Hall Ten Commandments monument surfaces in North Carolina," AP, January 20, 2004.

58. Susan Jones, "Ten Commandments Return to Alabama Judicial Building," CNSNews. com, February 06, 2004.

59. Kyle Wingfield, "Alabama governor unveils Capitol display including Ten Commandments," Associated Press, September 10, 2003.

60. Jones, "Ten Commandments Return," CNSNews.com, February 06, 2004.

61. Exodus 20:4; see "Editorial: God Reigns-Even in Alabama; Let's not make the Commandments into a graven image," *Christianity Today* 47/10 (October 2003), 35.

62. Jeffrey Gettleman, "Ten Commandments Supporters Rally On," *The New York Times*, August 24, 2003; Robert Marus and Greg Warner, "Moore: Defender of faith or dangerous demagogue?" *Associated Baptist Press*, August 26, 2003.

spective, the federal courts can be viewed as iconoclasts trying to keep their temples pure from foreign influences. But the iconoclastic controversies between the supporters and opponents of images that have periodically erupted in Jewish, Christian and Muslim history have generally resulted in replacing one set of images with another, and this case is no exception.[63]

The public display of iconic texts *per se* is not seriously in question in the current debate, only their appropriate location. That too has been characteristic of iconoclastic controversies, but an even better analogy to the current conflict can be found in ancient struggles for the supremacy of one image over others. Ancient gods were patrons of particular temples and states, and the placement and relative positions of their images in ancient Near Eastern temples reflected the political status of kings and cities. Victorious kings would place the gods of conquered cities in subordinate positions before their own patron deity. A biblical story about such iconic rivalries can be found in 1 Samuel 5, in which Israel's Ark of the Covenant refuses to let itself be subordinated to a Philistine cult statue. The iconic struggle over the Ten Commandments in contemporary America is not about whether to have iconic texts, and even less about whether to enshrine the commandments or the Constitution. It is rather about *where* to enshrine them and *how* to represent their relative position and status.

Rarely mentioned in the media frenzy over the Alabama case was the fact that the Alabama State Judicial Building already contained an iconic text, a bronze copy of the Bill of Rights.[64] Moore and his supporters want the Constitution to bow before the Ten Commandments and the Bible. In their words, they want the courts "to acknowledge God." The federal courts refuse to compromise the Constitution's symbolic supremacy over the U.S. government and society. Their rulings defend the sanctity of a national icon, the Constitution, and its temples, the courts. Both sides are engaged in a battle for the symbolic supremacy of their iconic texts. In Alabama, the granite commandments have come and gone, but the bronze Bill of Rights remains.

Because Western culture has for so long privileged texts over images, many readers' immediate reaction to this account may be to dismiss the entire conflict as superficial, as masking the "real" battles about how to interpret these important texts, the Bible and the Constitution. This reaction stems from the belief that interpretive issues in law and theology are more important than is symbolism, which functions simply as an inexact shorthand for these underlying issues.

---

63. Bruno Latour, *Iconoclash*, 4.

64. Roy Hoffman, "Alabama Ten Commandments monument is gone, not forgotten," *Religion News Service*, January 10, 2004.

From the perspective of the comparative study of iconic texts, however, such appeals to the semantic dimension of texts look like one more interpretation of the iconic nature of these books and texts as metaphors for political and religious authority (see Chapter 8). To claim greater reality or significance for the words of texts than for their physical forms and images paradoxically enhances the unique characteristics of texts that make them such potent icons in the first place. Books and texts have been invested with iconic status by long and widespread usage. The fact that some become particularly prominent in certain times and places does not mitigate the iconic function of all texts.

So we cannot avoid the symbolic import of texts, nor the fact that some have greater iconic appeal than others. A society can choose which ones to promote and "enshrine." That is exactly what the conflict over Ten Commandments monuments is about. At stake in its outcome is the fundamental issue of how the U.S. government will represent iconicly its relationship to various religious ideas and to the many different religions represented within the American population.

8

Book Aniconism
The Codex, Translation and Beliefs about Immaterial Texts

> Women and little children suspend Gospels from their necks as a powerful
> amulet, and carry them about in all places wherever they go. Rather do thou
> write the commands of the Gospel and its laws upon thy minds. Here there
> is no need of gold or property, or of buying a book.[1]

As previous chapters have noted, the study of iconic books has been
neglected by academic scholarship. Drawing attention to this gap raises the
question of why this research has not been done before. There are deeper
reasons than just academic myopia. There is an old and powerful resistance
in both academic and popular culture to seriously considering the significance of the material forms and uses of books.

Book Aniconism

Dorina Miller Parmenter recounted the story of a professor at a Christian
College who dropped a bible on the floor in front of his class and then deliberately stepped on it. He scandalized his pious students, but his purpose was
orthodox according to his Christian theology. His point was that the material book of scripture does not matter, only the meaning of its text matters.
The real Bible is an immaterial text that finds many and varied manifestations as physical books.

His actions and words expressed a belief in what I call "book aniconism."
The word "aniconism" describes movements and ideologies that discourage
the use of images (icons) in one way or another. It most commonly describes
religious doctrines that maintain that God cannot be seen and should not
be depicted by the visual arts—beliefs prominent to varying degrees in the
history of Judaism, Christianity, and Islam. Book aniconism, then, refers to
the belief that what matters about texts is their semantic meaning, not their

---

1. John Chrysostom, *Homily on the Statues* 19.14, in NPNF, ser. 1, vol. 9, 470; cited by Parmenter, "Iconic Book," 80-81.

visual appearance or material form. Book aniconism is frequently supported by a belief in immaterial texts.

Parmenter summarized studies that have documented this attitude as a dominant force in religious studies, in anthropology, and even in art history.[2] Though the humanities have recently rediscovered the bodily and material aspects of their subjects, this emphasis has not done much yet to refocus society's attention from words and their meanings. Instead, the weight of modern history has strengthened belief in immaterial texts. The Protestant Reformation, the Enlightenment, and many scientific and technological transformations have each reemphasized the translatability and transferability of human knowledge. A belief in immaterial texts now undergirds the "knowledge economy" and the marketing of "information technology." The whole culture has become enchanted by "virtual" texts in "the cloud." This rhetoric disguises the internet's physical infrastructure of screens, optical cables, server farms, and energy grids. Mass media and the marketing of digital technology obscure the materiality of texts now more than ever before.

My colleagues in the Iconic Books Project and SCRIPT have credited this blind spot variously to modernist[3] and orientalist[4] denigrations of superstition, to the humanities' failure to consider how illiterate people use written texts,[5] and to literate biases generally: Brian Malley observed that "efficacious" use of the Bible "is quite alien to us, the compulsively literate, and so such practices tend to be neglected in the study of the Bible's reception."[6] Many have singled out the influence of the Protestant Reformation's emphasis on the Bible alone.[7] Some have observed the same tendencies in non-Western and premodern traditions: Joanne Waghorne noted that iconic book practices deviate from orthodox Brahmin practice and have been encouraged in India by Christian and Muslim influence, and also by ancient Tamil book culture.[8] Katharina Wilkens observed the on-going conflict between "literacy ideologies" in Islamic cultures.[9]

2. Parmenter, "Iconic Book," 63–66; Parmenter, "Material Scriptures."

3. Myrvold, "Engaging with the Guru," 262.

4. Suit, "*Muṣḥaf* and the Material Boundaries," 192–193; Svensson, "Relating, Revering, and Removing," 32.

5. Yoo, "Possession and Repetition," 300, 302–303.

6. Malley, "Bible in British Folklore," 315.

7. Parmenter, "The Iconic Book," 65; idem, "A Fitting Ceremony," 55–56; Svensson, "Relating, Revering, and Removing," 32; Kinnard "It Is What It Is (Or Is It?)," 152, following Schopen, "The Phrase."

8. Waghorne, "Birthday Party for a Sacred Text," 283, 286, 289, 297.

9. Wilkens, "Infusions and Fumigations," 121–127.

Parmenter observed the anti-materialism promoted by an emphasis on the word and on oral transmission in a wide variety of religious traditions.[10] I argue in Chapters 1 and 9 that scribal and scholarly authority is rooted in the semantic dimensions of texts alone, and is often undermined by expressive and iconic ritualization. Scholars of every time and culture therefore have a vested interest, usually subconscious, for denigrating the importance of texts' expressive and, especially, iconic dimensions.

The view that what matters about a text is only what it says may seem like a rationalist, modern perspective, but it actually dates back to ancient times. It was common among Christian intellectuals already in the fourth and fifth centuries C.E. Jerome, the Christian hermit and translator of the Bible into Latin, complained about people who collected Gospels written in gold on purple parchment in jeweled bindings rather than reading them.[11] His contemporaries, the desert fathers, worried about the presence of "many fine books" in their remote retreats,[12] as also did Augustine and the Council of Laodicea. John Chrysostom, in the passage quoted at the beginning of this chapter, expressed the view of most theologians and humanistic scholars ever since, that what matters about books is their semantic meaning. That belief fuels scholars' translation efforts and their production of sermons and commentaries that search for the Bible's original meaning and apply it to contemporary circumstances. From their perspective, too much attention to the material form of the book, its iconic dimension, interferes with understanding and internalizing its message. This old and authoritative precedent in Christian tradition fuels the resistance of the modern scholars cited by Parmenter, as well as of Christian clergy who have long tried to suppress "magical" uses of scripture.[13]

Believers in the immateriality of sacred texts are quick to criticize people who value the material form and appearance of scripture. They denounce reverence for the material book as a form of superstition, of magic, even of idolatry. They claim that ritualizing the iconic dimension of scriptures interferes with true religious piety which should focus on spiritual rather than material realities. This attitude is book aniconism. Unlike acts of book destruction or desecration (biblioclasm) that attack a tradition by destroying its book, book aniconism develops within a religious tradition as an attempt to purify and protect it. However, like the iconoclasts of medieval

---

10. Parmenter, "Material Scripture."

11. Jerome, *Ep.* 22:32; also *Preface to Job*, PL 28: 1142.

12. Larson, "Gospels as Imperialized Sites of Memory," 384, citing the *Apophthegmata Patrum.*

13. See the examples cited by Malley, "The Bible in British Folklore."

Byzantium or early modern Protestants who destroyed images to reform Christianity, book aniconists view ritualizing a book's iconic dimension as at best a distraction and at worst a perversion of true religion, which should instead express itself internally as belief and faith.

Some support for the belief in the immateriality of texts, or at least of scripture, can be found in the Bible itself. The prophet, Jeremiah, predicted that the people of Israel would enjoy direct revelation of God's law unmediated by people or books:

> I will make a new covenant with the house of Israel and the house of Judah. It will not be like the covenant that I made with their ancestors .... I will put my law within them, and I will write it on their hearts; and I will be their God, and they shall be my people. No longer shall they teach one another, or say to each other, "Know the LORD," for they shall all know me.[14]

The apostle Paul echoed Jeremiah while strengthening the suspicion of written scripture:

> You are a letter of Christ, prepared by us, written not with ink but with the Spirit of the living God, not on tablets of stone but on tablets of human hearts ... ministers of a new covenant, not of letter but of spirit; for the letter kills, but the Spirit gives life.[15]

Thus Paul sharpened Jeremiah's complaint into a dichotomy between living spirit and dead letter, and set the stage for his book aniconist successors.

Chapter 6 showed that the Bible also provides explicit support for ritualizing its iconic dimension. For believers in the immateriality of texts, however, the dichotomy between semantic meaning and material text represents the mystical dichotomy between the human spirit and body. This analogy between books and people is reflected widely in religious thought and in book rituals far beyond Christianity.[16] Just as ascetics direct attention away from the body and towards the spirit, theologians direct attention away from the physical book and towards its contents. They do not destroy physical books because the material form is required as a container for its words, but they emphasize the words. They are unlikely to pay much attention to the fact that their own book practices contradict their belief in book aniconism: intellectuals are often very attached to their book collections! But that proclivity usually gets dismissed as personal idiosyncrasy.[17]

---

14. Jeremiah 31: 31–34 NRSV, quoted in Hebrews 8:9–10, 10:16.

15. 2 Corinthians 3:3, 6 NRSV.

16. See the essays in Myrvold, *Death of Sacred Texts* and Chapter 10 below.

17. It was frequently lampooned by eighteenth- and nineteenth-century satirists. See, for example, T. F. Dibdin, *The Bibliomania or Book Madness: Containing Some Account of the History, Symptoms, and Cure of this Fatal Disease* (1809), 59 ff.

Book aniconists insist that any container, any textual form, is as good as another so long as it conveys the meaning of the words to readers.

Many religious traditions share this tendency to believe in the immateriality of sacred texts. Most literate cultures nurture book aniconists, usually scholars and sages who criticize iconic book practices. Here I cite just a few examples to illustrate the cultural range and antiquity of these criticisms.

The medieval Jewish philosopher, Maimonides, criticized the use of amulets containing the written name of God as "utterly senseless."[18] Several centuries later, an Iberian rabbi, Duran, celebrated the decoration and embellishment of Bible codices as analogous to Solomon's decoration of the Temple, but still criticized wealthy Jewish families who thought that "possessing these books is sufficient as self-glorification, and they think that storing them in their treasure-chests is the same as preserving them in their minds."[19]

Many Islamic authorities have disparaged the use of amulets containing Qur'anic verses. Others have approved well-intentioned "prophetic medicine" that manipulates verses, including ingesting them, for physical health. Wilkens summarized this traditional debate:

> The use of magic, *sihr*, is one of the most contentious issues in the field of Qur'anic medicines, talismans and incantations. Al-Suyūṭī himself cites contradictory *ḥadīths* from Aḥmad ibn Ḥanbal, saying at one point that drinking a Qur'anic potion for medicinal purposes is "well and good" but that wearing amulets is an "abomination."[20]

Today, public discourse about proper Islamic practice usually denigrates amulets and Quranic potions, while their private use continues to flourish.[21]

The medieval Buddhist monk, Dōgen, who introduced Zen Buddhism to Japan, told a story approvingly about a monk who burned his whole collection of scriptures (*sutras*) and commentaries when he realized they would not lead him to enlightenment.[22] Dōgen nevertheless also mandated ceremonies of reading sutras by which monks ritualize Buddhist scriptures in expressive and iconic dimensions. His instructions included how monks should sit by rank, the distribution of scriptures and their collections accompanied by bows, the circumambulation of the donor during the recitation, and the ritual assignation of the reading's merit by posting a writ-

---

18. Maimonides, *Guide to the Perplexed* 1.61.

19. Stern, "Hebrew Bible in Europe in the Middle Ages," 267–268.

20. Wilkens, "Infusions and Fumigations," 125, citing Cyril Elgood, "Tibb-ul-Nabbi or Medicine of the Prophet," *Osiris* 14 (1962), 33–192 [155–157].

21. Wilkens, "Infusions and Fumigations," 127.

22. Dōgen. *Shōbōgenzō: The True-Dharma Eye Treasury* (tr. Gudo Wafu Nishijima and Chodo Cross; Berkeley: BDK America, 2007), 111.

ten notice.[23] Dōgen's attitude was book aniconic rather than biblioclastic: he did not advocate the destruction or avoidance of scriptures, only that they be used for their proper purpose. In Zen thought, enlightenment can only be found beyond the semantic meaning of the scriptural text and even beyond language itself.

Book aniconic criticisms also get voiced in modern secular cultures. For example, political commentators have long criticized Americans for invoking their "constitutional rights" when they have only a vague recollection of the text of the U.S. Constitution, if they have ever read it at all.[24] Today, advocates of digital texts embrace book aniconism with zealous fervor. For example, in 2011 James Gleik dismissed fears of digitization as "sentimentalism, and even fetishization." Citing the $21 million auction price of a copy of the Magna Carta as "odd," he asked "Why is this tattered parchment valuable? Magical thinking. It is a talisman. The precious item is a trick of the eye." He justified this conclusion by his belief in the immateriality of texts: "The real Magna Carta, the great charter of human rights and liberty, is available free online, where it is safely preserved. It cannot be lost or destroyed." His only evidence for the permanence of digital media was the age-old analogy between people and books: "An object like this — a talisman — is like the coffin at a funeral. It deserves to be honored, but the soul has moved on."[25]

This widespread belief in immaterial texts involves complicated philosophical issues of both epistemology and ontology. On the one hand, it seems very strange to claim immaterial permanence for human artifacts. On the other hand, the exact reproduction of a text in different books and digital media is empirically verifiable. That cannot be said for other popular beliefs, such as the endurance or transmigration of human souls after the death of their bodies.

Rather than pursuing these philosophical issues here,[26] I want to point out instead that modern beliefs in the immateriality of texts and book aniconism have been reinforced by two traditional practices with Christian scriptures. As we have seen, Christian theologians share a tendency towards book aniconism with intellectuals in other religious traditions. But book

---

23. Dōgen. *Shōbōgenzō*, 348–352.

24. Meyer, *Myths in Stone*, 85–86.

25. James Gleick, Books and Other Fetish Objects, *The New York Times Sunday Review*, July 16, 2011.

26. See Watts, "Books as Sacred Beings," *Postscripts*, forthcoming. For "container" as a fundamental metaphor of human thought and action, see George Lakoff and Mark Johnson, *Metaphors We Live By* (2nd edition; Chicago, IL: University of Chicago Press, 2003), 29–30, 58–60.

aniconism and belief in the immateriality of texts are widespread among lay Christians as well. Despite high regard for the Bible, popular devotional practice has not developed standardized etiquettes for the proper handling and storage of scripture like those among Jews, Muslims, Sikhs, Buddhists and Jains. Concerns about proper handling of bibles is often regarded as unwarranted by lay people and clergy alike.[27] Unlike devotees of many other scriptural religions, relatively few Christians worry about polluting or desecrating their copies of scripture.

There is a theological explanation for Christian's lack of concern for their material bibles. It maintains that belief in Jesus Christ as the bodily incarnation of the Word of God displaces concerns for the material scripture. Instead, concerns regarding pollution and desecration get focused on holy sites and, in some traditions, on the holy bread and wine used in the ritual of the Eucharist. However, the studies of Brown and Parmenter show that Christian designation of both Christ and Bible as "Word of God" has often led to equating them in theology and in art.[28] Christians' lack of concern for the purity and integrity of bibles therefore requires further explanation.

Christian belief in the immateriality of the Bible has been reinforced by two distinctive ritual practices with books. Christians have, from the very beginning, ritualized their scripture's iconic dimension in un-prestigious forms and its expressive dimension in multiple vernacular languages. The physical forms of Christian books and the vernacular languages in which they are read reinforce a belief in immaterial texts among Christians, and among their secular Western successors.

The Aniconic Codex: Notebook Religion

Early Christians adopted the codex for their religious documents and books. A codex is the form that almost all books take today: separate sheets of paper (or papyrus or parchment, etc.) are folded and bound together at the fold. Christian preference for the codex was unusual, because Greeks and Romans used codices primarily as notebooks. They kept their prestigious texts in the form of scrolls. Contrary to this cultural valuation of scrolls over codices, Christians preferred to produce their books as codices, especially the texts they regarded as scripture. Already by the second century, their codices included books of their Old Testament, the Greek translation of Jewish scriptures, as well as the Gospels and Paul's letters.[29]

---

27. Nevertheless, the concern does appear among Christians, as Parmenter has documented ("A Fitting Ceremony," 55–70).

28. Brown, "Images to Be Read"; Parmenter, "Iconic Book."

29. Larry W. Hurtado, *The Earliest Christian Artifacts: Manuscripts and Christian Origins* (Grand

Early Christians bound similar materials together, so one codex might hold Paul's letters while another might hold four gospels. The New Testament developed as a collection of four such volumes.[30] By the time the Roman Empire tolerated Christianity in the fourth century, the codex was already the iconic form of Christian scripture reflected in liturgy, art and imperial sponsorship.[31]

Historians speculate about why Christians adopted the codex for their scriptures. Common theories include the idea that they used codices for ease of cross reference. However, the practical advantages of codices seem to have been exaggerated, especially when their more complicated construction is taken into account.[32] A more likely suggestion is that Paul's letters were circulated in codices already in the first century (2 Peter 3:15–16), which privileged the codex in Christian imagination.[33] What is clear is that the codex quickly came to represent distinctively Christian books.[34]

Though codices replaced scrolls in the broader culture with the Christianization of the Roman Empire in the fourth century, Jews were much slower to adopt the codex form. They finally did so in the Middle Ages under the influence primarily of Islamic book culture which utilized codices from the start.[35] Synagogue rituals continue to use manuscript scrolls of the Torah and some other scriptures to this day.

Widespread adoption of the codex generated new ways of thinking about books or, more accurately, of thinking with books. Michel Melot described the epistemological change brought about by adopting the codex instead of the scroll as "thinking with the fold." Melot observed that the fold adds a third dimension to sheets.

> Thinking with the fold is not like thinking with the scroll. It occupies neither the same space nor the same time. The fold produces this prodigious transformation from a simple form into a complex form without adding anything

---

Rapids, MI: Eerdmans, 2006), 43–61.

30. David Trobisch, *The First Edition of the New Testament* (Oxford: Oxford University Press, 2000), 21; Tomas Bokedal, *The Formation and Significance of the Christian Biblical Canon* (London: Bloomsbury T. & T. Clark, 2014), 154.

31. Larson, "Gospels as Imperialized Sites of Memory."

32. Colin Henderson Roberts and T. C. Skeat, *The Birth of the Codex* (Oxford: Oxford University Press, 1983), 45–53.

33. Harry Y. Gamble, *Books and Readers in the Early Church: A History of Early Christian Texts* (New Haven: Yale University Press, 1995), 58–65.

34. Irven M. Resnick, "The Codex in Early Jewish and Christian Communities," *The Journal of Religious History* 17/1 (1992): 1–17 [4].

35. David M. Stern, "The First Jewish Books and the Early History of Jewish Reading," *Jewish Quarterly Review* 98/2 (2008): 163–202 [194–196].

at all. ... The fold divides spaces without separating them, at the same time distinct yet connected, two by two, front and back but also face to face or back to back, exterior and convex, interior and concave, two connected and two opposite. ... The book thus allows thinking continuity within discontinuity and discontinuity within continuity. The fold gives birth to a form of thought that is dialectical.[36]

As Lev Grossman put it, "The codex ... gave readers a power they never had before, power over the flow of their own reading experience."[37]

One of the "discontinuities within continuity" facilitated by the codex is the tendency to distinguish a book's contents from its material form. Rather than choosing between practical and ideological explanations for the Christian preference for codices,[38] we should remember that favoring "practicality" is itself an ideological position. Whatever the initial stimulus for doing so, Christians chose to produce their scriptures in the book form that the wider culture regarded as disposable and practical for notebooks, rather than in the scroll form that marked more valuable books. By favoring codices over scrolls, early Christians expressed in their material book practices the same tendency toward book aniconism that was voiced by Chrysostom and other early church leaders. Christians adopted the more "practical" codex for their scriptures rather than the valued and prestigious scroll because, in their view, only the meaning of the words mattered. The material form and look of the codex emphasized the importance of content over form. Eventually, however, their preference had the effect of turning the codex into the most iconic book form of all.

I will not devote more space to Christian adoption of the codex, because its development and impact has been widely discussed in recent scholarship. Another ancient Christian tendency, the desire to translate scripture into vernacular languages, has also reinforced book aniconism and the belief in immaterial texts. I will discuss this development in more detail because

---

36. "La pensée pliée n'est pas la pensée déroulée. Elle n'occupe ni le même espace ni le même temps. Le pli opère ce prodige de transformer une forme simple en une forme complexe sans rien y ajouter. ... Le pli divise les espaces sans les séparer, à la fois distincts et solidaires, deux à deux, recto-verso mais aussi face à face ou dos à dos, extérieurs et convexes, intérieurs et concaves, deux contigus et deux opposés. ... Le livre permet ainsi de penser le continu dans la discontinuité et le discontinu dans la continuité. Du pli naît alors une forme de pensée qui est celle de la dialectique" (Michel Melot, "Le livre comme forme symbolique," §13–14, Conférence tenue dans le cadre de l'Ecole de l'Institut d'histoire du livre, 2004; online at http://ihl.enssib.fr/le-livre-comme-forme-symbolique, accessed January 21, 2017). See also Michel Melot, *Livre* (Paris: L'Oeil Neuf, 2006), 39–55.

37. Lev Grossman, "From Scroll to Screen," *The New York Times Sunday Book Review*, September 2, 2011.

38. So Resnick, "Codex," 7.

there has been less recognition of the ideological impact of ritualized translation practices.

Aniconic Language: Vernacular Religion

Early Christian texts took a linguistic form that also expressed book aniconism. One of the most unusual features of Christian scripture when compared to the scriptures of other religious traditions is its linguistic mutability. Most scriptural religions value, even venerate, the original language of their scriptures.[39] A survey of the languages of scripture in various traditions will make this contrast clear.

The Languages of Jewish Scripture

Jewish history features competing claims for the ritual use of a scripture in its original language and in vernacular translations. The Jewish practices are highlighted by the contrasting choices of its younger sibling religions, Christianity and Islam.

The Jewish Torah consists of five books, Genesis, Exodus, Leviticus, Numbers and Deuteronomy—the Pentateuch. It first began to be ritualized as scripture in the fifth or fourth centuries B.C.E.[40] The Torah is written in Hebrew, the vernacular language of the people living in the kingdoms of Israel and Judah in the eighth to sixth centuries B.C.E. However, Aramaic was already replacing Hebrew as the vernacular by the end of the fifth century.[41] That means, then, that when the Torah was first being ritualized as a scripture, it was already being ritualized by a community that spoke a vernacular different from the language of the text. The scripture's language distinguished it as old and authoritative for ritual practice.[42]

The Torah was first translated into Greek by Egyptian Jews in the third century B.C.E. A Greek Torah would have symbolized the Hellenistic upperclass status of Jews within Ptolemaic Egyptian culture.[43] The practice of

39. John F. A. Sawyer, *Sacred Languages and Sacred Texts* (London: Routledge, 1999).

40. James W. Watts, "Using Ezra's Time as a Methodological Pivot for Understanding the Rhetoric and Functions of the Pentateuch," in *The Pentateuch: International Perspectives on Current Research* (ed. T. B. Dozeman, K. Schmid and B. J. Schwarz; Tübingen: Mohr Siebeck, 2011), 489–506.

41. Nehemiah 8: 7–8; 13: 23–24; Ingo Kottsieper, " 'And They Did Not Care to Speak Yehudit': On Linguistic Change in Judah During the Late Persian Period," in *Judah and the Judeans in the Fourth Century B.C.E.* (ed. Oded Lipschitz, Gary N. Knoppers, and Rainer Albertz; Winona Lake, IN: Eisenbrauns, 2007), 95–124.

42. Stefan Schorch, "The Pre-eminence of the Hebrew Language and the Emerging Concept of the 'Ideal Text' in Late Second Temple Judaism," in *Studies in the Book of Ben Sira* (ed. G. G. Xeravits and J. Zsengellér; Leiden: Brill, 2008), 43–54.

43. On the possible reasons for creating the Septuagint translation, see James Carleton Paget, "The Origins of the Septuagint," in *The Jewish-Greek Tradition in Antiquity and the*

reading Torah aloud in synagogue services in vernacular translations is also attested in rabbinic literature from the second through fifth centuries C.E. Though the rabbis preferred synagogue readings in Hebrew or for interlacing vernacular translations into the Hebrew readings, they admitted that many synagogues were reading Torah only in Greek.[44]

While earlier rabbinic texts were more open to the practice of reading Torah in Greek if no one in the congregation could read Hebrew, later texts from the third through fifth centuries tended to restrict the practice.[45] This debate continued through the Middle Ages into modernity. As Jewish denominations evolved in the nineteenth and twentieth centuries, their use or avoidance of vernacular languages in worship became a major distinguishing feature. Language choice as a means to engage the surrounding non-Jewish culture or to distinguish Jews from it remains a prominent issue in Jewish congregations to the present day.

The Languages of Zoroastrian and Manichean Scriptures

Zoroastrian tradition places great importance on the original language, Avestan, of their oldest scriptures. They were preserved primarily through oral recitation and tradition. When the language of the Avestas became archaic and poorly understood, this fact just served to emphasize their sacred status. The Avestas were eventually written down to aid in the training of priests, who must recite them from memory in ritual contexts. A new script was invented to write the Avestas to preserve their uniqueness in written form as well. Vernacular translations, the Zands, play a prominent role in Zoroastrian tradition, in written and oral form. But the tradition makes a clear distinction between the perfect Avestas and the necessarily flawed translations.[46]

Byzantine Empire (ed. J. K. Aitken and J. C. Paget; Cambridge: Cambridge University Press, 2014), 105–119 [117–119].

44. *m. Meg.* 2.1, *t. Meg.* 3:13, *y. Meg.* 4.3, 75a; see Willem Smelik, "Code-Switching: The Public Reading of the Bible," in *Was ist ein Text? Alttestamentliche, agyptologische and altorientalische Perspektiven* (ed. L. Morenz and S. Schorch; BZAW 362; Berlin: de Gruyter, 2007), 123-51 [134–137].

45. Philip Alexander, "The Rabbis, the Greek Bible and Hellenism," in *The Jewish-Greek Tradition in Antiquity and the Byzantine Empire* (ed. J. K. Aitken and J. C. Paget; Cambridge: Cambridge University Press, 2014), 229–246; for a more detailed discussion, see Willem F. Smelik, *Rabbis, Language and Translation in Late Antiquity* (Cambridge: Cambridge University Press, 2013).

46. Kianoosh Rezania, "Media Controversies in Zoroastrian Inter-Religious Debates of the Early Islamic Period," paper presentation to the conference, "Media of Scripture – Scripture as Media," of the Käte Hamburger Kolleg in the Center for Religious Studies, Ruhr University Bochum, December 10, 2015; see also Sawyer, *Sacred Languages and Sacred Texts*, 39–40, 74–75, 155–156.

The Zoroastrian's emphasis on oral recitation in the original Avestan language is highlighted by the contrary tendencies of a younger religion in the same region, Manichaeism. Its founder, Mani, wrote scriptures and encouraged their translation into every language possible in order to spread the new faith.[47]

The Languages of Christian Scripture

Jesus spoke Aramaic with his disciples, but Greek-speakers responded to the early Christian message more quickly and in much greater numbers than Aramaic-speakers. Christianity therefore quickly became a Hellenistic religious movement. It adopted the Greek translation of Jewish scripture as its own, and eventually added its own Greek writings to form the New Testament. As a result, Christians have not preserved the words of Jesus in the language in which he spoke them, except for a handful of scattered Aramaic phrases in the Gospels.[48]

By the end of Late Antiquity, the Greek Bible had been joined by translations into Latin, Syriac, Coptic, and Armenian.[49] Schisms then divided Medieval Christianity along linguistic lines.[50] In Western Europe, the religious influence of the Latin Bible and the central institution of the papacy provided a common religious and intellectual language. With the coming of the Renaissance, however, new interest in ancient philology and culture revived Christians' translational impulse. Protestant reformers championed vernacular translations in the sixteenth century, and Catholic and Protestant missionaries translated the Bible into hundreds of new languages—thousands by the end of the twentieth century.

One major effect of this enthusiastic use of scripture translations was to establish Christians and Christian scripture as decisively different from Jews and Jewish scripture. Embracing Greek and then other languages facilitated the development of their distinctive religious identity, in their own eyes and also in the eyes of Jews and others in the Roman Empire. John Sawyer summarized the results:

> The effect of translating Hebrew scripture into Greek was to construct a radically different text, one which, in the history of Christianity, virtually took the place of the Hebrew original as the Church's sacred text, and which the Jewish authorities soon rejected as alien.[51]

---

47. M 5494 (T II D 126 I); Rezania, "Media Controversies."

48. E.g. Mark 7:11, 34; 15:37.

49. Willard G. Oxtoby, " 'Telling in Their Own Tongues': Old and Modern Bible Translations as Expressions of Ethnic Cultural Identity," in *The Bible As Cultural Heritage* (ed. W. Beuken and S. Freyne; London: SCM, 1995), 24–35 [29–30].

50. John Sawyer, *Sacred Languages and Sacred Texts*, 86–89, 94–95.

51. Sawyer, *Sacred Languages and Sacred Texts*, 93.

New scripture translations have shaped the formation of Christian group identities ever since. Protestant vernacular translations standardized modern English and German, and contributed to national political projects.[52] European colonial empires, both Catholic and Protestant, wielded bible translation as a tool for cultural dominance and assimilation in the Americas, Africa and Asia.[53] Some indigenous cultures utilized colonial bible translations to mediate intra-religious factionalization.[54]

How do Christians justify changing the "word of God" into another language? The New Testament book of Acts provides a narrative rationale for Christian translations. Fifty days after Jesus' crucifixion, during the festival of Pentecost, his disciples

> were filled with the Holy Spirit and began to speak in other languages, as the Spirit gave them ability. Now there were devout Jews from every nation under heaven living in Jerusalem. And at this sound the crowd gathered and was bewildered, because each one heard them speaking in the native language of each. (Acts 2:4–6 NRSV)

This story depicts translation as an act of divine inspiration and has served to warrant further translation activity.[55] Nevertheless, churches have rarely claimed divine inspiration for their scripture translations. Translation activity has instead become a hallmark of Christian biblical scholarship.

The prototypical Christian biblical scholar is Jerome, the fourth-century hermit who produced the Latin "Vulgate" translation that became the official Bible of the Roman Church. Instead of working from the revered Septuagint Greek as many other church leaders preferred, he learned Hebrew and translated the Latin Old Testament directly from Jewish manuscripts. Jerome therefore established two precedents that have had long and growing influence over Christian scripture translation: the precedence

---

52. Sawyer, *Sacred Languages and Sacred Texts*, 170.

53. Oxtoby, "Telling in Their Own Tongues," 31–32.

54. As several studies of scripture use in Mayan Christian communities have shown: see Christine Kray, "The Summer Institute of Linguistics and the Politics of Bible Translation in Mexico: Convergence, Appropriation, and Consequence," in *Pluralizing Ethnography: Comparison and Representation in Maya Cultures, Histories, and Identities* (ed. J. M. Watanabe and E. F. Fischer; Santa Fe: School of American Research Press, 2004), 95–125 [117]; Christine Kovic, *Mayan Voices for Human Rights: Displaced Catholics in Highland Chiapas*, Austin: University of Texas Press, 2005; and C. Mathews Samson, "The Word of God and 'Our Words': The Bible and Translation in a Mam Maya Context," in *The Social Life of Scriptures: Cross-Cultural Perspectives on Biblicism* (ed. James S. Bielo; New Brunswick, NJ: Rutgers University Press, 2009), 64–79: "Maya Protestants in the Yucatan prefer Spanish as the language of worship and for their Bibles. ... [Evangelical, i.e. Protestant] identity is still one tightly tied to the text, to literacy, and generally to Spanish as the group presents itself to the outside world" (75).

55. Acts 2:16–21.

of the original Hebrew and Greek languages and the authority of philological expertise in translation. Jerome's precedent undermined appeals to Greek as Christianity's "original" language by establishing a bi-lingual original scripture and reinforcing the use of vernaculars in the liturgy of the churches. It also left Hebrew and, outside the Greek Orthodox churches, Greek to linguistic experts. Though this precedent's impact was muted in the Middle Ages when Jerome's own Vulgate Latin translation reigned supreme in Western Europe, Christian scholars have been celebrated since the Renaissance for their expertise in the original languages of scripture.

So, despite the Pentecost story, celebration of Christian Bible translations has tended to focus on human philological expertise combined with piety, rather than divinely inspired translations.[56]

The Language of Muslim Scripture

Islam takes the opposite approach regarding the language of its scripture. Muslims use the Arabic original of the Qur'an as their language of ritual, devotion and study. They commonly regard translations of the Qur'an as not the Qur'an at all, but as interpretations of its meaning in another language. Translation is permissible for the sake of those who do not have the means or opportunity to learn Arabic, but the real Qur'an is only in Arabic. Tetz Rooke summarized the reasoning that lies behind this famous tenet of the Muslim faith:

> An honoured dogma of Islam, known as ... 'i'jāz al-Qur'ān, is that the Koran is a linguistic miracle, inimitable and untranslatable. This dogma states that the Koranic text has such amazing stylistic and rhetorical fetures, that it is the most perfect example of ... eloquence that ever will be known, and thus constitutes the ultimate literary ideal. ... The Koran is recited aloud and memorized as miraculous sounds, as much as holy words. Since it is impossible to translate without losses the complete structure of the text, including its sounds and rhythm, a version of the Koran rendered in a foreign language is a translational impossibility. Exactly how and why is still a favoured research topic among Muslim scholars.[57]

William Graham observed the linguistic effects of Muslim veneration of the Arabic Qur'an:

> Because of the fundamental holiness of the words of the Qur'an, the classical Arabic language has taken on a sacrality felt in often quite visceral fashion

---

56. Watts, *Understanding the Pentateuch as a Scripture,* 186–189. Exceptions include some Christians' beliefs about the Latin Vulgate in Roman Catholicism and about the King James Version among some English-speaking Protestants.

57. Tetz Rooke, "Translation of Arabic Literature: A Mission Impossible?" in *Current Issues in the Analysis of Semitic Grammar and Lexicon II* (ed. L. Edzard and J. Retsö; Wiesbaden: Harrassowitz, 2006), 214–225 [219].

by the Muslim who knows it as the sublimely beautiful and untranslatable language of God's perfect revealed word, even if he or she speaks no Arabic.[58]

This emphasis on the Arabic of the Qur'an naturally goes hand-in-hand with its linguistic expression. The oral performance and reception of the Qur'an is the most characteristic and distinguishing feature of Muslim religious practice—a fact that is regularly emphasized by observing that the word, *al-Qur'an*, means "the recitation."[59]

The oral tradition of Qur'anic recitation, *qira'ah*, became a highly technical discipline aimed at preserving and transmitting the correct oral form. Muslim tradition has nevertheless grappled with linguistic change in the form of divergent traditions of recitation. Three centuries after the prophet Muhammed, Abu Bakr Ibn Muhjahid systematized rules for recitation and recognized seven different recitation traditions as authentic. Others have increased the number of approved approaches to ten or fourteen.[60]

All Muslims are expected to learn enough Arabic to recite at least the Qur'an's opening surah.[61] The Qur'an thus serves as a Muslim's prayer book as well as scripture. Arabic's precedence as the language of scripture and prayer makes it the first priority in Muslim education and the preferred language of theology and doctrine. As a result, native Arabic speakers have a clear advantage and exert disproportionate religious leadership due to the linguistic privilege granted to Arabic. Speakers of modern Arabic dialects, however, must also be trained in the grammar and cadences of the Qur'an, which is more than thirteen-hundred years old. Many Muslims may not completely understand the language they recite daily in prayer.

William Graham has suggested that the mono-lingual use of the Qur'an for oral recitation emphasizes "a nondiscursive understanding or meaning that is part of experience of overt encounter with the text itself."[62] He argued that a focus on semantic discourse alone fails to comprehend the religious experience of scriptures.

---

58. Graham, *Beyond the Written Word*, 85.

59. "The Qur'an has functioned primarily as a vocally transmitted text" (Graham, *Beyond the Written Word*, 88).

60. Graham, *Beyond the Written Word*, 99–100.

61. Graham, *Beyond the Written Word*, 103; for a summary of the history of debates over translating the Qur'an, see Meir M. Bar-Asher, " 'We have made it an Arabic Qur'an': the Permissibility of Translating Scripture in Islam in Contrast with Judaism and Christianity," in *Interpreting Scriptures in Judaism, Christianity and Islam: Overlapping Inquiries* (ed. M. Z. Cohen and A. Berlin; Cambridge: Cambridge University Press, 2016), 65–83.

62. Graham, *Beyond the Written Word*, 111.

It is in such reductionism that orientalist rationalism and Muslim conservatism and literalism walk the same path, for both prefer the precise words of the text, on the page, as the only legitimate object of interpretive interest.[63]

Nevertheless, the existence of conservative, literalistic movements within Muslim cultures reinforces a two-tier social hierarchy between native Arabic speakers and the speakers of other languages, who constitute the vast majority of Muslims in the world today.

The Languages of Asian Scriptures

Christianity's early and continuing commitment to translations, to the extent of not preserving Jesus' words in his original language, stands out sharply in contrast to Jewish and especially Muslim emphases on the original languages of their scriptures. This linguistic contrast between religions growing from common cultural roots also appears in Asia. I cannot survey the vast range of sacred texts in Hindu, Buddhist, Daoist, Confucian and Jain traditions. So I simply point out a contrast in how Buddhists and Hindus engage translations.

Buddhism is another large translational religion, and provides the closest analogy to Christianity's translation practices. The early collections of Buddhist scriptures were written in Pali, but the Gautama Buddha may have spoken another dialect, perhaps Magadhi Prakrit.[64] As in Christianity, this early tendency towards translation has reproduced itself repeatedly in Buddhist history with later scriptures (*sutras*) translated and composed in other languages. As in Latin Christianity, some Buddhist traditions (Therevada) sought unity around an ancient translational language, Pali. The Mahayana traditions, however, were transmitted primarily through translation into Chinese, Tibetan, and Japanese—a translation effort that dwarfed in size and scope anything attempted by Western religions, as Oxtoby noted:

> In the sheer magnitude of the enterprise, given the number of texts and the conceptual differences between Indian and Chinese culture, the translation of Buddhism from Indian languages into Chinese is probably the most impressive single translation activity in the history of religions.[65]

Early in the spread of Mahayana traditions, Buddhists reflected on the theory and manner of translation as a process of matching concepts in the

---

63. Graham, *Beyond the Written Word*, 112.
64. Fabio Rambelli, *A Buddhist Theory of Semiotics: Signs, Ontology, and Salvation in Japanese Esoteric Buddhism* (London: Bloomsbury, 2013), 82.
65. Oxtoby, "Telling in Their Own Tongues," 24–35 [34].

original and target languages.[66] Eventually the prestige of translational languages, especially Chinese, often led to venerating scriptures in Chinese rather than in the local vernacular, such as Korean.

India also gave birth to a religious tradition adamantly dedicated to preserving the original language of its scriptures. The Vedas continue to be chanted in the Sanskrit language by Brahmins, who have preserved the language in this form for perhaps three millennia. As is the case with Islam, their devotion to the original language of the scriptures is accompanied by an emphasis on their oral expression, in fact, their exclusively oral transmission through much of their history up until recent centuries.

This linguistic focus has raised sound to unique importance in Hindu practice and theory, as J. Gondo emphasized:

> The Indian aestheticians ... were ... of the opinion that the experiences of the poet, representing the hero of his work and that of the listener, reader, or, in general employer of the work are identical.... This consciousness of the presence of truth, of the divine, the eternal or ultimate reality in a work of art which has been created by a truly inspired artist, together with the almost universal belief that words, especially duly formulated and rhythmically pronounced words, are bearers of power, has given rise to the traditional Indian conviction that "formulas" are a decisive power: that whoever utters a mantra sets power in motion.... [Mantras] represent the essence of the "gods."[67]

Thomas Coburn summarized the issue: "Ultimate reality, on this view, ... is affirmed at least to have sound-form."[68] He argued that for Hindu practice, intelligible discourse is not the overriding concern:

> While it is tempting to assume that scriptures, either read or heard, serve a didactic role in human lives, the central fact here is that, for many Hindus, the holiness of holy words is not a function of their intelligibility. On the contrary, sanctity often appears to be inversely related to comprehensibility.[69]

This attitude was encouraged by the language of the scriptures. "Sanskrit was ... always an individual's second language, unintelligible to speakers of the many local vernaculars, but always, for one who knew it, the language of preference."[70]

---

66. Oral communication from Licia Di Giacinto.

67. J. Gonda, *The Vision of the Vedic Poets* (The Hague: Mouton & Co. 1963), 61, 63-64, 66, quoted in Thomas B. Coburn, " 'Scripture' in India: Towards a Typology of the Word in Hindu Life," *Journal of the American Academy of Religion* 52 (1984), 435–459 [442].

68. Coburn, " 'Scripture' in India," 443-44; also Graham, *Beyond the Written Word*, 70–71.

69. Coburn, " 'Scripture' in India," 1984, 445.

70. Coburn, " 'Scripture' in India," 1984, 446.

Nevertheless, many recitations, especially of the epics, also take place in vernacular translation. Some translations, such as Tulsi Das' sixteenth-century translation of the Ramayana into Hindi, have become favorite texts for oral performance as well, both as recitations and in dramas which often update the language and embellish the dialogues. In the case of the epics, then, Hindus have embraced translation to convey the meaning of the stories.[71]

Religious Polarization over Scripture Translations

These different approaches taken by religious traditions to the languages of their scriptures do not revolve around the decision to translate or not. Linguistic expertise in the original languages is prized by almost all traditions that venerate written or oral scriptures. All of them also allow people who cannot master the original language to read or hear the text in their own vernacular. The usual means for doing so is the oral sermon which paraphrases and interprets in the vernacular language the significance of the scriptures.

Instead, the different philosophies of language among religious traditions revolve around the practice of oral reading or recitation of the scriptures, that is, ritualizing their expressive dimension. A comparison of the different oral practices of religions shows that translation practices mark dividing lines between several large religious traditions around the globe. Religious traditions stemming from India as well as from the Middle East have evolved opposite attitudes about ritualized performances of translations. They stake the status of their scriptures on either their linguistic mutability or, conversely, on their immutability. The reproduction of this contrast at both ends of Eurasia indicates that consciousness of the other religion's practices and competition between traditions has probably played a large role in the development of these distinctive views of translations.

The ritualization of scripture translations also differentiates religious experience. As a consequence of their linguistic commitments to Hebrew or Arabic or Sanskrit scriptures, Jews, Muslims and Hindus worldwide have a common aural experience of how reading or reciting their scriptures *sound* and, especially in the Jewish and Muslim cases, a common visual experience of how the text of their scriptures *look*. Even people who cannot understand or read Arabic or Hebrew or Sanskrit recognize (sometimes mistakenly) the sound of these languages and the sight of their script as likely expressing scripture.

---

71. Coburn, " 'Scripture' in India," 1984, 450–452; also Barbara A. Holdrege, "From Sanskritization to Vernacularization: Subaltern Inscriptions of Bodies and Landscapes," in *Scripturalizing the Human: The Written as the Political* (ed. Vincent L. Wimbush; New York: Routledge, 2015), 176–192.

Christians and Buddhists worldwide have no such common experience with their co-religionists. The Christian case is the most extreme. Christianity's embrace of scriptural translations from the time of its origin has resulted in the fact that the Christian Bible cannot be recognized cross-culturally by the sound of its words or the sight of its script.[72]

Immaterial Texts

Christian churches nevertheless claim that religious identity and unity extend across these linguistic divisions. This doctrine gets affirmed as belief in "one catholic (i.e. universal) church," in the language of the ancient Apostles' and Nicene creeds that are still recited weekly in many Christian churches worldwide.[73] This belief depends on the epistemological claim that the form and the language of the scripture do not matter. The religion needs the meaning of the Bible's contents to be infinitely mutable to the senses of sight and sound in order to justify its claim that Christianity constitutes a single religion despite its many linguistic divisions.

Little scholarly attention has been devoted to the effects of Christian scriptures appearing in manifestly different forms and languages.[74] Christians insist on the essential singularity of their scripture as "the Bible" despite its manifestly pluriform languages, formats and media. Christians similarly insist on the singular identity of their religion, Christianity, despite rampant and enduring schisms.[75] Scripture and creed thus bequeath to Christian theology an insistence on the unity of the Church as a necessary demonstration of monotheistic faith and as essential to Christian identity.

This insistence requires a certain epistemological stance towards language and translation. Scripture and doctrine *must* be capable of being conveyed accurately and effectively in any language. Melot described this

---

72. Sometimes, consistency of form has provided some visual consistency that distinguishes bibles from other texts. Contemporary Christian publishing, however, has promoted a plurality of formats for bibles that may be eviscerating its visual stereotypes. See Timothy Beal, *The Rise and Fall of the Bible*, 2011.

73. This affirmation has not, of course, prevented groups and denominations from denying the Christian status of their rivals. They nevertheless maintain the principle of cross-cultural unity while excluding in practice some groups that claim Christian identity.

74. Biblical scholars usually engage the theme of "the unity of scripture" only by addressing the problem that the Christian Bible contains diverse and, in many places, contradictory contents. Exceptions include the recent exploration of the Bible's multiple formats by Beal, *Rise and Fall of the Bible*.

75. The latter finds expression already in Paul's claim, in the face of first-century factionalism, that there is only "one body and one Spirit, ... one hope ..., one Lord, one faith, one baptism," which is guaranteed by "one God and Father of all, who is over all and through all and in all" (Galatians 4:4–6) and was crystalized in the early creed's affirmation of "the holy universal (= catholic) church."

stance by comparison to computer science: "What the Christians invented is what a computer scientist would call the portability of the sacred text, its compatibility and fixity across any medium."[76] He argued that this Christian insistence had far-reaching implications for Western thought and culture. Melot grounded this epistemological innovation in Christianity's early adoption of the codex. I suggest that it depends also on Christians' ritual use of scripture translations.

Christian translations of Christ's words announced the portability of the sacred text across language and culture. They exhibited the incarnational doctrine at the root of the Christian message: a tradition that believes in the incarnation of divine word (*logos*) into human flesh (John 1) and then into bread and wine (John 8) will not find it difficult to grasp that scriptural words can be transmuted from one language, script and media to another. This belief in the permanence of the Christian message across changing oral and visual media fueled Christian enthusiasm for translation and for the codex, and later for printing, radio, television, and digital texts.

From there, it is a short step to imagine that reason and knowledge in general (also good translations of *logos*) are transparent between languages and across written media. Just as what counts for Christianity is the underlying truth of scripture and doctrine apart from linguistic differences, what counts for philosophy and science is the underlying truth of their propositions stripped of linguistic distinctives. Christian doctrine thus supports the epistemology necessary for philosophy and science or any other knowledge that claims universality across human cultures. But this academic epistemology arises out of the same needs as in religion: science and philosophy *need* to be able to ignore variables introduced by different languages, just as Christianity *needs* to ignore the schismatic tendencies of scriptural translation and mass publication. The existence of strong and traditional religious epistemologies to the contrary, especially Hindu and Muslim, therefore poses a profound challenge to this fundamental belief that doctrine and reason can transcend language.

Translation depends on a belief in the fixity of the message regardless of oral and written form. Fabio Rambelli observed that the Buddhist tendencies towards translation also involved an epistemological choice that seems to be rooted in the earliest parts of the tradition:

> The choice of the historical Buddha to preach in a dialect of the kingdom of Maghada, and especially the subsequent decision by the Buddhist elders to transcribe the Buddha's teachings in Pali, a vernacular language, and not in

---

76. "Ce que les chrétiens ont inventé, c'est ce qu'un informaticien appellerait la portabilité du texte sacré, sa compatibilité à n'importe quel support dont il demeure pourtant solidaire" (Melot, "Le livre comme forme symbolique," §10).

Sanskrit, traditionally the language of the learned and of religion, shows a refusal of the older Vedico-Upanishadic beliefs in the existence of an absolute language as the privileged site/vehicle of the Truth. ... The choice to privilege contents over expression, doctrines over the language that conveys them, was extremely important for the diffusion of Buddhism, since it allowed the translation of the sacred scriptures—an operation which is impossible when the doctrines are related to a sacred, absolute, and therefore immutable language. Esoteric Buddhism, however, because of its different attitudes toward language, emphasized the importance of original formulae in Sanskrit that were not to be translated.[77]

Regarding the latter, he added that "It is possible to consider the Buddhist theories on mantras as a special case of the human quest for a perfect language—one that tells the truth about the world but also ensures salvation."[78]

Rambelli's last observation alludes to various attempts to find or create the most basic or universal language, attempts that have not been limited to religious traditions. Modern research in linguistics and philosophy has sought a universal grammar underlying all human languages. It has attempted to translate human language into symbolic logic, and scientists have long celebrated mathematics as the language of the physical universe.[79] Underlying such attempts are presuppositions about the portability of knowledge from one language to another and across media.[80] These presuppositions are rooted in deep-seated religious epistemologies related to the languages of scriptures. Jacque Derrida recognized messianic intentions in the search for a perfect or "true" language which, he thought, is implied in every attempt at translation:

> This religious code is essential here. The sacred text marks the limit, the pure even if inaccessible model, of pure transferability, the ideal starting from which one could think, evaluate, measure the essential, that is to say poetic, translation. Translation, as holy growth of languages, announces the messianic end .... It puts us in contact with that "language of the truth" which is

77. Rambelli, *Buddhist Theory*, 82.

78. Rambelli, *Buddhist Theory*, 84.

79. Galileo Galilei, *Opere Il Saggiatore* (Rome, 1623), 171, and quoted many times since.

80. The contrary position, maintaining some form of linguistic relativism, has also been widely espoused in modern thought. Frequently termed the Sapir-Whorf hypothesis, it maintains that thought is constrained by the language of the thinker. The argument between linguistic relativists and advocates of universal grammar has been especially strong in linguistics, where it has been the subject of increasingly subtle experiments that suggest a mediating position indicating greater linguistic influence over some cognitive processes than over others. In philosophy, thinkers sympathetic to the relativist view have included Ludwig Wittgenstein (*Philosophical Investigations*, tr. G.E.M. Anschombe, Oxford: Blackwell, 1953) and W. V. O. Quine (*Word and Object*, Cambridge, MA: MIT Press, 1960).

the "true language". ... The sacred text assigns the task to the translator, and it is sacred inasmuch as it announces itself as transferable, simply transferable, to-be-translated.[81]

My comparative survey of religious attitudes towards translation shows persisting doubts about the epistemologies of language that undergird translation efforts. Other theories of language can be applied to scriptures, and are in fact applied by adherents of other religious traditions. Philosophers writing in Arabic in the tenth and eleventh centuries developed nuanced positions between linguistic determinism and universal language: al-Farabi and Avicenna approved Aristotle's goal of a universal logic, but also maintained that Arabic expressed some logical ideas better than Greek, while Greek worked better for others. They therefore advocated the construction of logic from the varied resources provided by multiple languages.[82]

Nevertheless, the belief in immaterial texts remains strong. Some Christian movements have occasionally gone so far as to assert the primacy of oral inspiration and tradition over written scripture in any language. With the world-wide spread of Christianity in recent centuries, these assumptions now inform some anti-Western, anti-colonial variants of the tradition. For example, the Friday Masowe Church in Zimbabwe rejects any use of the Bible because it is a material object. The movement instead proclaims the "living word" of God received through direct inspiration. Utilizing classic iconoclastic rhetoric modeled by the Bible itself (Isa. 44: 9–20), one of the church's prophets denounced the Bible because of its material form:

---

81. Jacques Derrida, "Des Tours de Babel," in *Difference in Translation* (tr. J. F. Graham; Ithaca, NY: Cornell University Press, 1985), 196, 202–203. A recognition of the epistemological problems with such theories of languages as "containers" of knowledge does not free modern thought from its debt to religious theories of translation. This is readily apparent from the essays on translation by Walter Benjamin and Jacque Derrida. Derrida identified this problem specifically with the translation of scripture: "for a poetic text or a sacred text, communication is not the essential" ("Tours de Babel," 180). Though both Benjamin and Derrida challenge the notion of communicable content between languages, their discussions were nevertheless indebted to Jewish and, especially, Christian traditions of scripture translation. This influence is recognizable in their summaries, such as Benjamin's assertion that, for certain great works, "In [their translations] the life of the originals attains its latest, continually renewed, and most complete unfolding" (Walter Benjamin, "The Task of the Translator" (1921), translated by Harry Zohn in *Walter Benhamin Selected Works, Volume 1: 1913-1926* [ed. M. Bullock and M. W. Jennings; Cambridge, MA: Harvard Belknap, 1996], 253-2563 [255]) and Derrida's claim that "The translation will be a moment in the growth of the original, which will complete itself in enlarging itself" ("Tours de Babel," 188). It is hard to imagine a Muslim or Hindu philosopher describing the Qur'an or Vedas as completed through their translation.

82. Allan Bäck, "*Islamic Logic?*" in *The Unity of Science in the Arabic Tradition: Science, Logic, Epistemology and their Interactions* (ed. Shahid Rahman, Tony Street, Hassan Tahir; New York: Springer, 2008), 255–279 [264–271].

What is the Bible to me? Having it is just trouble. Look, why would you read it? It gets old. Look again. After keeping it for some time it falls apart, the pages come out. And then you can take it and use it as toilet paper until it's finished.[83]

Most Christians, including other Christian apostolics in Zimbabwe, find this statement outrageous, yet it is simply an extreme form of the book aniconism that has dominated Christian thought, if not Christian practice, since antiquity. This view asserts that form and material do not really matter so long as scripture's semantic meaning is made known. The Masowe Church takes that principle further in pursuit of an entirely "immaterial faith," but it has many antecedents in European Protestantism, such as the early English Puritan who asserted that "nothing spiritual can be present when there is anything material and physical."[84] For Christians who really believe this, the Bible must be regarded as essentially immaterial or else rejected altogether with the Masowe Christians. Matthew Engelke observed,

> What counts as material or immaterial, what makes materiality or immateriality valuable, and whether those valuations stand as bridges or barriers to the experience of the divine are, in the end, the stuff of historical and theological contestation.[85]

Christian thought and practice thus provides one important root for contemporary fascination with virtual texts, as was recognized by Alan Kaufman in his screed against digital books:

> Not since the advent of Christianity has the world witnessed so sweeping a change in the very fabric of human existence. Behind the hi-tech revolution is an idea of Progress that in many regards resembles the premises of Christianity itself. The superseding of the new way over the old, of the New

---

83. Matthew Engelke, *A Problem of Presence: Beyond Scripture in an African Church* (Berkeley: University of California, 2007), 2.

84. Engelke, *Problem of Presence*, 21; also 8. See also Elisa Heinamaki, "Proving the Inner Word: (De)materializing the Spirit in Radical Pietism," in *Christianity and the Limits of Materiality* (ed. Minna Opas and Anna Haapalainen; London: Bloomsbury, 2017), 187–209.

85. Engelke, *Problem of Presence*, 28. Engelke argued that secularized forms of the belief in immaterial texts appear in the invention of symbolic logics and Saussurian linguistics which fueled a "separation of language from the material world," which itself built on typical Western "separation of mind from body." This belief finds obvious expression in contemporary popular culture in advocacy of "virtual" digital texts in place of physical ones. Engelke appealed for a return to C. S. Pierce's theory of signs (C. S. Pierce, "On A New List of Categories" [1867], in *The Writings of Charles S. Peirce: A Chronological Edition* [6 vols.; Peirce Edition Project; Bloomington, IN: Indiana University Press, 1982], 49–58; see discussion in Watts, "Scripture's Indexical Touch," 174) rather than Saussure's in order to dispose of "the facile but commonplace claim that to take things as 'signs' is to reduce the world to discourse and its interpretation, to give in to the totalizing imperative to render all things meaningful" (Engelke, *Problem of Presence*, 32–33).

Testament over the Old Testament, the discrediting of the traditional as inferior or even evil, a sense of powerful excitement about the revolutionary, and of course, most importantly, the promise of heavenly immortality over the temporal limitations of the wasting physical body—the accursed haptic book versus the blessed Holy Ghostly Internet—all these earmark the hi-tech pogrom against the book.[86]

The Challenge of Iconic Books

An ancient Christian need lies at the root of "modern" faith in the infinite mutability of information, text and data, that is, in the immateriality of texts. The Iconic Books Project tests the universality of this principle. It points out that writing was invented to serve as physical evidence of economic transactions (Chapter 6) and that book rituals continue to legitimize social institutions of all sorts (Chapter 3). It therefore questions beliefs in the infinite mutability of textual forms and in immaterial texts. By pointing out the function of ritualized expression in inspiring individuals and groups, it questions the infinite translatability of textual effects.

The Iconic Books Project also raises the possibility that textual mutability varies across the iconic, expressive, and semantic dimensions (Chapter 1). Even if it is the case that the semantic meaning of a text is mutable across different languages, that does not mean that its performative effects when read aloud or enacted through theater will be the same in different languages and cultures, nor that its iconic ritualization will produce the same effects in different scripts and textual forms. The Iconic Books Project has stimulated comparative research to examine whether the experience of inspiration and legitimacy produced by ritualizing the expressive and iconic dimensions of scriptures vary by language, script and textual form. It questions whether the belief in infinite textual mutability applies even to the ritualized semantic dimension of preaching, teaching, interpretation, and commentary. The historic Christian tendency towards schism along linguistic lines indicates that the religious authority produced by ritualizing the semantic dimension of scripture has, in fact, proven vulnerable to linguistic change.

The Iconic Books Project therefore puts book aniconism and the belief in immaterial texts on the agenda for academic analysis and discussion. This move is in sympathy with Bruno Latour's efforts to analyze the endemic iconoclasm of modern culture:

---

86. Alan Kaufman, "The Electronic Book Burning," *Evergreen Review* 120 (October 2009), http://www.evergreenreview.com/120/electronic-book-burning.html (accessed January 6, 2017).

Instead of iconoclasm being the meta-language reigning as a master over all other languages, it is the worship of iconoclasm itself which, in turn, is interrogated and evaluated. From a resource, iconoclasm is being turned into a topic.[87]

Similarly, beliefs in immaterial texts and book aniconism should be acknowledged and turned into a topic, rather than being allowed to reign as the unstated premises behind academic investigations of almost every kind and also behind the text creation, publishing, collecting, and disposal policies of libraries, publishers, universities, denominations, and nations.

---

87. Latour, "What is Iconoclash?" 17.

9

Mass Literacy and Scholarly Expertise

On January 3rd, 2007, U.S. Representative Keith Ellison took the oath of office on a Qur'an once owned by Thomas Jefferson. Ellison was the first Muslim elected to the Congress of the United States. His intention to take the oath on a Qur'an aroused a storm of controversy in a country accustomed to seeing only bibles in this role. Ellison responded by using Thomas Jefferson's Qur'an for this purpose. This textual relic placed a nationalistic stamp on these particular volumes of Muslim scripture because of their association with an American founding father.

On May 21st, 2009, U.S. President Barack Obama went to the Rotunda of the National Archives to give a speech about his plans to close the detention center at Guantánamo Bay, Cuba. The setting allowed him to use the relic manuscript of the U.S. Constitution as a backdrop while he addressed a television audience about constitutional law and terrorism. His picture standing in front of the Constitution visually buttressed his claim of defending the rights guaranteed by that document.

One might expect that rising rates of literacy would gradually shift the cultural emphasis from the iconic to the semantic dimensions of texts. As more people learn to read, the contents of texts would presumably take on greater importance than their visual forms. That is the way the story is usually told, for example, of the development of ancient Judaism. In the fifth and fourth centuries B.C.E, priests authorized by the iconic ritual texts of the Torah wielded supreme authority in Jerusalem. A thousand years later, however, rabbinic scholars had displaced priests as the religious and, sometimes, secular leaders of the Jews.[1] Jack Goody concluded

---

1. See, for example, Martin Hengel, *Judaism and Hellenism* (Philadelphia: Fortress, 1974), 1: 78–83; Shaye J. D. Cohen, *From the Maccabees to the Mishnah* (Philadelphia: Westminster, 1987), 75, 101–102, 160–162; Joachim Schaper, "The Theology of Writing: The Oral and the Written, God as Scribe, and the Book of Deuteronomy," in *Anthropology and Biblical Studies: Avenues of Approach* (ed. Louise J. Lawrence and Mario I. Aguilar; London: T. & T.

that, as a result, "alphabetic religions spread literacy and ... literacy spread these religions."[2]

This claim reflects a rhetoric of popularized textuality that is a prominent feature of Judaism, Christianity and Islam. The temples of Babylon, Egypt, and Rome kept their most sacred texts for priests, or even the gods, alone. In contrast to such esoteric religions, Judaism, Christianity and Islam published their texts openly. Their scriptures, the Torah, the Gospels, and the Qur'an, themselves require religious leaders to make every effort to publish their contents:

> Every seventh year, ... you shall read this law before all Israel in their hearing. Assemble the people—men, women, and children, as well as the aliens residing in your towns—so that they may hear and learn to fear the Lord your God and to observe diligently all the words of this law.
> (Deuteronomy 31:10–12 NRSV; cf. 6:6–7)

> Go therefore and make disciples of all nations, ... teaching them to obey everything that I have commanded you.
> (Matthew 28:19-20 NRSV; cf. John 20:31)

> O Messenger! proclaim the (message) which hath been sent to thee from thy Lord. If thou didst not, thou wouldst not have fulfilled and proclaimed His mission. (Surah 5:67, Yusufali translation)

Many historians find here a major water-shed in religious and cultural development, what Jan Assmann called "the transition from cult religion to book religion."[3] However, such characterizations allow the *ideal* of universal access to scripture and scriptural interpretation preached by these religions to obscure the social *reality* of how they actually organized their rituals, institutions and surrounding communities. In fact, the increasing ritualization of Torah in all three dimensions (iconic, expressive, and semantic) seems to have supported the rise to power of the Jewish priests who also monopolized temple rituals.[4] It played a role in giving them unprecedented political as well as religious authority in the mid- and later Second Temple period.

Elsewhere too—and still today—the spread of popular literacy has not displaced learned elites, but instead strengthened and empowered them. Jack Goody observed that religious institutions have usually dominated

---

Clark. 2004), 144; Jan Assmann, *Religion and Cultural Memory* (tr. R. Livingstone; Stanford: Stanford University Press, 2006), 122–138.

2. Goody, *Logic of Writing*, 4.

3. Assman, *Religion and Cultural Memory*, 128.

4. Watts, "Using Ezra's Time," 489–506; Watts, *Understanding the Pentateuch as a Scripture*, 190, 231–235.

scribal and scholarly education in most cultures, despite some prominent exceptions: "the kind of separation between the priest and the teacher, between the religious orders and written accomplishment that occurred in Greece, and to a lesser extent in China, has been a rare feature of literate civilizations."[5] At the same time, as cultures became more literate, iconic texts continued to play important roles both in religion (e.g. the Torah, Bible, Qur'an) and in politics (e.g. the Twelve Tables, the Magna Carta, the U.S. Constitution). Modern mass literacy turns out to be compatible with both the expertise of scholars and the ritualization of iconic texts.

Many scholars view such practices as a stage on an evolutionary spectrum between illiteracy and full literacy. Joachim Schaper, for example, commented that in ancient Judah, "writing is still a numinous act."[6] But for very many people alive today, including cultural elites who take oaths on scriptures and stockpile books in expensive libraries, "writing is still a numinous act." Every one of the forms of iconic textuality in the ancient Near East (Chapter 6) continues to be reproduced in modernity, though in different proportions. If monumental inscriptions do not cover every inch of our public buildings, they still appear especially on government buildings and libraries to legitimize these institutions and also to point to the huge collections of books and other documents inside. Books remain a prominent feature of portraiture, especially of civic, academic and religious portraiture. They also show up frequently in other kinds of art and illustration. Processions with books held high continue to be a standard feature of many Jewish, Christian, Sikh, and Buddhist rituals, while protestors waving scriptures have been prominent in recent political news from America, the Middle East and Asia (Chapters 5 and 7). And while myths of supernatural books appear commonly only in fantasy novels, art and movies, the divine nature of scriptures remains a potent point of theological contention between sects and denominations.[7] Differences in emphasis and practice do not reflect different levels of cultural development, but rather the ideological stakes that different social groups have in books and other written texts.

Nineteenth and twentieth-century scholarship belittled such iconic book practices as folkloric or superstitious, but that attitude was not new. Fourth-century Christian scholars were already criticizing other Christians who valued Gospel books for their pretty appearance rather than reading them, and that critique has been maintained by preachers and professors ever

5. Goody, *Logic of Writing*, 18.

6. Schaper, "Theology of Writing," 112.

7. Dorina Miller Parmenter, *The Iconic Book: The Image of the Christian Bible in Myth and Ritual*, Ph.D. Dissertation, Syracuse University, 2009.

since (Chapter 8). They are less likely to criticize public manipulation of iconic books in political and judicial oath ceremonies and on public monuments, since those manipulating these textual icons tend to be powerful or rich. Even here, scholars treat the iconic dimension as second- or third-best, something that must be accommodated because of cultural traditions but should not be privileged. Scholars' socially mandated focus is on the more prestigious semantic dimension. More than anyone else, it is scholars who look down on iconic manipulation of texts as folk custom or superstition.

As William Graham has argued, historians have "seriously short-changed both ourselves and our field of study by ignoring or minimizing the 'sensual' aspects of religious life."[8] Though much has changed on that score in the study of religion since he wrote those words, the study of scriptures and other written texts has not. This near-universal dismissal of iconic textuality is unexamined at best and prejudicial at worst.

This blindness to the iconic function of texts is restricted to academic scholars. Politicians, by contrast, have frequently proven adept at manipulating the iconic dimensions of books and texts for political purposes. Their examples range from the conventional manipulation of sacred books while taking an oath of office to the extraordinary staging of the scenes described at the beginning of this chapter. In these instances, politicians manipulated national and religious iconic texts intelligently and expertly to persuade their audience in their favor. They received, however, no help from academic theories of iconic texts, which are rare and not widely known. These political examples show that only scholars suffer from this blind spot about iconic books and texts. It is not the result of levels of literacy, social development, or intelligence.

The interactions between ritualizing texts' iconic and semantic dimensions undermine common models of gradual evolution from oral to literate cultures.[9] That is because advances in book making and printing technology created more opportunities for ritualizing books' iconic dimension at the same time that they increased people's access to semantic interpretation. It is also because mixed goals have motivated book production from antiquity to the present. Will Tuladhar-Douglas observed that "there are many ways of being literate" and concluded from his survey of early Mahayana Buddhist text production that

> The consubstantiation of the physical object and the sacred scripture generated an utterly new kind of object, the written relic that demanded its own replication. This was a literacy, and it was this literacy and not any other

8. Graham, *Beyond the Written Word*, 164.
9. E.g. Ong, *Orality and Literacy*.

that drove forward a chain of mechanical innovations that gave to us reading and writing humans the invention of printing.[10]

Recognizing that the iconic dimension of texts was fundamental to the invention of writing (Chapter 6) and that iconic ritualization has driven book production and use as much as semantic interpretation and expression—these realizations rehabilitate the views of many indigenous peoples who, upon first encounter, regarded Westerners' books and texts as objects of power.[11] That accurate insight into the function of iconic texts in modern religions, nations and empires could not be recognized by colonizers blinded by anti-ritualistic prejudices to their own iconic practices.

Why does rising literacy and increasing popular access to texts empower scholarly elites? Because in literate societies, the scholars' authority exemplifies a universal ideal that is nevertheless unattainable except for a small minority. That was certainly true when Deuteronomy first espoused this ideal.[12] As literacy spreads, the skills necessary to earn the status of expert scholars ironically increase as well. The multiplication and accumulation of texts creates the need for summaries, commentaries, and synopses, in other words, for the products of rabbinic and scholastic learning that only very few people will ever have the time or resources to master, much less produce.[13] Thus while literacy spreads and produces more texts, textual expertise gets concentrated in relatively few hands. Literate religious groups often try to expand the circle of textual participation by allocating performance (reading, recitation, memorization) to a wider, but still privileged circle.[14] But the authority of the lector, the cantor and the hafiz is usually subordinate to that of the scholar.

Why does iconic textuality persist despite increasing literacy and access to texts? Because it provides non-experts control over texts and whatever social and religious power they may possess. Unlike semantic interpretation and public performance for which one should defer to the inner circles of expert scholars and often also to the wider circles of trained readers, artists and performers, physical texts can be owned and manipulated by non-specialists whether literate or not.[15] Venerating a material text lies entirely within the control of the individual. In antiquity and still today, textual

---

10. Tuladhar-Douglas, "Writing and the Rise of Mahayana," 270, 272.

11. Wimbush, *White Men's Magic*, 48–73.

12. Schaper, "Theology of Writing," 109.

13. Goody, *Logic of Writing*, 162.

14. See Chapter 1 above, and Yohan Yoo, "Public Scripture Reading Rituals in Early Korean Protestantism: A Comparative Perspective," *Postscripts* 2 (2006): 226–240.

15. Yoo, "Possession and Repetition."

amulets are common and widespread.[16] Already by the last two centuries B.C.E., Jews were placing phylacteries (*tifillin*) containing excerpts from the Torah on their foreheads and forearms during prayers and affixing similar containers (*mezuzot*) on their doorposts.[17] Many ancient Christians carried scrolls that mixed scriptural texts, especially the words of Jesus, with magical formulas.[18] Already in the seventh-century battle at Siffin between Muslim armies, one side displayed Quranic verses on spears to pressure the other side to agree to arbitration.[19] Still today, people of many ethnic and religious backgrounds revere Arabic Qur'anic texts as powerful amulets.

Why has this lacuna in scholarship persisted for so long? As scholars of humanistic texts, we do not like to admit our own dependence on political and economic forces and their influence on our scholarship, even as nations try to leverage their investment in universities into greater economic productivity and competitive advantages in the so-called "information economy." We especially do not like to admit that the status and appeal of our favorite texts may depend as much or even more on iconic factors than on their semantic meaning.[20] Hence scholarly ignorance about iconic texts: it allows us to be in denial of the social conditions of our own livelihood. We insist that a text's real meaning lies in its semantic interpretation alone, which we are the experts at elucidating. But many of our texts mediate power and legitimacy in ways that semantic and even performative interpretation cannot understand or control.

The study of iconic books and texts will not change the power relationships mediated by texts. However, comparative and historical study of the functions of books and texts in the iconic dimension, as well as in the dimensions of expression and semantic interpretation, will enable us to describe those forces more clearly and understand better our own role in ritualizing books and texts. They will hopefully provide analytical tools that will help us employ all three textual dimensions more wisely and constructively in the future.

---

16. Malley, "Bible in British Folklore," 315–347.

17. Cohn, *Tangled Up in Text*, 2008.

18. Theodore de Bruyn, *Making Amulets Christian: Artefacts, Scribes, and Contexts* (Oxford: Oxford University Press, 2017).

19. Edward D. A. Hulmes, "Siffin, Battle of," in *The Encyclopedia of Islamic Civilization and Religion* (ed. I. A. Netton; Oxon: Routledge, 2008), 836.

20. See further Carr, *Writing on the Tablet of the Heart*, 294–297, and Solibakke, "Pride and Prejudice of the Western World," 347–360.

Why Books Matter
Preservation and Disposal

In 2009, worries about the future of books hit home at the university where I work. The university library announced plans to dispose of some materials and move many more books to a commercial storage facility across the state in order to free space in the stacks for new acquisitions. These plans came soon after renovations transformed two of the library's seven floors from book stacks into a coffee shop, a computer commons, "collaborative learning spaces" (i.e. tables with chairs), and classrooms. So the announcement of deacquisitions and off-site storage plans prompted an uproar among faculty members in the humanities, producing 113 faculty signatures (including mine) on two letters of protest. Faculty in the sciences and social sciences soon circulated their own protest letters in solidarity with the humanists' initiatives. A student petition against the plan garnered more than 1,000 signatures. All demanded greater consultation and collaboration in developing library collections and policies. The library responded with its own letters and policy papers, claiming that it has always sought input, especially from faculty.[1]

Beyond the argument over input, however, the dueling documents revealed a conceptual gap between the library's administrators on the one hand and the faculty and student protestors on the other. Comparing the professors' letters and the librarians' policy papers showed that their subjects were completely different. The library focused on "information"—how and by whom it is accessed, distributed, analyzed and used. The faculty's letters almost never mentioned that word; only the social scientists used it at all. Their letters focused instead on the importance of reading physical books and documents, browsing stacks and viewing fold-out charts and

---

1. See Jennifer Epstein, "A Win for the Stacks," *Inside Higher Ed* (November 13, 2009), https://www.insidehighered.com/news/2009/11/13/syracuse (accessed 6/13/2015); and Jennifer Howard, "In Face of Professors' 'Fury,' Syracuse U. Library Will Keep Books on Shelves," *Chronicle of Higher Education* (November 12, 2009), http://chronicle.com/article/In-Face-of-Professors-Fury/49133/ (accessed June 13, 2015).

maps. The library's letters emphasized collaborative learning while the professors focused on the needs of solitary researchers. The library invoked utility while the faculty worried about recruitment and institutional prestige. The different subjects of the dueling documents show that this dispute involved very different ideas about books.

The whole affair could be dismissed as one more academic tempest in a teapot were it not for the much wider debates over the role of libraries on college campuses, over the state of book publishing and marketing, and, of course, over the future of the book itself. Like most long-standing social institutions, libraries are more than just mechanisms for providing particular services. They symbolize a cultural ideal. But libraries exemplify that ideal only by virtue of the books they house. Questions about the roles of libraries are, at bottom, questions about the significance of books.

Missing from these debates was any serious discussion of the values that modern societies invest in books. Because my university hosts the Iconic Books Project, an interdisciplinary research program aimed at documenting and analyzing precisely this set of issues across history and diverse cultures, I followed the library debate with particular interest. It prompted me to imagine how an iconic books perspective can help us understand the values attached to browsing stacks, to physical books, to book disposal, and to library architecture.

The Importance of Browsing

Complaints against both digitized texts and off-site storage of library books frequently evoke the experience of browsing library shelves. Faculty members report the benefit of getting an overview of an entire subject contained in a collection. They repeat stories of finding just what they were looking for in the book *next* to the one they came into the stacks to collect. They celebrate how browsing stacks can produce random juxtapositions that neither cataloguing systems nor their own research plans anticipate, yet which provide the key to resolving their problem or to setting their research onto a new and more productive path. For them, this kind of browsing is not possible with either a catalog or an internet "browser" because its success depends on the physical juxtaposition of books on a shelf.

The open-stack library that makes browsing possible manifests an old idea. The notion that the contents of texts should be randomly accessible has slowly grown in strength over three thousand years. It decisively shapes the physical forms of books as well as libraries.

Ancient Egyptian and Mesopotamian libraries were owned by temples and royal courts that strictly limited access to only their priests and officials. When new religions made knowledge of their sacred texts public instead of keeping them secret, public reading and interpretation became a standard element in Jewish, Christian and Muslim worship.

At first, religious books were scrolls whose pages were sewn together edge to edge. Scrolls must be read sequentially, either the whole text at once or sections over a series of sessions. In synagogue services, Torah scrolls are still read sequentially over a year. The scroll form makes it hard to compare different parts of the same book, and it cannot be opened randomly.

Ancient Christians adopted a different technology for their sacred books, one that folds and binds together sheets of parchment or paper on the fold (see Chapter 8). This "codex" is the form that almost all books take today. The codex allows you to skip from one part of the book to another easily, to compare different sections, to read in any order that you want, and even to read randomly by letting the book fall open. People of various religious traditions still use random access to find in scriptures a message appropriate to their circumstances.

Peter Stallybrass argued that digital texts extend the power of the codex, because they increase the ability to cross-reference and book mark that the codex first made possible.[2] He pointed out that the discontinuous reading encouraged by online searches and hypertext merely extends reading practices perfected by codex genres such as dictionaries, encyclopedias, directories, and lists of all sorts. He did not, however, take random access into account. Ironically, digital versions of these genres do not permit browsing to the degree that their paper predecessors did.

The public library movement of the nineteenth and twentieth centuries made volumes of literature and information much more widely available, often in the form of open-stacks libraries that allow the public to browse the shelves. Open stacks multiply the advantages of codex technology. You can access as many volumes as you can lay your hands on in any way you wish, including randomly. Ben Ratliff described the experience as "grazing around, letting the shelves make the connections for me."

> Doing it the inefficient way, you use the senses. You look at a row of spines, imprinted with butch, ultra-legible white or black type; your eye takes in more at any time than can be contained on a computer screen. You hold the books in your hand and feel the weight and size; the typography and the paper talk to you about time. ... You can also create luck in any given spot: You turn your head to the opposing row of books. A different subject area can arise, perhaps only partly to do with your areas of interest. This is non-link-based browsing. You can discover, instead of being endlessly sought.[3]

2. Peter Stallybrass, "Books and Scrolls: Navigating the Bible," in *Books and Readers in Early Modern England: Material Studies* (ed. J. Andersen and E. Sauer; Philadelphia: University of Pennsylvania Press, 2012), 42–79 [42–47].

3. Ben Ratliff, "Grazing in the Stacks of Academe," *The New York Times*, June 26, 2012.

Open stacks represent the reader's complete control over the physical process and sequence of reading. To refuse such access by storing volumes off-site or on-line feels like imposing the textual strait-jacket of a scroll on readers who have become accustomed to the freedom of a codex.

Attention to the physical forms of texts reminds us that reading is an embodied practice. You must hold a book physically, brace it with your hands or put in on a table, position your body in certain ways and, of course, focus your eyes in order to read. Working on computers or e-readers requires different physical activities that have provided much fodder to debates about e-books.

But here I want to point out that visiting a library is also an embodied practice. Walking into the building, navigating the stacks, sitting in carrels to study your finds, and checking out and carrying away the most promising books comprise physical routines that have long characterized the scholar's lifestyle. The convenience of electronic texts and computerized catalog searches that deliver texts to you is offset by constricting the physical scope of your research activities to your own desk and computer. This loss may be felt especially keenly by faculty and students in the humanities whose research already tends to be the most individualistic of all the university disciplines and, therefore, the most isolating. For them, trips to the library have traditionally provided a physical research activity that some may be sorry to see go.

Material Books and the Desire for Textual Permanence

Books represent more, however, than just the reader's control over the reading process. They are powerful cultural symbols. Books matter because they are material manifestations of our culture's ideals: educational ideals, political ideals, philosophical ideals, and religious ideals. They represent our best hopes for ourselves. But ideals can be hard to remember, much less live by. Books seem to preserve our values in physical form. They are material manifestations of whatever we hold most dear. And when we struggle to know what that is, we can read books to remember what we've forgotten.

To a great degree, therefore, the cultural significance of books involves *old knowledge*. They represent our desire for old knowledge even while publishing new information. The publishing business, of course, wants new products to sell. Professors, especially those in the humanities, want to write and sell books. Research universities require them to do so. As a result, more books are published every year than the year before, and research libraries find themselves losing ground and floor-space in the effort to keep up. But unlike chain bookstores, libraries owe their cultural prestige to their role in preserving old books as much as in acquiring new ones.

Many fields of the humanities as well as qualitative fields in the social sciences promulgate old knowledge preserved in books. Of course, human-

Chapter 10 • Why Books Matter

ists also conduct creative research, use electronic resources and expect the most recent intellectual trends to appear on their library's shelves. But our teaching tends to be book-centered and many of those books are old. In courses in literature, philosophy, history, and religion, students' work consists mostly of reading books, often primary texts. Distinguishing primary from secondary sources is a hallmark of humanistic research that emphasizes the importance of reading authors from diverse times and cultures. Many professors in such classes teach book in hand, modeling by their own performance a text-centered way of thinking. Explicit in such performances is the assertion that these old texts still have important things to say to contemporary students. Implicit is the hope that, in this or another book, we may find forgotten wisdom that could benefit us and our society.

Such pedagogies reflect wider cultural commitments. Human cultures tend to vest some material objects with important, even transcendent, meanings. Objects like national flags, religious art, and grave markers evoke powerful emotions and motivate the behavior of very many people, no less today than in the past.

Books also evoke powerful emotions and symbolic connotations. That is most obviously the case for religious scriptures. The Torah, Bible and Qur'an, to name only three, function as icons not only for Jews, Christians and Muslims. They also serve as powerful symbols of those religions within the wider culture. But many other books also exhibit iconic qualities, if not to the same degree. The image of the book (codex) appears in art and other visual media to represent knowledge and learning. It is a conventional prop in the portraits of scholars and writers. Many universities put images of books on their institutional seals and web-pages.

Material books evoke a semi-sacred feeling in many people. They will therefore go to great lengths to avoid destroying them. The cultural roots of this antipathy run deep. Memories of cultural loss because of mass book destructions lie at the roots of both Chinese and Western cultures: the first Quin emperor ordered the destruction of most forms of literature in 213 B.C.E, while Roman troops accidentally burned the library of Alexandria in 48 B.C.E. Historians debate the accuracy of both stories, but that has not lessened their cultural significance. Conflict between and within religious traditions has frequently included destroying books and attacking their owners. These were also infamous practices of totalitarian governments and political movements in the twentieth century. As a result, book burning remains one of the most outrageous activities in contemporary culture, closely followed by attempts to ban books from libraries or bookstores.

From a practical point of view, all of this is inexplicable. Books are very common and widely distributed commodities. The destruction of one copy or even many copies will not seriously threaten the availability of mass-marketed books. But such practical observations do nothing to lessen the iconicity of books. Most religious scriptures are even more widely distributed, often in very inexpensive form, and are so common that the destruction of tens of thousands of copies would not seriously affect access to their texts. Yet news of scripture desecrations arouses great fury and catches the attention of the world's news media (Chapter 5). The iconic status of books in contemporary culture is unaffected by their ubiquity or commercial value.

So research libraries in the twenty-first century find themselves in a difficult predicament. On the one hand, the ever-rising number of academic publications and ever-expanding scope of scholarly interests puts enormous pressure on their budgets and their shelf space. It is understandable that the advent of electronic texts might look like a timely technological fix to these woes. On the other hand, the broader society privileges research libraries—and the universities that support them—as conservators of intellectual culture. The prestige of a university is often crudely calculated by the sheer number of volumes in its collections. (Even more extreme examples of the social priority on book conservation can be found in national depository libraries like the U.S. Library of Congress and the British Library.)

E-books do not serve this desire to preserve culture very well. Electronic texts are an ephemeral textual medium, like chalk boards. And like chalk boards, preserving electronic texts depends on frequent copying, though they are much easier to reproduce. They show absolutely no promise for permanence, either physically (on various kinds of computer hardware all of which suffers rather rapid physical decline and even more rapid technological obsolescence) or culturally (due to ever-changing software that overwhelms the human expertise needed to operate older systems). The widespread hope that constant copying and upgrades will preserve e-texts long term shows remarkable ignorance of human history. When physical, economic, and political systems can all be disrupted on a catastrophic scale—as they were several times in the twentieth century alone—systems that depend on electrical power and digital communication networks cannot be trusted as reliable long-term repositories of cultural memories.

The university library has served the function of cultural repository for centuries. Though its collections can also be destroyed by war and other catastrophes, books at least do not require dedicated electrical technologies in order to work. They only need a human eye and a mind that understands the language and script they contain, and even that knowledge can often be reconstructed after being lost. As Robert Darnton argued,

> there is something to be said for both visions, the library as a citadel and the Internet as open space. ... Google Book Search, the largest undertaking of them all, will [not] make research libraries obsolete. On the contrary, Google will make them more important than ever. ... the totality of world literature—all the books in all the languages of the world—lies far beyond Google's capacity to digitize. ... Electronic enterprises come and go. Research libraries last for centuries. Better to fortify them than to declare them obsolete, because obsolescence is built into the electronic media. ... The obsession with developing new media has inhibited efforts to preserve the old. We have lost 80 percent of all silent films and 50 percent of all films made before World War II. Nothing preserves texts better than ink imbedded in paper .... The best preservation system ever invented was the old-fashioned, pre-modern book.[4]

Books preserved in libraries of various kinds have proven to be the most reliable, flexible, and portable technology for long-term cultural preservation for the last two thousand years. That is why books symbolize the preservation of cultural ideals and why they carry so much cultural prestige. Libraries that abandon the role of book preservation lose the prestige that goes with it.

Non-Disposable Books

Books are hard to throw away. Though produced in mass quantities at low prices like so many other disposable commodities, books exert a grip on our imaginations that ensures special treatment. Many families socialize their children from an early age to cherish and collect books, even before they are able to read them for themselves. Public education reinforces and universalizes this socialization. Libraries are venerated as the "hearts" of schools and universities. Mass media celebrates authors for their creativity and scholars for their expertise, documented by the titles of books they have written and, often, by displaying their most recent book. Governments invest resources in archival depositories to ensure that all the books produced in their countries are preserved. So, disposing of books transgresses inhibitions reinforced by family, school, media and government.

Even secular books such as novels and encyclopedias gain non-disposable status by being ritualized. They may be ritualized along one or more dimensions. In the case of novels, it is their interpretation in the semantic dimension that is most frequently ritualized through exposition in school

---

4. Robert Darnton, "The Library in the New Age," *The New York Review of Books*, June 12, 2008.

and university classes and commentary in book reviews and other forms of literary analysis. The more a particular book receives semantic ritualization, the greater its status as literature becomes. Poetry is frequently ritualized in the expressive dimension by public readings. Publication of collectors' editions of "classic" literature in leather bindings ritualizes works of literature in the iconic dimension by making them appear valuable and venerable. Other genres also elicit one or another of these kinds of ritualization to establish their texts as worthy of preservation and dissemination.

Nevertheless, books must be thrown away. They are produced in such quantities that they cannot all be preserved nor are they all needed or valued. Their pages and bindings wear out or, more commonly these days, their contents go out-of-date. It is cheaper to buy a new copy than repair an old one and more useful to buy a revised edition than to continue using the old version. Yet the ubiquity of old reference books and tattered paper-backs in rummage sales and used book stores testifies to the cultural inhibition on disposing of books. A librarian tells me that because of public outrage at reports of libraries throwing out books, she and her colleagues have carried their worn-out, duplicate or out-of-date copies to the garbage dumpster at night, under the cover of darkness.[5]

Destroying books arouses deep antipathies stoked by memories of political and religious suppression by book burnings. Such concerns do not just reflect modern political history, such as the bonfires of the Nazi party. Memories of ancient book burnings lie at the roots of Chinese culture as well as the Jewish and Christian religions.[6] Less frequently remembered is the fact that suppression of books succeeded in virtually destroying the Manicheans.[7] Concerns over the possible loss of texts have manifested themselves historically in the apocalyptic eschatologies of both Indian Jains and Japanese Buddhists.[8] Older yet are the anathemas inscribed in ancient Near Eastern royal inscriptions and religious epics against anyone who might destroy or modify their texts—evidence that concern for textual preservation may be as old as the textualization of narrative itself.

---

5. Wendy Bousfield, personal communication.

6. For Chinese, see *Shiji* 87: 6b-7a in William Theodore de Bary, ed., *Sources of East Asian Tradition: Premodern Asia.* (New York: Columbia University Press, 2008), 117–118; for Jewish, see 1 Maccabees 1:56–57 in the Bible's Apocrypha; for Christian, see the discussion by Daniel Sarefield, "The Symbolics of Book Burning: The Establishment of a Christian Ritual of Persecution," in W. E. Klingshirn and L. Safran, *The Early Christian Book* (Washington, DC: Catholic University of America Press, 2007), 159–173.

7. Zsuzsanna Gulácsi, *Mediaeval Manichaean Book Art* (Leiden: Brill, 2005), 30.

8. Balbir, "Is a Manuscript an Object," 107–124; Moerman, "Death of the Dharma," 71–90.

Expressions of outrage over the intentional or unintentional destructions of libraries—such as the burning of the library of ancient Alexandria in 48 B.C.E. or the collapse of the Cologne city archives in 2009[9]—usually focus on the loss of information. To address this concern, university and government libraries build more and larger buildings to house collections exploding in size due to the growth of book publishing in the late twentieth and early twenty-first centuries. These buildings have recently come to include warehouses for off-site storage that measure shelf-space by the kilometer.[10] The inaccessibility of books in such facilities led one journalist to comment that "they're our era's equivalent of pharaonic tombs ... time capsules ..."[11]

The urge for book preservation is not constrained much by the fact that some texts are so ubiquitous that their complete loss is unimaginable, such as the scriptures of several large religions. This observation suggests that factors other than information preservation are at work here. The concern for book preservation involves respect for cultures, veneration of traditions, and, at its root, the preservation of cultural values. There is therefore an inherent tension in most literate cultures between the idea of a book or enduring text on the one hand and the possibility of its disposal or destruction on the other.

Of course, there are certain kinds of media, some in book (codex) form, that are designed to be disposable and are easily treated that way, such as newspapers, magazines, and telephone books. Thinking about such disposable media casts the distinctive iconic nature of non-disposable books into sharper relief.

There is nothing new about disposable written media. They have existed since the invention of writing. In fact, writing was probably invented in ancient Sumer with short-term use in mind, namely to produce sales receipts in malleable and reusable clay (Chapter 6). Ancient scribes also wrote letters and receipts on shards of broken pottery (ostraca). Other transient written media have included wax tablets and chalk boards. The invention of movable-type printing in Europe was quickly employed to mass-produce disposable broadsheets containing news, advertisements and songs. The mutability of today's digital texts therefore has very old precedents.

Why can some texts and books be disposed of easily while others cannot? The telephone book provides an instructive example of the difference between disposable and non-disposable books. The difference does not lie

---

9. Andrew Curry, "Archive Collapse Disaster for Historians," *Spiegel,* March 4, 2009.

10. Stuart Jeffries, "Inside the Tomb of Tomes," *Guardian,* November 24, 2007.

11. Geoff Manaugh, "The Future Warehouse of Unwanted Books," BLDG/BLOG, December 1, 2007. http://bldgblog.blogspot.com/2007/12/future-warehouse-of-unwanted-books.html (accessed January 23, 2017).

in either the number of copies published or in the degree to which they are instantly recognizable. The phone book's physical and economic ubiquity over the twentieth century is undeniable, as Paul Collins noted in 2008:

> The humble phone book spent the 20th century as the prince of print jobs. … The phone book is the one book guaranteed to be present in every household, no matter how little else the occupants read. Even in a vacant apartment, you'll still find old phone books in the kitchen cabinet. … Last year, according to the industry group the Yellow Pages Association, approximately 615 million directories were printed in the United States alone, generating revenues of $13.9 billion.[12]

But he also pointed out that "the phone book's ubiquity has given it an invisibility. … Despite being the most popular printed work ever, there's never been a single scholarly monograph on the phone book."

Collins' observations go to the heart of what makes a book iconic: cultural attention focused by rituals. Rituals are practices that draw attention, in this case to books, to make people conscious of how they are using and reading them (see Chapter 1). Religious processions with scriptures, political oath ceremonies, and textual amulets all ritualize the physical form and image of books or other texts. But people also ritualize books—that is, they draw sustained and conscious attention to them—by interpreting their meaning (in scholarly articles and monographs, among many other media) and also by performing the text through recitations, songs, art, theater, and film. People in different cultures, times and places ritualize different books to different degrees along each of the iconic, semantic, and expressive dimensions.

Phone books, however, are ritualized in none of these dimensions. Not only does their semantic form and cultural significance remain uninterpreted, but the idea of "performing" their text or contents ritually is ludicrous.[13] As to their physical form, no one protests if they are burned, mutilated, or otherwise destroyed (unless it is out of concern for environmental impact). By the analysis employed here, phone books are among the most disposable of books.

Thinking about disposable books may also help us grasp the likely effects of transforming texts into digital media. To the degree that a book simply serves as an information source, it can be replaced by computer searches without readers feeling any loss. Online phone directories are now readily available and have almost replaced material phone books entirely. Sacred

---

12. Paul Collins, "The Book of the Undead: Why won't phone books die?" *Slate*, March 21, 2008.

13. Which is exactly what some comics and actors have done: see The Phone Book on Public Radio Exchange (PRX), online at https://www.prx.org/series/35653-the-phone-book (accessed January 23, 2017).

texts have also been adapted for the new media, but with very different prospects for the material books. Biblical texts, for example, were digitized and marketed in electronically searchable forms even before phone books (Chapter 4). The difference between phone books and bibles lies not in the degree to which they have been transformed and accepted in electronic form, but rather in the fact that the disappearance of physical bibles is unimaginable because of their ritual uses. It is very unlikely that e-readers will ever replace traditional codices in liturgical processions and other ritual uses in the iconic dimension, because computers and other kinds of e-readers do not represent particular texts but are generic containers for any content.[14] As a result, the transformation of scripture into electronic texts has elicited no protests from the devout that I can find, unlike the widely voiced concerns that meet the transformation of literary texts into electronic form. To the degree that people ritualize books and other texts along the iconic dimension, that is, to the degree that they pay conscious attention to how they look and feel, how they carry them and their own posture as they read them, such iconic books will remain major features of human cultures. The iconic status of various kinds of material books preserves and even enhances their appeal in an age of digital information.[15]

Non-disposable books are supposed to preserve their contents for the future. In contrast to disposable texts, concern for preservation has always motivated the production of iconic texts. These concerns appear explicitly in many ancient texts that prohibit their own destruction and mandate their preservation and even oral reproduction.[16]

Written texts have always served not only to transmit information, but also to provide evidence of the age and reliability or variability of information, to show whether it has changed or not. Writings' role as physical evidence goes back to the origins off writing as receipts (Chapter 6) and is still basic to historical research of all kinds. The internet is very good at providing information in the present, but it exists in an eternal now that makes it much harder to tell how the information has changed over time. The rare exceptions, such as Wikipedia's "show edits" mode and the Wayback

---

14. Though some people try to do so: former Microsoft executive, Suzi LeVine, took her oath of office in 2014 as the U.S. ambassador to Switzerland and Liechtenstein by placing her hand on an e-reader open to the U.S. Constitution (Eric Levenson, "New U.S. Ambassador Swore Her Oath on an E-Reader," *The Atlantic*, June 2, 2014).

15. Anderson, "Scriptures, Materiality, and the Digital Turn."

16. On the Lotus Sutra, see Moerman, "Death of the Dharma," 71–90, and on such colophons in medieval Jain texts, see Balbir, "Is a Manuscript," 107–124. For examples from ancient Near Eastern texts, see the conclusion of the ancient Babylonian Erra epic in Foster, *Before the Muses*, 910–911; Deuteronomy 6:6–9 and 31:11–12 in the Hebrew Bible; and the New Testament book of Revelation 22:18–19.

Machine, simply highlight the rest of the web's atemporal presentation of information.

Books preserve knowledge, culture and religion. Books therefore play a central role in forming and reproducing individual and corporate identity. Authors create an authorial voice in their works that replaces their embodied personas in the minds of readers and has the potential to long outlast them. Cultures establish and perpetuate the canon of their "greatest" authors to claim their voices as authentic representatives of the culture. Sacred texts establish the authoritative voice of a religious tradition and implicitly or explicitly represent it as the voice of deity. By internalizing and reproducing these voices, readers identify themselves with that culture and/or religion. By claiming the books, they define their own identities. Preserving books then becomes vital to preserving religious and cultural identity.

Texts by their nature reinforce a widespread human tendency to distinguish material form from essential nature. Readers distinguish the "contents" of a text—it's linguistic form and thematic message—from the particular material in which they find it. In this sense, texts readily transcend the material book in which they are read (Chapter 8).

Such textual transcendence bears a more than analogous relationship to religious transcendence. Though individual copies of texts may wear out or be destroyed, the transcendent texts can last forever so long as copies are reproduced and/or preserved. Their potential for infinite reproduction and eternal preservation provides a practical and demonstrable form of immortality.

Disposing of Sacred Texts

In 2010, Kristina Myrvold edited a collection of essays, *The Death of Sacred Texts*, with the subtitle, "the ritual disposal and renovation of texts in world religions."[17] Separate chapters by different authors described how Jews, Muslims, Christians, Japanese Buddhists, Hindus, Jains, and Sikhs ritualize the disposal of sacred texts. The collection demonstrated a pervasive cultural concern for the "proper" disposal of scriptures amidst the wide diversity of ritual practices and beliefs. These essays prompted me to reflect on the problem of how to dispose of sacred texts and, for that matter, of books in general.

The disposal ceremonies described in *The Death of Sacred Texts* ritualize the iconic dimension of sacred texts. The chapters document both a widespread concern for ritual disposal of scriptures as well as the great variety

---

17. Kristina Myrvold, ed., *The Death of Sacred Texts: Ritual Disposal and Renovation of Texts in World Religions* (London: Ashgate, 2010).

among religious traditions regarding both the form of the rituals and the frequency with which they are actually performed. And expressing concerns about how to dispose of sacred texts does not necessarily translate into routine performance of disposal rituals.[18]

Nevertheless, some common themes show up in discussions of scripture disposal from almost every religious tradition. The most prominent is an analogy between the disposal of a sacred text and of a human body. Muslims, Jews, and Christians urge burial of worn-out sacred texts because burial represents the respectful ritual for treating the dead. Sikhs provide a "respected pyre" for cremating sacred texts in a ceremony explicitly analogous to a funeral. When Jains, Hindus and some Jewish rabbis distinguish scripture disposal from human burial on purity grounds, the analogy to funerals nevertheless remains operative in how they distinguish the disposal rituals from ordinary funerals. In the case of medieval Japanese Buddhists, concerns for the afterlife often motivated the elaborate reproduction and preservative burial of sacred texts.

Ordinary funerals provide a ritual means for emphasizing the continuing value of this particular human life and of human life in general, despite the destruction of the material body. Its destruction raises anxieties about the preservation of the person's transcendent soul or value. The habit of treating books as material incarnations of transcendent meanings makes them particularly powerful symbols of this conundrum. The ritual establishment of transcendent value despite material destruction lies at the heart of scripture disposal ceremonies, so they also tend to take funerary form. Conversely, afterlife beliefs often invoke the trope of textual permanence in the form of a heavenly "Book of Life" or something similar that preserves the names of the saved and/or a record of every person's deeds. This theme of afterlife expectations permanently inscribed in supernatural texts appears among Jews, Daoists, Christians, Muslims and Sikhs.[19]

The other common theme that appears in these essays involves analogies between sacred texts and bodily relics, in which books are treated ritually like relics (see Chapter 3 above). I must observe here that such practices are hardly limited to religious traditions. Secular institutions regularly treat particular books (and other objects) in precisely the same manner, though they avoid the religious vocabulary of "relic" and "veneration." The most prominent secular reliquaries are museums and libraries, though private collections also perform this function. The objects they collect and display

18. As was noted by Svensson, "Relating, Revering, and Removing," 31–54; by Parmenter, "A Fitting Ceremony," 55–70; and by Balbir, "Is a Manuscript," 107–124.

19. Parmenter, "The Bible as Icon," 298–310.

or store attain their status either as intrinsically rare or important or from their association with important people and events, but they call them "collector's items" instead.

Historically, of course, museums and secular libraries developed out of religious institutions which they continue to imitate, for the most part unconsciously. As has often been observed, they function as shrines of national or secular culture.[20] When museums and libraries put books on exhibit, they remove them from ordinary use, just like sacred texts treated as relics (Chapter 3). Display ritualizes their iconic dimension to the point that the text can no longer function in the semantic or expressive dimensions. Here belief in the transcendent nature of a book's contents allows people to distinguish it from its particular material incarnation. So long as the contents are readily available in non-relic copies, the relic text can be exhibited for its historical importance and/or distinctive material form.

My point is that the book practices of religious communities can be understood as extensions of the book practices of their wider cultures. These practices reflect the inherent understanding of books and other texts as physical repositories of meanings and values that transcend their particular material form. Religious communities generally elaborate and exaggerate the ritualization of books found in secular culture, though not always in the same ways. Traditions for handling other sacred objects without desecrating them inform how sacred texts get handled. Religious groups with established traditions of relic veneration find such practices particularly applicable to relic texts.

One might suppose, however, that the ritual production of sacred texts purely for the sake of burying them must exceed any possible secular analogue. Max Moerman described the medieval Japanese practice of writing elaborate copies of the Lotus Sutra in order to bury them in funeral ceremonies. The goal was to preserve them through the coming time of ignorance of the Dharma, as well as to offer the individual who sponsored their creation hope for an afterlife. Burial in this case represents not disposal but eschatological preservation, a kind of "time capsule" as Moerman noted.[21] However, exactly the same language was used by Geoff Manaugh to describe the British Library's warehouse to store "nil to low use material."[22]

---

20. See Gretchen Buggeln, Crispin Paine, and S. Brent Plate, "Religion in Museums, Museums as Religion," in *Religion in Museums: Global and Multidisciplinary Perspectives* (New York: Bloomsbury, 2017), 1–8.

21. Moerman, "The Death of the Dharma," 72.

22. Geoff Manaugh, "The Future Warehouse of Unwanted Books," BLDG/BLOG, December 1, 2007. http://bldgblog.blogspot.com/2007/12/future-warehouse-of-unwanted-books.html (accessed January 23, 2017).

Similarly, *The Guardian* described it as "262 linear kilometres of high-density, fully automated storage in a low-oxygen environment ... meticulously constructed to house things that no one wants," hence a "tomb of tomes."[23] The stated rationale behind laws establishing copyright libraries is, of course, the preservation of information, which though currently unwanted might someday be needed. The status of "someday" in that rationalization is more than vaguely eschatological. Positively apocalyptic is the Long Now Foundation's efforts to preserve a record of 1,500 human languages etched microscopically on a nickel "Rosetta disk" designed to last 50,000 years—ten times the entire history of written language to date.[24]

By the labels "eschatological" and "apocalyptic," I do not mean to denigrate the fears of information loss that motivate these projects. As a fully socialized member of twenty-first-century Western culture, I too find the prospect of an information apocalypse very likely and am convinced of the real harm of widespread language extinctions. Just like medieval Japanese Buddhists, we inhabitants of contemporary secular cultures fear the loss of our cultural capital in the near future. Some of us are making expensive and time-consuming efforts to preserve it in more or less inaccessible forms.

Applications of modern technology and engineering to these problems are not new. In the early years of the nuclear arms race, the U.S. Constitution and Declaration of Independence were moved into the Rotunda of the National Archives in Washington, DC, where they could be displayed under protective glass during the day and lowered into bomb-proof vaults under the building at night (Chapter 7). The Ancient Biblical Manuscripts Center in Claremont, California, stores archival copies of its microfilm and digital files in a vault deep in the Sierra Nevada Mountains. These facilities were built to withstand both natural and human threats to the documents' preservation. In 2011, the Internet Archive, a project to preserve historical digital collections and make them accessible online in the Wayback Machine, added a physical archive capable of storing ten million books to back up its digital files.[25] I suspect that such examples of extreme measures for text preservation can be multiplied many times over.

These examples show that veneration and preservation of the material text remains an essential aspect of the cultural function of books.

23. Stuart Jeffries, "Inside the Tomb of Tomes," *Guardian,* November 24, 2007.

24. Alexander Rose, "Macro to micro etching," The Long Now Foundation Blog, November 3, 2008. http://blog.longnow.org/2008/11/03/macro-to-micro-etching/ (accessed January 23, 2017)

25. Brewster Kahle, "Why Preserve Books? The New Physical Archive of the Internet Archive," *Internet Archive Blogs,* June 6, 2011. http://blog.archive.org/2011/06/06/why-preserve-books-the-new-physical-archive-of-the-internet-archive/ (accessed January 23, 2017).

Preservation of physical books and other texts remains a secular as well as religious eschatological concern. Lay and scholarly interests unite around the cause of text preservation, though often the particular books of concern are different. While the American public is more likely to be interested in the manuscripts of the nation's founding documents in the elaborate Rotunda, professional historians are likely to be interested in more obscure documents in the National Archives' vaults. The financial stability of libraries and museums often depends on their skill at catering to both interests. So, the Archives' building in Washington has two main entrances: on one side is the grand entrance for tourists while on the opposite side of the building is an equally impressive entrance for researchers.

Scholars, despite their interpretive authority, have rarely been able to enforce attention to the semantic dimension of scriptures alone. Powerful lay interests usually insist on some socially privileged book rituals, such as their use for political and judicial oath ceremonies, because manipulation of the iconic text conveys political and religious legitimacy (Chapter 9). In many cultures, wealthy lay sponsors supply the funding to create and maintain sacred texts, often in hopes of specific recognition in this life and/or the next. They also play key roles in the rituals surrounding their disposal. A Sikh businessman took the initiative to develop and fund an institution for reverently cremating sacred texts of the Sikh and other religious traditions.[26] A Pakistani Muslim began storing worn-out copies of the Qur'an in a mountain tunnel in 1992. Now its more than 2.5 million volumes have turned the site into a popular shrine.[27] Such book preservation efforts draw the attention of the religiously devout and of secular media alike.

Architectural Values

The rococo library of Admont Stift is often celebrated as one of the most beautiful libraries in the world. This Benedictine monastery was founded in the eleventh century in a wide valley in the Austrian alps. Today, it claims to be the largest monastic establishment in Austria, with considerable land holdings and many businesses including a winery and apothecary. Its buildings appear relatively modern, due to a devastating fire in 1865 that required almost complete rebuilding, and its prosperity is evident from its up-to-date facilities for visitors.

The baroque library of Admont Stift survived the nineteenth-century fire intact. Its large hall claims to be the longest of any monastery library

---

26. Myrvold, "Making the Scripture a Person," 134–136.

27. Hannah Al-Othman, "Pictured: Incredible underground shrine," DailyMail.com 21 January, 2017. http://www.dailymail.co.uk/news/article-4143086/Incredible-shrine-old-copies-Koran-buried.html (accessed 12/27/2017).

worldwide, and its shelves hold 70,000 volumes. The library was finished in 1776 and its white paint, floral decorations and ceiling frescoes reflect the rococo style of the period. The frescoes depict the uniting of scientific, humanistic and religious learning and reflect eighteenth-century enlightenment thought with an authoritarian Hapsburg orientation. When I visited in 2016, the library had been recently refurbished and looked like new.

From the extensive facilities for visitors, including up-to-date ticket counters, restrooms, parking lots, and a restaurant, it appears that the library attracts many tourists. They are encouraged by the single admission price to also visit the museums of art and natural history in the same building. The art collection provides a concise survey of changes in artistic styles from medieval through renaissance and baroque to rococo, before focusing on the monastery's ecclesiastical treasures: reliquaries, vestments, chalices, and so forth.

The natural history museum is more extensive. It proves to be a deliberate reproduction of a "cabinet of curiosities." The monastery had extensive collections that perished in the 1865 fire. The monks subsequently rebuilt a remarkable collection of stuffed or pickled wild-life, pinned insects, botanical specimens and minerals. One room presents a multi-media and child-friendly introduction to the local natural environment. But most of the museum preserves an older approach that emphasizes cataloguing and comparing species.

The museums of natural history and art join with the Admont Stift library in projecting the Benedictine ideal of the pursuit of learning, all learning, as a form of devotion. The library shelves contain books on secular subjects in its south end and theological subjects in its north end, while saving the central rotunda for scripture and its ancient interpretation. The museums, then, extend this vision of universal scholarship centered around scripture to include artifacts and specimens.

But whereas the museums' architecture and decoration are entirely functional, the library's rococo style is quite ornate. Why the contrast?

A clue to the answer can be found in reliquaries displayed in the monastery's art museum. Many are made of gold and silver and decorated with jewels—all to display and preserve small bodily relics, maybe a piece of bone or hair or cloth. A reliquary proclaims the extraordinary significance of the apparently mundane objects it contains. The most elaborate in Admont Stift's treasury is a "monstrance" for displaying the host—the wheat wafer transformed by a priest's blessing into the body of Christ and presented to congregants during the ritual of the Eucharist. A thin wheat wafer would be placed inside this gilded stand decorated with 2,175 gemstones to emphasize the superlative value of the host.

Figure 7.   The rococo library of Admont Stift, a Benedictine monastery on the Enns River in Austria.

The rococo library functions like this monstrance. It proclaims the super-lative value of its contents—in this case, of its books. By the eighteenth cen-tury, books had become common objects. Against the tendency to think of them as mundane, the rococo library encases them in rich art and decora-tion to show every visitor the importance of its contents. The library is a reliquary that emphasizes the treasure of religious, cultural and scientific knowledge that it contains.

Libraries, as repositories of material books, continue to function today as powerful symbols of the ideals of free thought, empowerment, culture and counter-culture, with or without the architecture. A "People's Library" sprang up at the Occupy Wall Street protest in New York in 2011 and was frequently highlighted in news coverage of the event. The media interest reflected the sentiment of the protestors that the library was somehow rep-resentative of their movement. "Literacy, Legitimacy and Moral Authority" read the sign above the library's donations box. After police evicted the protestors, ruined books were displayed in front of the New York Public Library to portray the suppression of the movement.[28] In the same month

---

28. Occupy Wall Street Library, https://peopleslibrary.wordpress.com/ (accessed January 22, 2017).

Figure 8.   A monstrance (a reliquary for the Eucharistic host) in the monastery museum
            of Admont Stift.

that the Occupy library was scattered, *The New York Times* described the
Read/Write Library in Chicago that collects "anything from university press
to handmade artists' books to zines made by thirteen-year-olds."[29] It also
highlighted the 12,000 libraries opened in villages around the world by the
charity, Room to Read.[30] These stories show that books and libraries continue to function as powerful material symbols of people's hopes for a more
equitable, enlightened and peaceful world.

Libraries often use their special exhibits to shape cultural values. For
example, several major Western libraries tried to counter anti-Muslim prej-

29. Juan-Pablo Veleznov, "An Unusual Library Finds a New Home," *The New York Times*,
    November 12, 2011.

30. Nicholas Kristof, "His Libraries, 12,000 So Far, Change Lives," *The New York Times*,
    November 5, 2011.

udices after 9/11 by displaying beautiful manuscripts of Jewish, Christian, and Muslim scriptures side-by-side. First there was "Torah, Bible, Coran: Livres de parole" at the Bibliothèque nationale de France in 2005, followed by "Sacred" at the British Library in 2007, and "Three Faiths: Judaism, Christianity, Islam" at the New York Public Library in 2010. These exhibits of amazing manuscripts and printed books from each of the three Western religions were deliberate efforts to demonstrate what these three religions have in common.[31]

On today's university and college campuses, library buildings manifest the culture's symbolic investments in the books they contain. It is a very old religious idea that books of scripture convey some of their importance to the buildings that house them. A synagogue is holy because of the sacred Torah scrolls it contains, a Sikh *gurdwara* is a shrine for the Guru Granth Sahib, and a mosque is holy to many Muslims because of its Qur'ans. Buddhists as well as Christians have frequently treated books of scripture just like the relics of saints, and the boxes and buildings that contain them as reliquaries. Library architecture often reflects this tradition by imitating Greek temples or Gothic churches. University professors and administrators frequently claim that the library is the heart and soul of the university, but university crests show that their real referents are the books inside those libraries.

This architecture and rhetoric do not make casual claims. They tie the university's identity to material artifacts—books—that exemplify learning and wisdom, in contrast to other campus architecture—such as the football stadium—that emphasizes very different cultural values. Library policies therefore evoke heated debates because the cultural identity of universities in general, and of the humanities in particular, are at stake. Books matter because they are the icons for such values. A university without a book-stuffed library is a university without a soul.

At my university, the debate in 2009 led to somewhat more funding for the libraries. The main library still lacks books on its first two floors, but the books that were removed are stored at a new facility less than two miles from the center of campus. The two-story reading room of an older library building has been renovated to provide a very stately space for quiet reading and study. These developments are heartening acknowledgments of the university library as a symbol of academic values and as the protector of the material forms of our values—our books. Yet the argument over whether and how to redefine that role continues. In 2017, the new university librarian on my campus was quoted in the student newspaper as saying:

---

31. Edward Rothstein, "Abraham's Progeny, and Their Texts," *The New York Times*, October 22, 2010.

Bird [Library] was built to hold large collections of physical objects and accommodate growth, but the library is no longer collections-focused. ... Bird is 'the heart of the campus.' You only need to walk into this building at 8 o'clock at night to see that we've been very successful at providing a space for students to socialize and study.[32]

By contrast, Alberto Manguel in 2015 described concisely the cultural function of libraries as three-fold: "as preservers of the memory of our society, as providers of the accounts of our experience and the tools to navigate them — and as symbols of our identity."

Since the time of Alexandria, libraries have held a symbolic function. For the Ptolemaic kings, the library was an emblem of their power; eventually it became the encompassing symbol of an entire society, a numinous place where readers could learn the art of attention which, Hannah Arendt argued, is a definition of culture. But since the mid-20th century, libraries no longer seem to carry this symbolic meaning and, as mere storage rooms of a technology deemed defunct, are not considered worthy of proper preservation and funding.

Manguel listed the many ways that librarians are diversifying their services to remain relevant and fundable in the current political and cultural climate. But he argued that, "If we change the role of libraries and librarians without preserving the centrality of the book, we risk losing something irretrievable."

Every economic crisis responds, first of all, by cutting funds to culture. But the dismantling of our libraries and changing their nature is not simply a matter of economics. Somewhere in our time, we began to forget what memory—personal and collective—means, and the importance of common symbols that help us understand our society.[33]

Conscious of our heritage from previous generations, we cherish old texts as relics that connect us to the past. Conscious of our own mortality, we hope that "our" books will live on indefinitely. Depending on the kind of texts in question, they represent an author's hopes for immortality, a nation's desire for permanence, or a religion's claim to eternal truth. The traditional codex book makes these hopes realistically possible and verifiably true of many texts that have been preserved for centuries and even millennia.

You might think that the transcendental quality of texts would render their individual material manifestations inconsequential, that when

---

32. Kennedy Rose, "Bird Library was built 45 years ago. Now, the building's future is uncertain under the Campus Framework plan," *The Daily Orange*, September 26, 2017.

33. Alberto Manguel, "Reinventing the Library," *The New York Times*, October 23, 2015.

texts appear in very many copies, destruction of individual copies would not threaten their existence and so receive little resistance. This practical observation conflicts, however, with the deeply engrained socialization that books represent essential cultural and religious values. As a result of this pervasive socialization, a book's symbolic value has very little to do with calculations of its utility. Most human societies teach people to believe that books incarnate the values of their culture and religion, and should therefore be cherished, preserved, and reproduced. That is why books matter.

Bibliography of Books and Academic Articles

Alexander, Philip. 2014. "The Rabbis, the Greek Bible and Hellenism." In *The Jewish-Greek Tradition in Antiquity and the Byzantine Empire*, edited by J. K. Aitken and J. C. Paget, 229–246. Cambridge: Cambridge University Press. https://doi.org/10.1017/cbo9780511736223.020

Anderson, Brad. "Scriptures, Materiality, and the Digital Turn: The Iconicity of Sacred Texts in a Liminal Age." *Postscripts*. forthcoming.

Arnold, Philip P. 1995. "Paper Ties to Land: Indigenous and Colonial Material Orientations to the Valley of Mexico." *History of Religions* 35: 27–60. https://doi.org/10.1086/463406

———. 2002. "Paper Rituals and the Mexican landscape." In *Representing Aztec Ritual: Performance, Text, and Image in the Work of Sahagún*, edited by Eloise Quiñones Keber, 227–250. Boulder: University Press of Colorado. https://doi.org/10.2307/25063108

———. 2013. "Indigenous 'Texts' of Inhabiting the Land: George Washington's Wampum Belt and the Canandaigua Treaty." In *Iconic Books and Texts*, edited by J. W. Watts, 361–372. Sheffield: Equinox. First published in *Postscripts* 6: 277–289. https://doi.org/10.1558/post.v6i1-3.277

Bar-Asher, Meir M. 2016. "'We have made it an Arabic Qur'an': the Permissibility of Translating Scripture in Islam in Contrast with Judaism and Christianity." In *Interpreting Scriptures in Judaism, Christianity and Islam: Overlapping Inquiries*, edited by M. Z. Cohen and A. Berlin, 65–83. Cambridge: Cambridge University Press. https://doi.org/10.1017/cbo9781107588554.004

Assmann, Jan. 1997. *Das kulturelle Gedächtnis: Schrift, Erinnerung und politische Identität in frühen Hochkulturen*. Munich: Beck. https://doi.org/10.17104/9783406703409

———. 2006. *Religion and Cultural Memory*. Translated by R. Livingstone. Stanford, CA: Stanford University Press.

Ayoub, Mahmoud M. and Vincent J. Cornell. 2005. "Qur'an: Its Role in Muslim Practice and Life." *Encyclopedia of Religion*, 2nd ed., 11: 7570–7574. Farmington Hills, MI: Macmillan Reference.

Bäck, Allan. 2008. "Islamic Logic?" In *The Unity of Science in the Arabic Tradition: Science, Logic, Epistemology and their Interactions*, edited by S. Rahman, T. Street, and H. Tahir, 255–279. New York: Springer. https://doi.org/10.1007/978-1-4020-8405-8_9

Balbir, Nalini. 2010. "Is a Manuscript an Object or a Living Being? Jain Views on the Life and Use of Sacred Texts." In *The Death of Sacred Texts: Ritual Disposal and Renovation of Texts in World Religions*, edited by K. Myrvold, 107–124. London: Ashgate. https://doi.org/10.4324/9781315615318

Beal, Timothy. 2011. *The Rise and Fall of the Bible: The Unexpected History of an Accidental Book*. New York: Houghton Mifflin Harcourt.

———. 2011. "Reception History and Beyond: Toward the Cultural History of Scriptures." *Biblical Interpretation* 19: 357–372. https://doi.org/10.1163/156851511x595530

———. 2013. "The End of the Word as We Know It: The Cultural Iconicity of the Bible in the Twilight of Print Culture." In *Iconic Books and Texts*, edited by J. W. Watts, 207–224. Sheffield: Equinox. First published in *Postscripts* 6: 165–184. https://doi.org/10.1558/post.v6i1-3.165

Bell, Catherine. 1992. *Ritual Theory and Ritual Practice*. New York: Oxford University Press.

———. 1997. *Ritual: Perspectives and Dimensions*. New York: Oxford University Press.

Bellah, Robert N. 1967. "Civil Religion in America." *Dædalus* 96(1): 1–21.

Benjamin, Walter. 1996 [1921]. "The Task of the Translator," translated by Harry Zohn in *Walter Benhamin Selected Works*, Volume 1: 1913–1926, edited by M. Bullock and M. W. Jennings, 253–263. Cambridge, MA: Harvard Belknap.

Bibb, Bryan. 2017. "Readers and their E-Bibles: the Shape and Authority of the Hypertext Canon." In *The Bible in American Life*, edited by P. Goff, *et al.*, 256–265. New York: Oxford University Press. https://doi.org/10.1093/acprof:oso/9780190468910.003.0021

Bidderman, Shlomo. 1995. *Scripture and Knowledge: An Essay on Religious Epistemology*. Leiden: Brill.

Bokedal, Tomas. 2014. *The Formation and Significance of the Christian Biblical Canon*. London: Bloomsbury T. & T. Clark.

Broo, Måns. 2010. "Rites of Burial and Immersion: Hindu Ritual Practices on Disposing of Sacred Texts in Vrindavan." In *The Death of Sacred Texts: Ritual Disposal and Renovation of Texts in World Religions*, edited by K. Myrvold, 91–106. London: Ashgate. https://doi.org/10.4324/9781315615318

Brown, Michelle. 2003. *The Lindisfarne Gospels: Society, Spirituality and the Scribe*. London: British Library.

———. 2013. "Images to Be Read and Words to Be Seen: The Iconic Role of the Early Medieval Book." In *Iconic Books and Texts*, edited by J. W. Watts, 93–118. Sheffield: Equinox. First published in *Postscripts* 6: 39–66. https://doi.org/10.1558/post.v6i1-3.39

Brown, Peter. 1982. "Relics and Social Status in the Age of Gregory of Tours." In *Society and the Holy in Late Antiquity*, 222–250. Berkeley: University of California Press.

Bruyn, Theodore de. 2017. *Making Amulets Christian: Artefacts, Scribes, and Contexts*. Oxford: Oxford University Press.

Buggeln, Gretchen, Crispin Paine, and S. Brent Plate, eds. 2017. *Religion in Museums: Global and Multidisciplinary Perspectives*. New York: Bloomsbury. https://doi.org/10.1080/10477845.2017.1415072

Camp, Claudia V. 2013. "Possessing the Iconic Book: Ben Sira as Case Study." In *Iconic Books and Texts*, edited by J. W. Watts, 389–406. Sheffield: Equinox. First published in *Postscripts* 6: 309–329. https://doi.org/10.1558/post.v6i1-3.309

Cantwell, Cathy. 2017. "Seeing, Touching, Holding, and Swallowing Tibetan Buddhist Texts." In *Sensing Sacred Texts*, edited by J. W. Watts, 137–160. Sheffield: Equinox. First published in *Postscripts* 8: 137–160. https://doi.org/10.1558/post.32531

Carr, David M. 2005. *Writing on the Tablet of the Heart: Origins of Scripture and Literature*. Oxford: Oxford University Press.

Coburn, Thomas B. 1984. "'Scripture' in India: Towards a Typology of the Word in Hindu Life." *Journal of the American Academy of Religion* 52: 435–459. https://doi.org/10.1093/jaarel/52.3.435

Cohen, Shaye J. D. 1987. *From the Maccabees to the Mishnah*. Philadelphia, PA: Westminster.

Cohn, Yehudah B. 2008. *Tangled Up in Text: Tefillin and the Ancient World*. Providence, RI: Brown University. https://doi.org/10.1017/s0364009410000474

Corwin, Edward S. 1936. "The Constitution as Instrument and Symbol." *The American Political Science Review* 30(6): 1071–1085. https://doi.org/10.2307/1948289

Dalley, Stephanie. 1998. *The Legacy of Mesopotamia*. Oxford: Oxford University Press.

De Bary, William Theodore, ed. 2008. *Sources of East Asian Tradition: Premodern Asia*. New York: Columbia University Press. https://doi.org/10.1007/s12140-009-9085-0

Derrida, Jacques. 1985. "Des Tours de Babel." In *Difference in Translation*, translated by J. F. Graham. Ithaca, NY: Cornell University Press.

De Simini, Florinda. 2016. *Of Gods and Books: Ritual and Knowledge Transmission in the Manuscript Cultures of Premodern India*. Berlin: De Gruyter. https://doi.org/10.1515/9783110478815

Dōgen. 2007. *Shōbōgenzō: The True-Dharma Eye Treasury*. Translated by Gudo Wafu Nishijima and Chodo Cross. Berkeley, CA: BDK America. https://www.bdkamerica.org/digital/dBET_T2582_Shobogenzo1_2009.pdf

Douglas, Mary. 1966. *Purity and Danger*. London: Routledge.

Drogin, Marc. 1989. *Biblioclasm: The Mythical Origins, Magic Powers, and Perishability of the Written Word*. Savage, MD: Rowman & Littlefield.

Elgood, Cyril. 1962. "Tibb-ul-Nabbi or Medicine of the Prophet." *Osiris* 14: 33–192. https://doi.org/10.1086/368625

Elitzur, Zeev. 2013. "Between the Textual and the Visual: Borderlines in Late Antique Book Iconicity." In *Iconic Books and Texts*, edited by J. W. Watts, 135–150. Sheffield: Equinox. First published in *Postscripts* 6: 83–99. https://doi.org/10.1558/post.v6i1-3.83

Engelke, Matthew. 2007. *A Problem of Presence: Beyond Scripture in an African Church*. Berkeley: University of California. https://doi.org/10.1163/157338310x537635

Foster, Benjamin R. 2005. *Before the Muses: An Anthology of Akkadian Literature*. 3rd ed. Bethesda, MD: CDL.

———. 2007. *Akkadian Literature of the Late Period*. Münster: Ugarit.

Frevel, Christian. 2018. "On Instant Scripture and Proximal Texts: Some Insights into the Sensual Materiality of Texts and their Ritual Roles in the Hebrew Bible and Beyond." In *Sensing Sacred Texts*, edited by J. W. Watts, 57–79. Sheffield: Equinox. First published in *Postscripts* 8: 57–79. https://doi.org/10.1558/post.32631

Gamble, Harry Y. 1995. *Books and Readers in the Early Church: A History of Early Christian Texts*. New Haven, CT: Yale University Press. https://doi.org/10.1086/ahr/102.3.794

Ganz, David. 2018. "Touching Books, Touching Art: Tactile Dimensions of Sacred Books in the Medieval West." In *Sensing Sacred Texts*, edited by J. W. Watts, 81–114. Sheffield: Equinox. First published in *Postscripts* 8: 81–114. https://doi.org/10.1558/post.32702

Gardella, Peter. 2014. *American Civil Religion: What Americans Hold Sacred*. Oxford: Oxford University Press. https://doi.org/10.1007/s13644-015-0212-7

Geary, Patrick. 1986. "Sacred commodities: the circulation of medieval relics." In *The Social Life of Things: Commodities in Cultural Perspective*, edited by A. Appadurai, 169–191. Cambridge: Cambridge University Press. https://doi.org/10.1017/cbo9780511819582.008

Gedicks, Frederick. 2012. "American Civil Religion: an Idea Whose Time is Past." *George Washington International Law Review* 41: 891–908.

Gomez, Michael A. 2003. "The Preacher-Kings: W. E. B. Du Bois Revisited." In *African Americans and the Bible: Sacred Texts and Social Textures*, edited by Vincent L. Wimbush, 501–513. New York: Continuum.

Gonda, J. 1963. *The Vision of the Vedic Poets*. The Hague: Mouton & Co.

Goody, Jack. 1971. "The Impact of Islamic Writing on the Oral Cultures of West Africa." *Cahiers d'etudes africaines* 11: 455–166. https://doi.org/10.3406/cea.1971.2796

———. 1986. *The Logic of Writing and the Organization of Society*. Cambridge: Cambridge University Press.

Graham, M. Patrick. 2013. "The Tell-Tale Iconic Book." In *Iconic Books and Texts*, edited by J. W. Watts, 165–186. Sheffield: Equinox. First published in *Postscripts* 6: 117–141. https://doi.org/10.1558/post.v6i1-3.117

Graham, William A. 1987. *Beyond the Written Word: Oral Aspects of Scripture in the History of Religion*. Cambridge: Cambridge University Press.

———. 2005. "Scripture." *Encyclopedia of Religion*, 2nd ed., 12: 8194–8205. New York: Macmillan.

———. 2013. "'Winged Words': Scriptures and Classics as Iconic Texts." In *Iconic Books and Texts*, edited by J. W. Watts, 33–46. Sheffield: Equinox. First published in *Postscripts* 6: 7–22. https://doi.org/10.1558/post.v6i1-3.7

Grey, Thomas C. 1984. "The Constitution as Scripture." *Stanford Law Review* 37(1): 1–25.

Griffiths, Paul J. 1999. *Religious Reading: the Place of Reading in the Practice of Religion*. Oxford: Oxford University Press.

Gulácsi, Zsuzsanna. 2005. *Mediaeval Manichaean Book Art*. Leiden: Brill.

Hayward, C. T. R. "Scripture in the Jerusalem Temple." In *The New Cambridge History of the Bible: From the Beginnings to 600*, edited by J. C. Paget and J. Schaper, 321–344. Cambridge: Cambridge University Press. https://doi.org/10.1017/cbo9781139033671.018

Heinamaki, Elisa. 2017. "Proving the Inner Word: (De)materializing the Spirit in Radical Pietism." In *Christianity and the Limits of Materiality*, edited by Minna Opas and Anna Haapalainen, 187–209. London: Bloomsbury.

Hengel, Martin. 1974. *Judaism and Hellenism*. Philadelphia: Fortress.

Heyman, George. 2006/2008 "Canon Law and the Canon of Scripture." *Postscripts* 2: 209–225. https://doi.org/10.1558/post.v2i2.209

Holdrege, Barbara A. 2003. "Beyond the Guild: Liberating Biblical Studies." In *African Americans and the Bible: Sacred Texts and Social Textures*, edited by Vincent L. Wimbush, 138–159. New York: Continuum.

———. 2015. "From Sanskritization to Vernacularization: Subaltern Inscriptions of Bodies and Landscapes." In *Scripturalizing the Human: The Written as the Political*, edited by Vincent L. Wimbush, 176–192. New York: Routledge.

Hurtado, Larry W. 2006. *The Earliest Christian Artifacts: Manuscripts and Christian Origins*. Grand Rapids: Eerdmans. https://doi.org/10.1017/s002204690700303x

Hurvitz, Leon, trans. 1976. *Scripture of the Lotus Blossom of the Fine Dharma (The Lotus Sutra)*. New York: Columbia University Press. https://doi.org/10.2307/602344

Jaffee, Martin S. 2005. "Torah." *Encyclopedia of Religion*, 2nd ed., 13: 9230–9241. Farmington Hills, MI: Macmillan Reference.

Joselit, Jenna Weissman. 2017. *Set In Stone: America's Embrace of the Ten Commandments*. New York: Oxford University Press.

Jung, Carl. 2009. *The Red Book: Liber Novus*. Ed. Sonu Shamdasani. New York: W. W. Norton.

Kafka, Ben. 2009. "Paperwork: the State of the Discipline." *Book History* 12: 340–353. https://doi.org/10.1353/bh.0.0024

Kammen, Michael. 1994. *A Machine that Would Go of Itself: The Constitution in American Culture*. New York: Alfred A. Knopf. https://doi.org/10.1086/ahr/93.1.215

Kaufman, Alan. 2009. "The Electronic Book Burning," *Evergreen Review* 120 (October). http://www.evergreenreview.com/120/electronic-book-burning.html (accessed Januray 6, 2017).

Keane, Webb. 2013. "On Spirit Writing: Materialities of Language and the Religious Work of Transduction," *Journal of the Royal Anthropological Institute* 19: 1–17. https://doi.org/10.1111/1467-9655.12000

Kessler, Edward. 2004. *Bound By the Bible: Jews, Christians and the Sacrifice of Isaac*. Cambridge: Cambridge University Press. https://doi.org/10.1017/s0364009405260178

Kieschnick, John. 2000. "Blood Writing in Chinese Buddhism." *Journal of the International Association of Buddhist Studies* 23: 177–194.

Kinnard, Jacob N. 1999. *Imaging Wisdom: Seeing and Knowing in the Art of Indian Buddhism*. Surrey: Curzon.

———. 2002. "On Buddhist 'Bibliolaters': Representing and Worshiping the Book in Medieval Indian Buddhism." *The Eastern Buddhist* 34(2): 94–116.

———. 2013. "It Is What It Is (Or Is It?): Further Reflections on the Buddhist Representation of Manuscripts." In *Iconic Books and Texts*, edited by J. W. Watts, 151–164. Sheffield: Equinox. First published in *Postscripts* 6: 101–116.

Kort, Wesley. 1996. *Take, Read: Scripture, Textuality and Cultural Practice*. College Park, PA: Pennsylvania State University Press. https://doi.org/10.1177/004057369905500416

Kosso, Peter. 1992. *Reading the Book of Nature: An Introduction to the Philosophy of Science*. Cambridge: Cambridge University Press.

Kottsieper, Ingo. 2007. "'And They Did Not Care to Speak Yehudit': On Linguistic Change in Judah During the Late Persian Period." In *Judah and the Judeans in the Fourth Century B.C.E.*, edited by Oded Lipschitz, Gary N. Knoppers, and Rainer Albertz, 95–124. Winona Lake, IN: Eisenbrauns. https://doi.org/10.1086/basor27805150

Kovic, Christine. 2005. *Mayan Voices for Human Rights: Displaced Catholics in Highland Chiapas*. Austin: University of Texas Press. https://doi.org/10.1017/s0022216x07003859

Kray, Christine. 2004. "The Summer Institute of Linguistics and the Politics of Bible Translation in Mexico: Convergence, Appropriation, and Consequence." In *Pluralizing Ethnography: Comparison and Representation in Maya Cultures, Histories, and Identities*, edited by J. M. Watanabe and E. F. Fischer, 95–125. Santa Fe: School of American Research Press. https://doi.org/10.7202/011754ar

Lake, Kirsopp, ed. 1911. *Codex Sinaiticus Petropolitanus. The New Testament, The Epistle of Barnabas and the Shepherd of Hermas.* Oxford: Clarendon Press.

Lakoff, George and Johnson, Mark. 2003. *Metaphors We Live By.* 2nd ed. Chicago, IL: University of Chicago Press.

Larson, Jason T. 2013. "The Gospels as Imperialized Sites of Memory in Late Ancient Christianity." In *Iconic Books and Texts*, edited by J. W. Watts, 373–388. Sheffield: Equinox. First published in *Postscripts* 6: 291–307. https://doi.org/10.1558/post.v6i1-3.291

Latour, Bruno. 2002. "What is Iconoclash?" In *Iconoclash: Beyond the Image Wars in Science, Religion, and Art*, edited by Bruno Latour and Peter Weibel, 16–40. Karlsruhe: Center for Art and Media. https://doi.org/10.2307/3177388

Lerner, Max. 1937. "Constitution and Court as Symbols." *The Yale Law Journal* 46(8): 1290–1319.

Levering, Miriam. 1989. "Scripture and its Reception: A Buddhist Case." In *Rethinking Scripture: Essays from a Comparative Perspective*, edited by M. Levering, 58–101. Albany: State University of New York Press. https://doi.org/10.1017/s0364009400002713

Levinson, Sanford. 1988. *Constitutional Faith.* Princeton, NJ: Princeton University Press.

Lévi-Strauss, Claude. 1981. *The Naked Man.* Translated by J. and D. Weightman. New York: Harper and Row. (Original French, 1971).

Levtow, Nathaniel B. 2011. "Text Production and Destruction in Ancient Israel: Ritual and Political Dimensions." In *Social Theory and the Study of Israelite Religion*, edited by Saul M. Olyan, 111–139. Atlanta, GA: SBL. https://doi.org/10.2307/j.ctt32bz5t.10

Lieberman, Stephen J. 1990. "Canonical and Official Cuneiform Texts: Towards an Understanding of Assurbanipal's Personal Tablet Collection." In *Lingering Over Words: Studies in ancient Near Eastern literature in Honor of William J. Moran*, edited by Tzvi Abusch *et al.*, 305–336. Harvard Semitic Monographs 37. Atlanta, GA: Scholars Press. https://doi.org/10.1163/9789004369559_020

Liverani, Mario. 1995. "The Deeds of Ancient Mesopotamian Kings." In *Civilizations of the Ancient Near East*, edited by J. M. Sasson, 2353–2365. New York: Scribners.

Loner, Shawn. 2013. "Be-Witching Scripture: The Book of Shadows as Scripture within Wicca/Neo-Pagan Witchcraft." In *Iconic Books and Texts*, edited by J. W. Watts, 273–292. Sheffield: Equinox. First published in *Postscripts* 2: 273–292. https://doi.org/10.1558/post.v2i2.273

Long, Burke. 2003. *Imagining the Holy Land: Maps, Models and Fantasy Travels.* Bloomington, IN: Indiana University Press. https://doi.org/10.1017/s0364009404390215

Love, Velma. 2003. "The Bible and Contemporary African American Culture I." In *African Americans and the Bible: Sacred Texts and Social Textures*, edited by Vincent L. Wimbush, 49–65. New York: Continuum.

MacKenzie Brown, C. 1986. "Purāṇa as Scripture: From Sound to Image of the Holy Word in the Hindu Tradition." *History of Religions* 26(1): 68–86. https://doi.org/10.1086/463061

Madigan, Daniel A. 2001. *The Qur'an's Self Image: Writing and Authority in Islam's Scripture*. Princeton, NJ: Princeton University Press. https://doi.org/10.2307/j.ctv346ptt

Malley, Brian. 2004. *How the Bible Works: An Anthropological Study of Evangelical Biblicism*. Walnut Creek, CA: AltaMira. https://doi.org/10.1080/10508610701572887

———. 2013. "The Bible in British Folklore." In *Iconic Books and Texts*, edited by J. W. Watts, 315–347. Sheffield: Equinox. First published in *Postscripts* 2: 241–272.

Marty, Martin. 1982. "America's Iconic Book." In *Humanizing America's Iconic Book*, edited by Gene M. Tucker and Douglas A. Knight, 1–23. Chico, CA: Scholars Press.

May, Natalie N., ed. 2012. *Iconoclasm and Text Destruction in the Ancient Near East and Beyond*. Chicago, IL: Oriental Institute.

McDannell, Colleen. 1994. *The Christian Home in Victorian America, 1840–1900*. Bloomington: Indiana University Press. https://doi.org/10.2307/3166098

Melanchthon, Monica Jyotsna. 2005. "Dalits, Bible, and Method." SBLForum, December. http://www.sbl-site.org/Article.aspx?ArticleId=459

Melot, Michel. 2004. "Le livre comme forme symbolique." Conférence tenue dans le cadre de l'Ecole de l'Institut d'histoire du livre. http://ihl.enssib.fr/le-livre-comme-forme-symbolique

———. 2006. *Livre*. Paris: L'Oeil Neuf. https://doi.org/10.1484/j.at.3.63

Meyer, Jeffrey F. 2001. *Myths in Stone: Religious Dimensions of Washington DC*. Berkeley: University of California Press.

Mittlebeeler, Emmet V. 2003. "Ten Commandments." In *The Encyclopedia of American Religion and Politics*, edited by P. A. Djupe and L. R. Olson, 434. New York: Facts on File.

Moerman, D. Max. 2010. "The Death of the Dharma: Buddhist Sutra Burials in Early Medieval Japan." In *The Death of Sacred Texts: Ritual Disposal and Renovation of Texts in World Religions*, edited by K. Myrvold, 71–90. London: Ashgate. https://doi.org/10.4324/9781315615318

Myrvold, Kristina. 2010. "Making the Scripture a Person: Reinventing Death Rituals of Guru Granth Sahib in Sikhism." In *The Death of Sacred Texts: Ritual Disposal and Renovation of Texts in World Religions*, edited by K. Myrvold, 125–146. London: Ashgate. https://doi.org/10.4324/9781315615318

———. 2013. "Engaging with the Guru: Sikh Beliefs and Practices of Guru Granth Sahib." In *Iconic Books and Texts*, edited by J. W. Watts, 261–281. Sheffield: Equinox. First published in *Postscripts* 6: 201–224. https://doi.org/10.1558/post.v6i1-3.201

Myrvold, Kristina, ed. 2010. *The Death of Sacred Texts: Ritual Disposal and Renovation of Texts in World Religions*. London: Ashgate. https://doi.org/10.1163/15685152-1018b0006

Myrvold, Kristina and Dorina Miller Parmenter, eds. 2019. *Miniature Books: Production, Print, and Practice*. Sheffield: Equinox. First published in *Postscripts* 9 (2018).

Nasr, Seyyed Hossein. 2002. "The Spiritual Message of Islamic Calligraphy." In *Religion, Art, and Visual Culture*, edited by S. Brent Plate, 112–117. New York: Palgrave. Excerpted from Nasr, S. H. 1987. *Islamic Art and Spirituality*. Albany: State University of New York Press. https://doi.org/10.1525/jung.1.1988.8.2.97

Nelson, Robert S. and Margaret Olin, eds. 2003. *Monuments and Memory, Made and Unmade*. Chicago, IL: University of Chicago Press.

Nesbitt, Eleanor. 2005. "Guru Granth Sahib." *Encyclopedia of Religion*, 2nd ed., 6: 3715–3718. Farmington Hills, MI: Macmillan Reference.

Ong, Walter. 1982. *Orality and Literacy*. Abingdon: Routledge.

Oxtoby, Willard G. 1995. "'Telling in Their Own Tongues': Old and Modern Bible Translations as Expressions of Ethnic Cultural Identity." In *The Bible As Cultural Heritage*, edited by W. Beuken and S. Freyne, 24–35. London: SCM.

Paget, James Carleton. 2014. "The Origins of the Septuagint." In *The Jewish-Greek Tradition in Antiquity and the Byzantine Empire*, edited by J. K. Aitken and J. C. Paget, 105–119. Cambridge: Cambridge University Press. https://doi.org/10.1017/cbo9780511736223.011

Parmenter, Dorina Miller. 2009. "The Bible as Icon: Myths of the Divine Origins of Scripture." In *Jewish and Christian Scripture as Artifact and Canon*, edited by C. A. Evans and H. D. Zacharias, 298–310. London: T. & T. Clark.

———. 2009. The Iconic Book: The Image of the Christian Bible in Myth and Ritual. Ph.D. Dissertation, Syracuse University.

———. 2010. "A Fitting Ceremony: Christian Concerns for Bible Disposal." In *The Death of Sacred Texts: Ritual Disposal and Renovation of Texts in World Religions*, edited by Kristina Myrvold, 55–70. London: Ashgate. https://doi.org/10.4324/9781315615318

———. 2013. "Iconic Books from Below: The Christian Bible and the Discourse of Duct Tape." In *Iconic Books and Texts*, edited by J. W. Watts, 225–238. Sheffield: Equinox. First published in *Postscripts* 6: 185–200. https://doi.org/10.1558/post.v6i1-3.185

———. 2013. "The Iconic Book: The Image of the Bible in early Christian Rituals." In *Iconic Books and Texts*, edited by J. W. Watts, 63–92. Sheffield: Equinox. First published in *Postscripts* 2: 160–189. https://doi.org/10.1558/post.v2i2.160

———. 2015. "Material Scripture." In *The Oxford Encyclopedia of the Bible and the Arts*, edited by T. Beal. Biblical Studies. Oxford: Oxford University Press. http://www.oxfordbiblicalstudies.com/print/opr/t454/e97

———. 2018. "How the Bible Feels: The Christian Bible as Effective and Affective Object." In *Sensing Sacred Texts*, edited by J. W. Watts, 27–38. Sheffield: Equinox. First published in *Postscripts* 8: 27–38. https://doi.org/10.1558/post.32589

Pasulka, Diana Walsh. 2006/2008. "Premodern Scriptures in Postmodern Times." *Postscripts* 2: 293–315. http://doi.org/10.1558/post.v2i2.293

Paul, Shalom. 1973. "Heavenly Tablets and Books of Life." *Journal of the Ancient Near Eastern Society* 5: 343–353.

Pickstock, Catherine. 1998. *After Writing: The Liturgical Consummation of Philosophy.* Oxford: Blackwell. https://doi.org/10.1017/s003693060005688x

Plate, S. Brent. 2013. "Looking at Words: the Iconicity of the Page." In *Iconic Books and Texts*, edited by J. W. Watts, 119–133. Sheffield: Equinox. First published in *Postscripts* 6: 67–82. http://doi.org/10.1558/post.v6i1-3.67

———. 2018. "What the Book Arts Can Teach Us About Sacred Texts: The Aesthetic Dimension of Scripture." In *Sensing Sacred Texts*, edited by J. W. Watts, 5–26. Sheffield: Equinox. First published in *Postscripts* 8: 5–26. https://doi.org/10.1558/post.32516

Quine, W. V. O. 1960. *Word and Object.* Cambridge, MA: MIT Press.

Rambelli, Fabio. 2013. *A Buddhist Theory of Semiotics: Signs, Ontology, and Salvation in Japanese Esoteric Buddhism.* London: Bloomsbury. https://doi.org/10.5040/9781472541840

Rapp, Claudia. 2007. "Holy Texts, Holy Men and Holy Scribes: Aspects of Scriptural Holiness in Late Antiquity." In *The Early Christian Book*, edited by W. E. Klingshirn, and Linda Safran, 194–222. Washington, DC: Catholic University of America Press. https://doi.org/10.2307/j.ctt2853v4.17

Rappaport, Roy A. 1999. *Ritual and Religion in the Making of Humanity.* Cambridge: Cambridge University Press.

Rakow, Katja. 2017. "The Bible in the Digital Age: Negotiating the Limits of 'Bibleness' of Different Bible Media." In *Christianity and the Limits of Materiality*, edited by Minna Opas and Anna Haapalainen, 101–121. London: Bloomsbury. https://doi.org/10.5040/9781474291798.0013

Resnick, Irven M. 1992. "The Codex in Early Jewish and Christian Communities." *The Journal of Religious History* 17(1): 1–17. https://doi.org/10.1111/j.1467-9809.1992.tb00699.x

Rezania, Kainoosh. 2015. "Media Controversies in Zoroastrian Inter-Religious Debates of the Early Islamic Period." Media of Scripture—Scripture as Media conference. Käte Hamburger Kolleg in the Center for Religious Studies, Ruhr University Bochum, December 10.

Roberts, Colin Henderson, and Skeat, T. C. 1983. *The Birth of the Codex.* Oxford: Oxford University Press.

Rooke, Tetz. 2006. "Translation of Arabic Literature: A Mission Impossible?" In *Current Issues in the Analysis of Semitic Grammar and Lexicon II*, edited by L. Edzard and J. Retsö, 214–225. Wiesbaden: Harrassowitz.

Rothberg-Halton, Francesca. 1984. "Canonicity in Cuneiform Texts." *Journal of Cuneiform Studies* 36: 127–144. https://doi.org/10.2307/1360053

Samson, C. Mathews. 2009. "The Word of God and 'Our Words': The Bible and Translation in a Mam Maya Context." In *The Social Life of Scriptures: Cross-Cultural Perspectives on Biblicism*, edited by J. S. Bielo, 64–79. New Brunswick, NJ: Rutgers University Press. https://doi.org/10.1111/j.1548-1352.2012.01253.x

Sarefield, Daniel. 2007. "The Symbolics of Book Burning: The Establishment of a Christian Ritual of Persecution." In *The Early Christian Book*, edited by W. E. Klingshirn and L. Safran, 159–173. Washington, DC: Catholic University of America Press. https://doi.org/10.2307/j.ctt2853v4.15

Sawyer, John. 1999. *Sacred Languages and Sacred Texts: Religion in the First Christian Centuries*. Abingdon: Routledge.

Schaeffer, Kurtis. 2009. *The Culture of the Book in Tibet*. New York: Columbia University Press.

Schaper, Joachim. 2004. "The Theology of Writing: The Oral and the Written, God as Scribe, and the Book of Deuteronomy." In *Anthropology and Biblical Studies: Avenues of Approach*, edited by Louise J. Lawrence and Mario I. Aguilar, 97–119. London: T. & T. Clark.

Schimmel, Annemarie. 1984. "Calligraphy and Islamic Culture." In *Religion, Art, and Visual Culture*, edited by S. Brent Plate, 106–111. New York, Palgrave, 2002. Excerpted from A. Schimmel, *Calligraphy and Islamic Culture*. New York: New York University Press. https://doi.org/10.1017/s0020743800023734

Schleicher, Marianne. 2009. "Artifactual and Hermeneutical Use of Scripture in Jewish Tradition." In *Jewish and Christian Scripture as Artifact and Canon*, edited by Craig A. Evans and H. Daniel Zacharias, 48–65. London: T. & T. Clark.

———. 2010. "Accounts of a Dying Scroll: On Jewish Handling of Sacred Texts in Need of Restoration or Disposal." In *The Death of Sacred Texts: Ritual Disposal and Renovation of Texts in World Religions*, edited by Kristina Myrvold, 11–30. London: Ashgate. https://doi.org/10.4324/9781315615318

———. 2018. "Engaging all the Senses: On Multi-sensory Stimulation in the Process of Making and Inaugurating a Torah Scroll." In *Sensing Sacred Texts*, edited by J. W. Watts, 39–56. Sheffield: Equinox. First published in *Postscripts* 8: 39–56. https://doi.org/10.1558/post.32694

Schmandt-Besserat, Denise. 1995. "Record Keeping Before Writing." In *Civilizations of the Ancient Near East*, edited by Jack M. Sasson, 2097–2106. Farmingham, MA: Scribner's.

Schopen, Gregory. 1975. "The Phrase '*sa prthivipradesas caityabhuto bhavet*' in the *Vajracchediku*: Notes on the Cult of the Book in Mahayana." *Indo-Iranian Journal* 17: 147–181. https://doi.org/10.1163/000000075790079574

Schorch, Stefan. 1972. "The Pre-eminence of the Hebrew Language and the Emerging Concept of the 'Ideal Text' in Late Second Temple Judaism." In *Studies in the Book of Ben Sira*, edited by G. G. Xeravits and J. Zsengellér, 43–54. Leiden: Brill. https://doi.org/10.1163/ej.9789004169067.i-273.20

Schott, Siegfried.1972. "Thoth als Verfasser heiliger Schriften." *Zeitschrift für Ägyptische Sprache und Altertumsurkunde* 99: 20–25. https://doi.org/10.1524/zaes.1972.99.1.20

Schussler Fiorenza, Elizabeth. 1999. *Rhetoric and Ethic: The Politics of Biblical Studies.* Minneapolis, MN: Augsburg Fortress.

Setzer, Claudia and David A. Shefferman. 2011. *The Bible in American Culture: A Sourcebook.* New York: Routledge.

Shopshire, James M., Ida Rousseau Mukenge, Victoria Erickson, and Hans a Baer. 2003. "The Bible and Contemporary African American Culture II: Report on a Preliminary Ethnographic Project." In *African Americans and the Bible: Sacred Texts and Social Textures*, edited by Vincent L. Wimbush, 66–80. New York: Continuum.

Siker, Jeffrey S. 2017. *Liquid Scripture: The Bible in the Digital World.* Minneapolis, MN: Fortress.

Smelik, Willem F. 2007. "Code-Switching: The Public Reading of the Bible." In *Was ist ein Text? Alttestamentliche, agyptologische und altorientalische Perspektiven*, edited by L. Morenz and S. Schorch, 123–151. Beihefte zur Zeitschrift für die alttestamentliche Wissenschaft 362. Berlin: de Gruyter. https://doi.org/10.1515/9783110924336

———. 2013. *Rabbis, Language and Translation in Late Antiquity.* Cambridge: Cambridge University Press.

Smith, Jonathan Z. 1987. *To Take Place: Toward Theory in Ritual.* Chicago, IL: University of Chicago Press. https://doi.org/10.1017/s0360966900040421

———. 1987. "The Domestication of Sacrifice." In *Violent Origins*, edited by R. G. Hamerton-Kelly, 191–235. Stanford, CA: Stanford University Press.

———. 1998. "Canons, Catalogues and Classics." In *Canonization and Decanonization*, edited by A. van der Kooij and K. van der Toorn, 295–311. Leiden: Brill. https://doi.org/10.18874/jjrs.26.1-2.1999.216-220

Smith, Wilfred Cantwell. 1971. "The Study of Religion and the Study of the Bible." *Journal of the American Academy of Religion* 39: 131–140. Reprinted in 1989 in *Rethinking Scripture: Essays from a Comparative Perspective*, edited by M. Levering, 18–28. Albany, NY: State University of New YorkPress. https://doi.org/10.1017/s0364009400002713

———. 1989. "Scripture as Form and Concept: Their Emergence for the Western World." In *Rethinking Scripture: Essays from a Comparative Perspective*, edited by M. Levering, 29–57. Albany, NY: State University of New York Press. https://doi.org/10.1017/s0364009400002713

Solibakke, Karl Ivan. 2013. "The Pride and Prejudice of the Western World: Canonic Memory, Great Books and Archive Fever." In *Iconic Books and Texts*, edited by J. W. Watts, 347–360. Sheffield: Equinox. First published in *Postscripts* 6: 243–259. https://doi.org/10.1558/post.v6i1-3.261

Stam, Deirdre C. 2013. "Talking about 'Iconic Books' in the Terminology of Book History." In *Iconic Books and Texts*, edited by J. W. Watts, 47–60. Sheffield: Equinox. First published in *Postscripts* 6: 23–38. https://doi.org/10.1558/post.v6i1-3.23

Stern, David M. 2008. "The First Jewish Books and the Early History of Jewish Reading," *Jewish Quarterly Review* 98(2): 163–202. https://doi.org/10.1353/jqr.0.0005

Stolow, Jeremy. 2010. *Orthodox by Design: Judaism, Print Politics, and the ArtScroll Revolution*. Berkeley: University of California Press. https://doi.org/10.1017/s0364009411000183

Suit, Natalia K. 2013. "Muṣḥaf and the Material Boundaries of the Qur'an." In *Iconic Books and Texts*, edited by J. W. Watts, 189–206. Sheffield: Equinox. First published in *Postscripts* 6: 143–163.

———. 2015. "Enacting 'Electronic Qur'ans': Tradition Without a Precedent." Material Religions web blog, 18 November. http://materialreligions.blogspot.com/2015/11/enacting-electronic-qurans-tradition.html

Svensson, Jonas. 2010. "Relating, Revering, and Removing: Muslim Views on the Use, Power, and Disposal of Divine Words." In *The Death of Sacred Texts: Ritual Disposal and Renovation of Texts in World Religions*, edited by Kristina Myrvold, 31–54. London: Ashgate. https://doi.org/10.4324/9781315615318

———. 2017. "Hurting the Qur'an – Suggestions Concerning the Psychological Infrastructure of Desecration." *Temenos* 53(2): 243–264.

Toorn, Karel van der. 1997. "The Iconic Book: Analogies Between the Babylonian Cult of Images and the Veneration of the Torah." In *The Image and the Book: Iconic Cults, Aniconism and the Rise of Book Religion in Israel and the Ancient Near East*, edited by K. van der Toorn, 229–248. Louven: Peeters. https://doi.org/10.1177/030908929802307711

Trobisch, David. 2000 [1996]. *The First Edition of the New Testament*. Oxford: Oxford University Press.

Tuladhar-Douglas, Will. 2009. "Writing and the Rise of Mahayana Buddhism." In *Die Textualisierung der Religion*, edited by Joachim Schaper, 250–272. Tubingen: Mohr Siebeck.

Velten, Hans Rudolf. 2012. "Performativity and Performance." In *Travelling Concepts for the Study of Culture*, edited by Ansgar Nunning and Birgit Neumann, 249–266. Berlin: de Gruyter.

Vismann, Cornelia. 2008. *Files: Law and Media Technology*. Stanford, CA: Stanford University Press. https://doi.org/10.1525/lal.2010.22.1.199

Waghorne, Joanne Punzo. 2013. "A Birthday Party for a Sacred Text: The Gita Jayanti and the Embodiment of God as the Book and the Book as God." In *Iconic Books and Texts*, edited by J. W. Watts, 283–298. Sheffield: Equinox. First published in *Postscripts* 6: 225–242. https://doi.org/10.1558/post.v6i1-3.225

Watts, James W. 2004. "Ten Commandments Monuments and the Rivalry of Iconic Texts." *Journal of Religion & Society* 6. http://moses.creighton.edu/jrs/2004/2004-13.pdf. Revised as Chapter 7 this volume.

———. 2005. "Ritual Legitimacy and Scriptural Authority." *Journal of Biblical Literature* 124(3): 401–417. Reprinted in 2007 as "The Rhetoric of Scripture." In *Ritual and Rhetoric in Leviticus,* 193–217. Cambridge: Cambridge University Press. https://doi.org/10.2307/30041032

———. 2009. "Desecrating Scriptures." A case study for the Luce Project in Religion, Media and International Relations. Syracuse University. Revised as Chapter 5 above. http://sites.maxwell.syr.edu/luce/jameswatts.html

———. 2010. "Disposing of Non-Disposable Texts: Conclusions and Prospects for Further Study." In *The Death of Sacred Texts: Ritual Disposal and Renovation of Texts in World Religions,* edited by K. Myrvold, 147–159. London: Ashgate. Revised as part of Chapter 10 above. https://doi.org/10.4324/9781315615318

———. 2011. "Using Ezra's Time as a Methodological Pivot for Understanding the Rhetoric and Functions of the Pentateuch." In *The Pentateuch: International Perspectives on Current Research,* edited by T. B. Dozeman, K. Schmid and B. J. Schwarz, 489–506. Tübingen: Mohr Siebeck.

———. 2012. "Relic Texts." Iconic Books Blog. June 8. http://iconicbooks.blogspot.com/2012/06/relic-texts.html. Revised as Chapter 3 above.

———. 2013. "Ancient Iconic Texts and Scholarly Expertise." In *Iconic Books and Texts,* edited by J. W. Watts, 407–418. Sheffield: Equinox. First published in *Postscripts* 6: 331–344. Revised as parts of Chapters 5 and 9 above. https://doi.org/10.1558/post.v6i1-3.331

———. 2013. "The Three Dimensions of Scriptures." In *Iconic Books and Texts,* edited by J. W. Watts, 9–32. Sheffield: Equinox. First published in *Postscripts* 2: 135–159. Revised as Chapter 1 above.

———. 2013c. "The Political and Legal Uses of Scripture." In *The New Cambridge History of the Bible: From the Beginnings to 600,* edited by J. C. Paget and J. Schaper, 345–364. Cambridge: Cambridge University Press. https://doi.org/10.1017/cbo9781139033671.019

———, ed. 2013. *Iconic Books and Texts.* Sheffield: Equinox.

———. 2016. "From Ark of the Covenant to Torah Scroll: Ritualizing Israel's Iconic Texts." In *Ritual Innovation in the Hebrew Bible and Early Judaism,* edited by N. MacDonald, 21–34. Beihefte zur Zeitschrift für die alttestamentliche Wissenschaft 468. Berlin: dse Gruyter. https://doi.org/10.1515/9783110368710-004

———. 2017. *Understanding the Pentateuch As A Scripture.* Chichester: Wiley Blackwell.

———. 2018. "Scripture's Indexical Touch." In *Sensing Sacred Texts*, edited by J. W. Watts, 173–184. Sheffield: Equinox. First published in *Postscripts* 8: 173–184. https://doi.org/10.1558/post.32671

———, ed. 2018. *Sensing Sacred Texts*. Sheffield: Equinox.

———. "Books as Sacred Beings." *Postscripts.* forthcoming.

Wilkens, Katharina. 2018. "Infusions and Fumigations—Literacy Ideologies and Therapeutic Aspects of the Qur'an." In *Sensing Sacred Texts*, edited by J. W. Watts, 115–136. Sheffield: Equinox. First published in *Postscripts* 8: 115–136. https://doi.org/10.1558/post.32508

Williams, Megan Hale. 2006. *The Monk and the Book: Jerome and the Making of Christian Scholarship*. Chicago, IL: University of Chicago.

Wimbush, Vincent L. 2003. "Introduction: Reading Darkness, Reading Scriptures." In *African Americans and the Bible: Sacred Texts and Social Textures*, edited by Vincent L. Wimbush, 7–22. New York: Continuum.

———. 2012. *White Men's Magic: Scripturalization as Slavery*. Oxford: Oxford University Press.

Wittgenstein, Ludwig. 1953. *Philosophical Investigations*. Translated by G.E.M. Anschombe. Oxford: Blackwell.

Yoo, Yohan. 2006. "Public Scripture Reading Rituals in Early Korean Protestantism: A Comparative Perspective." *Postscripts* 2: 226–240. https://doi. org/10.1558/post.v2i2.226

———. 2013. "Possession and Repetition: Ways in which Korean Lay Buddhists Appropriate Scriptures." In *Iconic Books and Texts*, edited by J. W. Watts, 299–313. Sheffield: Equinox. First published in *Postscripts* 6: 243–259. https://doi.org/10.1558/post.v6i1-3.243

———. 2018. "Neo-Confucian Sensory Readings of Scriptures: the Reading Methods of Chu Hsi and Yi Hwang." In *Sensing Sacred Texts*, edited by J. W. Watts, 161–172. Sheffield: Equinox. First published in *Postscripts* 8: 161–172. https://doi.org/10.1558/post.32267

INDICES

AUTHOR INDEX

Subject Index

Figures indicated by italic page numbers.

Printed in Australia
AUHW010824240619
313780AU00002B/2